Social and Political Theatre in 21st-Century Britain

Methuen Drama Engage offers original reflections about key practitioners, movements and genres in the fields of modern theatre and performance. Each volume in the series seeks to challenge mainstream critical thought through original and interdisciplinary perspectives on the body of work under examination. By questioning existing critical paradigms, it is hoped that each volume will open up fresh approaches and suggest avenues for further exploration.

Series Editors

Mark Taylor-Batty
Senior Lecturer in Theatre Studies, Workshop Theatre,
University of Leeds, UK

Enoch Brater
Kenneth T. Rowe Collegiate Professor of Dramatic Literature &
Professor of English and Theater, University of Michigan, USA

Titles

Adaptation in Contemporary Theatre
by Frances Babbage
ISBN 978–1–4725–3142–1

Authenticity in Contemporary Theatre and Performance
by Daniel Schulze
ISBN 978–1–3500–0096–4

Beat Drama: Playwrights and Performances of the 'Howl' Generation
edited by Deborah R. Geis
ISBN 978–1–472–56787–1

Brecht in Practice: Theatre, Theory and Performance
by David Barnett
ISBN 978-1-4081-8503-2

Drama and Digital Arts Cultures
by David Cameron, Michael Anderson and Rebecca Wotzko
ISBN 978-1-4725-9220-0

The Contemporary American Monologue: Performance and Politics
by Eddie Paterson
ISBN 978-1-472-58501-1

Watching War on the Twenty-First Century Stage: Spectacles of Conflict
by Clare Finburgh
ISBN 978-1-472-59866-0

Theatre in the Dark: Shadow, Gloom and Blackout in Contemporary Theatre
edited by Adam Alston and Martin Welton
ISBN 978-1-4742-5118-1

Theatre of Real People: Diverse Encounters from Berlin's Hebbel am Ufer and Beyond
by Ulrike Garde and Meg Mumford
ISBN 978-1-4725-8021-4

Social and Political Theatre in 21st-Century Britain

Staging Crisis

Vicky Angelaki

Series Editors
Enoch Brater and Mark Taylor-Batty

Bloomsbury Academic
An imprint of Bloomsbury Publishing Plc

B L O O M S B U R Y
LONDON · OXFORD · NEW YORK · NEW DELHI · SYDNEY

Bloomsbury Methuen Drama

An imprint of Bloomsbury Publishing Plc

Imprint previously known as Methuen Drama

50 Bedford Square	1385 Broadway
London	New York
WC1B 3DP	NY 10018
UK	USA

www.bloomsbury.com

BLOOMSBURY and the Diana logo are trademarks of Bloomsbury Publishing Plc

First published 2017

© Vicky Angelaki, 2017

British Library Cataloguing-in-Publication Data

A catalogue record for this book is available from the British Library.

ISBN:	HB:	978-1-474-21317-2
	PB:	978-1-474-21316-5
	ePDF:	978-1-474-21319-6
	ePub:	978-1-474-21318-9

Library of Congress Cataloging-in-Publication Data

A catalog record for this book is available from the Library of Congress.

Series: Methuen Drama Engage

Cover design by Louise Dugdale
Cover photograph © Marc Brenner

Typeset by Integra Software Services Pvt. Ltd.
Printed and bound in Great Britain

For Dimitris

Contents

Acknowledgements

This book began many years ago as an idea and, as is the case with all projects of this kind, it had to wait patiently for some time for other books, journals, articles and so on to happen so that this, too, might begin to materialize in its own time. During this period new writing saw a remarkable growth; the binary between alternative and mainstream became forever blurred; the form that political theatre was likely to follow became radically redefined. The writing of this book took place in many different locations, including central London, where I lived for part of this period. I benefitted from the city and its lived experience, which facilitated a consideration of social, political, financial, environmental and many other crises on such a large and illuminating scale, heightening the density of emotion and range of problematics that the texts discussed in this book contend with.

On a more tangible note, I wish to thank Mark Dudgeon at Bloomsbury for his support to the project. I would also like to extend warm thanks to the editors of the series in which this book is published, Mark Taylor-Batty and Enoch Brater, for their very positive, supportive and encouraging response to this book from the proposal stages. I am grateful to the peer reviewers for their valuable and constructive feedback. I must thank the University of Birmingham for granting me one term's research leave. I thank very sincerely Liz Tomlin and the cohorts of Drama finalists who took my modules Theatre and Social Crisis and Playwright's Theatre for their enthusiasm and energy.

Thank you, very warmly, to colleagues in British and international universities who invited me to present papers relating to my research as it developed – especially colleagues at NUI Galway, Royal Holloway, Sorbonne – Paris IV, University of Kent, University of Konstanz, University of York. One of these universities was, of course, also the University of Reading, where I moved in 2016, and I thank my new colleagues very much for their warm response to my research and to this book as it continued to develop in my new post.

Thank you to my mentors and frequent collaborators Elizabeth Sakellaridou, Chris Megson, Dan Rebellato and Elisabeth Angel-Perez, as well as to the broader community of CDE, the German Society for Contemporary Drama in English, for their continued support – especially but by no means exclusively Ute Berns, Julia Boll, Martin Middeke, Trish Reid, Christina Wald, Clare Wallace, Eckart Voigts and Heiner Zimmermann.

I also wish to thank the playwrights, directors, theatre artists and companies who have produced the work discussed in this book – work that is defiant and hopeful, even in its occasional darkness, because it is bold and forward facing. I thank Marc Brenner for the image of the Almeida production of *Carmen Disruption* by Simon Stephens directed by Michael Longhurst, set design by Lizzie Clachan, which has provided the cover of this book, and Louise Dugdale for the cover design. Every effort has been made to ensure that quotations included in this work fall within fair dealing regulations.

A heartfelt thanks to Maria, Vangelis, Nicolas, Deirdre, Tonia, Christos, Margaret, Vlasis and Jayne for their friendship. Above all, I am extremely fortunate to have the love and support of Vaso, Nikos, Manolis, Paulina, Akis and George. I can never possibly thank you enough. The final thank you is reserved for my husband Dimitris, to whom I dedicate this book. Thank you for your kindness, your fierce support, your faith, your spirit – then, now and always.

Vicky Angelaki,

2016

Introduction: Theatres of Crisis

Under normal circumstances, it might have been premature to write a book on social and political theatre in twenty-first-century Britain as we are only now transitioning to the second half of the new century's second decade. But defining normal has become more of a challenge, as an outcome of the manifold events that have become conflated into the term 'crisis': the key point of reference and concern of this book. Already, in the twenty-first century, societies globally have had rather a lot to contend with: watershed political moments; major military conflicts; threats to public safety; a dramatic increase in surveillance mechanisms; the digitization of lives; a social media revolution; a major financial downturn; climate change – and the list continues. It may not be possible for a single book to account for these phenomena exhaustively. It is important, nonetheless, to engage in conversation that problematizes some of the primary preoccupations for British society as captured in its theatre of the 2000s and 2010s. This has been the incentive for this book and the dialogue that it seeks to contribute to.

'Crisis' has been a recurring term in the post-2000 period and a buzzword that entered our contemporary lexicon in many different contexts with roots in three interconnected primary areas: political, environmental, financial. Of these, it is the latter that has dominated the modern use of a word that has been around since ancient times. In Greek, it denotes both a state of emergency and intellectual judgement. As a derivative noun of the verb *krīnein* (κρίνειν), crisis (modern Greek κρίση [krīsi], ancient Greek κρίσις [krīsis]) is defined by the *Oxford English Dictionary* (*OED*), in the usages most relevant to this book, as:

> **Pathol.** The point in the progress of a disease when an important development or change takes place which is decisive of recovery or death; the turning-point of a disease for better or worse; also applied to any marked or sudden variation occurring in the progress of a disease and to the phenomena accompanying it.

Or:

> **transf. and fig.** A vitally important or decisive stage in the progress of anything; a turning-point; also, a state of affairs in which a decisive change for better or worse is imminent; now applied esp. to times of difficulty, insecurity, and suspense in politics or commerce. (2016b)

The similarities between the two definitions are striking, making clear that the field or concern to which the term 'crisis' is applied is a patient of sorts – whether a person, or a community – teetering at the edge between improvement or decline, salvation or catastrophe. It is fascinating that even though in everyday discourse the term 'crisis' carries pejorative signification that allows little margin for hope, the dictionary definitions deviate from that. As we see in the *OED*, the definitions very much locate crisis in that indeterminate no man's land which represents the reconciliation of binaries, the moment of reckoning, the space where the intervention might still take place.

The theatre discussed in this book is also located in that as yet indeterminate territory that is as worrisome as it is promising and it captures the process of attempting a transition. The transition may not deliver immediate results, but it produces the possibility of change through dialogue and exposition that allow space for feeling and are not bound to rhetoric. The possibility of social change in twenty-first-century British theatre, certainly the kind that this book concentrates on, is accomplished by acknowledging the problem; by attacking it dialectically; by exposing the hues in humanity that render individuals more than the sum of their neoliberalist context and at the same time by addressing the conditioning factors which have limited our options. The artists whose work this book deals with are diverse, with distinctive writing and staging aesthetics, but they share the fact that they do not come to the issue at hand from a position of superiority and authority. They come to it, rather, from the imperative of exploration and honesty, and they extend to the audience an invitation to this experiential journey. The fact that there is no audience participation in the most limiting understanding of the term as a stage intervention of sorts does not mean that participation does not occur. It occurs because the work discussed in this book acknowledges crisis as a collective concern, one from which the contemporary playwright, as a citizen, does not exempt themselves. There is equality and democracy in plays such as the ones that this book discusses and it begins from the core dramaturgical device of stories in formation. Plot and events might be written and therefore predetermined but the form of these texts makes it clear that we are in a space of exchange where we are called to think, question, judge and be moved rather than consume a politically gratifying message that might reaffirm any given spectator's ideological or intellectual superiority in a way that might, in turn, generate complacency. These are plays that confuse, distract, disturb and imagine so that they might disrupt: first our expectations, then the dominant social and political narratives of neoliberalism and governmentality.

I have previously discussed the importance of such strategies at length focusing on one of the playwrights that this book also examines (Angelaki 2012). As *The Plays of Martin Crimp: Making Theatre Strange* argued with extensive reference to the phenomenology of theatre, affect, as opposed to effect, is a primary tool through which the impact of the play is created. 'Affect' as a term is built on intersubjectivity, empowering the spectator through dramaturgy that imagines them as an active agent. 'Effect', on the contrary, is a term that imagines the spectator as a receiver, or, worse yet, a recipient with limited and predetermined active agency, whether emotional, physical or intellectual. These distinctions are crucial, especially at a time when individualism has become a fraught term, tied to the narrative of neoliberalism. The subversive act of the plays discussed in this book is that they imagine the spectator as an individual in the sense of an elemental part of a community of spectators and citizens. And so they appeal to our sensibilities, our judgements, our capabilities of being involved in the broader historical narrative of our time not as mere observers. A key component of this process, as I also argued elsewhere (Angelaki 2012), is that the plays do not operate on the binary of the aesthetic versus the political: rather, they exist in the space between the two to create a new form of theatre responsive to the complexities of our time. As a consequence, social and political performance becomes redefined, moving further away from social realism and into a territory where formal experimentation and sensory richness are no longer seen as tropes of alternative stages but as methodologies that, in twenty-first-century British theatre, have infiltrated the mainstream. This marks a significant turn in contemporary theatre-making of the crisis era. The work discussed in this book sees the potential in crisis: it does not treat it as part of a binary, diametrically opposed to prosperity, but it probes the fluidity of our time, attempting to understand it better so as to see whether, and how, it might hold promise.

'Crisis', as a concept denoting social and political emergencies and dysfunctions, is such an all-encompassing term that it is important to be clear as to what this book specifically concentrates on. Even though the book takes on concerns of global impact, its primary area of focus is British society and theatre produced in this country from 2000 onwards. We have witnessed a radical change as to the experience of the everyday and the at-risk status of human life even in contexts previously treated as safe and in lifestyles typically seen as commonplace. Terms like 'terror' and 'terrorism' have become part of everyday vocabulary especially as in the first two decades of the twenty-first century the world has seen numerous attacks targeting civilians in major urban centres. Non-terrorism-related acts of sociopathy perpetrating violence have also continued, increasing in impact. Societies have often appeared divided, at the brink of major disruption as a result of rioting. The Western world, and, of course, Europe, has been divided by the stance different countries took to participating in extensive military operations. Most recently, we have witnessed an immigration and asylum-seeking crisis of extraordinary scale.

Each of these subjects invites a lot of ink to be spilled on discourses focusing on how theatre has responded to such events in Britain and of course worldwide. This is not the remit of this book. To discuss the contemporary Hydra of crisis in any meaningful way and make a claim to critical depth, this book, like any other, must define its territory quite specifically, acknowledging that it will form part of a broader conversation on the staging, social and political histories of the present, which will of course continue beyond it. The territory of this book, then, is the crisis exacerbated by the individualism of capitalism as proliferated by neoliberalism, as colonizing every aspect of human experience and as depicted in new plays produced on British stages from 2000 onwards, with a distinct focus on the post-2010 period, in the aftermath of the recession. In this period we have seen a dramatic increase in redundancies; in the cost of living; in the role of social media in everyday lives; in urban alienation and mental health issues; in voices calling for the understanding of our responsibilities towards the environment; in the fluidity of experience and uncertainty brought on by these factors. The theatre of crisis that this book concentrates on has absorbed these events, whose common thread is the economy, capitalism and neoliberalism; it has been affected by them to its thematic and formal core; it is now reflecting them back unto the society that produced them, the same one that is still in awkward stages of tentative recovery, with a possibility for change as much as for gliding back to the grips of capitalist excess. The plays discussed here capture the symptoms of crisis and the wavering; the knowledge and the difficulty; the promise and the compromise.

The title of this book proclaims a concern with 'theatre' and focuses on a category broadly defined as plays. It does so not with the intention of colonizing and claiming the field of theatre for one specific representational genre, however vast. It would be naïve to think that at a time when we are witnessing such a plethora of representational methods and performance events, playwriting can make any assertion as to its own primacy or might still be thought of as standing for any kind of anachronistic orthodoxy. But the book purposely uses the term 'theatre' in its title because it also actively discourages the segregation of plays into categories rigidly defined under terms such as 'text-based'. Whatever the value of such terms, located within the need to define sub-genres of theatre and representation more widely, there is a risk that must be acknowledged. The moment we begin thinking of the work of playwrights who have benefitted from fruitful collaborations with visionary directors and companies, leading to excellent examples of theatre-making as *Gesamtkunstwerk*, as playwriting defined narrowly, we begin to ignore that theatre is a medium of collaboration and mutual contextual impact in which the playwright is one, but far from the only, part of the process. In contemporary contexts where playwrights enjoy long, productive relationships with specific collaborators and/or partake in rehearsals on the democratic terms of creating a product of collective labour, assumptions that using 'theatre' to refer to work where a playwright has been crucial means that an entire genre is being claimed by one of its sub-genres are tenuous and problematic. Recently, Duška Radosavljević's *Theatre-Making: Interplay between Text and Performance in the 21st Century* (2013) made a contribution towards debunking this myth.

Having identified crisis in British society stemming from neoliberalism as represented in contemporary British theatre as the primary focal area of this book and the benchmark for selecting case studies in all eight main chapters, it is important to address what neoliberalism has stood for and what it still represents today, at a time when it is both a relic of itself, post-recession, and continues to be the dominant system. Britain entered the twenty-first century under Tony Blair's Labour government. The New Labour era produced a lifestyle along the same lines as in many affluent Western countries during the early 2000s: materialism, consumption, credit, mortgages. By the time Gordon Brown succeeded Blair as prime minister in 2007, the burst of the prosperity bubble was fast approaching and 2008 delivered the worst financial downturn in recent history. Its reverberations would continue for many countries well into the 2010s, leading to dramatic developments and austerity measures felt across Europe and especially in the Eurozone countries that came to be known under the derogatory PIIGS acronym (Portugal, Italy, Ireland, Greece, Spain). During this time, Britain transitioned to David Cameron and Nick Clegg's Conservative and Lib Dem Coalition Government (2010–2015) and subsequently to Cameron's Conservative Government following the 2015 general election. In early 2010 it was announced that Britain had come out of the recession, though only marginally (BBC 2010). More recently, in early 2016, London was ranked as the sixth most expensive place worldwide to live in on *The Economist* Cost of Living Index for 2015 (The Economist – The Data Team 2016).

In his seminal study David Harvey defines neoliberalism as 'a theory of political economic practices that proposes that human well-being can best be advanced by liberating individual entrepreneurial freedoms and skills within an institutional framework [...]' (Harvey 2005: 2). Writing over ten years ago, it might have been difficult for Harvey to predict the extraordinary change in digital media that has been implemented in the last decade. This renders observations such as the one he makes concerning 'technologies of information creation and capacities to accumulate, store, transfer, analyse, and use massive databases to guide decisions in the global marketplace' as pivotal to processes of neoliberalization and a new 'information society' especially prescient (Harvey 2005: 3–4). Such definitions of neoliberal practices will be crucial to the thematic concerns of the book over the following chapters. So will further observations that Harvey arrives at regarding certain staple areas. These include well-being and class:

> While personal and individual freedom in the marketplace is guaranteed, each individual is held responsible and accountable for

his or her own actions and well-being. This principle extends into the realms of welfare, education, health care [...]. Individual success or failure are interpreted in terms of entrepreneurial virtues or personal failings [...] rather than being attributed to any systemic property (such as the class exclusions usually attributed to capitalism). (Harvey 2005: 65–66)

Mobility of markets and, by extension, of people:

The free mobility of capital between sectors, regions, and countries is regarded as crucial. [...] State sovereignty over commodity and capital movements is willingly surrendered to the global market. (Harvey 2005: 66)

Community:

At the popular level, the drive towards market freedoms and the commodification of everything can all too easily run amok and produce social incoherence. The destruction of forms of social solidarity [...] leaves a gaping hole in the social order. (Harvey 2005: 80)

Labour and the environment:

The biases arise in particular out of the treatment of labour and the environment as mere commodities. In the event of a conflict, the typical neoliberal state will tend to side with a good business climate as opposed to either the collective rights [...] of labour or the capacity of the environment to regenerate itself. (Harvey 2005: 70)

The extensive quotations here are merited as these areas represent the central thematic stands of this book emerging in the ensuing chapters and Harvey's exposition of neoliberalist problematics helps establish the terms of the discussion.

The relationship between neoliberalism and theatre has recently been foregrounded most notably in the work of Jen Harvie. *Fair Play: Art, Performance and Neoliberalism* (2013) offers both a valuable discussion of the neoliberalist framework in today's Britain and an exploration of representational modes other than plays that have embodied the concept of socially geared practices including the work of visual artists as well as theatre companies and artistic organizations. The present book shares some of Harvie's contextual concerns, but moves in a different direction in terms of the specific kinds of performance that it foregrounds. Harvie's activist scholarship in *Fair Play* is relevant to setting the thematic parameters of my book, which is also concerned with

> [...] essentials of social life [that] are jeopardized by contemporary cultural trends which damage communication and prioritize self-interest. Communication may appear to be enhanced by contemporary technologies, [...] but in many ways they [... are] isolating individuals [...]. The kind of self-interest [...] actively cultivated by dominant neoliberal capitalist ideologies which aggressively promote individualism and entrepreneurialism and pour scorn on anyone unfortunate enough to need to draw on the safety net of welfare support. (2013: 2)

Harvie also provides a contemporary definition of the key term 'governmentality', which, traced back to Michel Foucault among other theorists, indicates how 'political ideologies such as neoliberalism are not principally imposed through top-down government "controls", but rather through [...] the dissemination of knowledge that people internalize so that they become self-governing' (2013: 3). And so, Harvie argues, 'naturalized governmentality' is produced (2013: 3). In their discussion of the term's development in Anglophone territories, Nikolas Rose, Pat O'Malley and Mariana Valverde specifically trace the roots of 'governmentality' in Foucault's 1970s discourse (2006: 83). Their citation of Foucault's description of governmentality as 'understood in the broad sense of techniques and procedures for directing human behavior. Government of children, government of souls and consciences, government of a household, of a state, or of oneself' is encompassing and resonant (Foucault 1997: 82; Rose, O'Malley, and Valverde 2006: 83). In their rigorous analysis Rose, O'Malley and Valverde also problematize the relationship between governmentality and neoliberalism, arguing that 'one of the attractions of governmentality has been its capacity to render neo-liberalism visible in new ways' (2006: 97), but that this has also led to some issues as to the blanket applicability of neoliberalism as a term. They describe the categorization of the Blair government as neoliberal as neglecting 'the architects of Blair's Third Way explicitly reject[ing] such a description' (Rose, O'Malley, and Valverde 2006: 97). This is despite the fact that 'elements of neo-liberal ways of thinking and acting can be found in most governing regimes and programs today' (Rose, O'Malley, and Valverde 2006: 97). The Third Way, linked to Anthony Giddens, is most simply defined as 'the old class-based divisions of left and right are now redundant' (Mellbye 2003). For Rose, O'Malley and Valverde the problematic in the indiscriminate use of the term 'neoliberalism' consists in that

> To describe certain techniques or even programs as neo-liberal indicates their lineage and provides a point of family resemblance with other postsocial governance. This may be useful at a certain level of generality, but it is not the same as describing diverse contemporary regimes or rationalities as neo-liberal. (2006: 97)

This is also broadly the approach that this book takes, in identifying certain traits, policies and behaviours as remnants of neoliberalism but also appreciating that we need to infuse the conversation with consistent references to sociology and to the contemporary context in order to appreciate how, even though the neoliberalist framework applies as conditioning factor, this, too, has become a hybrid. The new formulation, post-Third Way, post-recession and still in crisis territory might seem as post-ideological. However, all this means is that, as the plays discussed in this book show, we have transitioned to a time where institutional collapse and political saturation have enabled more distance between individual and society, more options for governmentality and a new mutation of the neoliberalist gene (see also Rose, O'Malley, and Valverde 2006: 98). Following the financial crisis, austerity and moderation (in consumption, in feelings, in expectations) have been presented as the certain path forward, with recovery and prosperity waiting at the other end. The forming narrative of the post-Blair era, then, once more, is based on the individual behaving according to set norms and responding to capitalist triggers. But as the playwrights whose work this book discusses show, there is nothing inspirational about such an aspiration. The personas and characters we encounter in these plays have absorbed their social context; they have been affected by the sensational collapse, as have the spectators – and so they are inhabiting that uncertain space of crisis, from where not only catastrophe, but perhaps also change might spring. It is not surprising, then, that in many of the plays discussed here individuals oscillate between anxiety and hope.

The main concerns of the book, intersecting in different chapters, converge in the neoliberalisms and governmentalities of our time, as well as in the tensions between the non-binary of private and public. They also develop in specific thematic sub-strands, all of which highlight different crises comprising the broader crisis. These concerns are: social and political fluidity leading to (inter)personal uncertainties; citizenship, community and responsibility; anti-capitalist resistance; class and violence; individual and environment; austerity; mobility and identity; therapy culture and insularity; urban alienation and mental health; science, industry and ethics. The economy features throughout as overarching concern and interconnecting thread. The emphasis of this book on the crossovers of society, politics and science in conjunction with theatre, responding to the interdisciplinary formal and thematic approaches that the plays themselves have taken, necessitates a sustained engagement with critical discourse emerging in the social sciences. The book, therefore, follows a methodology that is responsive to the structure and subject matter of the texts discussed. This requires a broader dialogue with relevant sociological perspectives, which are distinct and yet speak to each other, sharing their imperative of locating the individual within the collective narrative in a time of flux. Illuminating the concerns of the book with appropriate critical and theoretical contextualization, therefore, is necessarily a composite matter because of the range and complexity of the matters at hand. Within this enquiry, the work of Zygmunt Bauman, Carlo Bordoni,

Robert H. Frank, Frank Furedi, Richard Sennett and John Urry is particularly significant in establishing primary parameters. Additional references to the work of scholars in the fields of interdisciplinary sociology, philosophy and theatre studies allow me to further probe specific thematic nuances in chapters as necessary.

The book begins with a chapter focusing on Caryl Churchill's recent work, which sets the tone for areas that the remainder of the book goes on to explore. Churchill's continuous formal innovation in the context of a thematic range that evidences sustained engagement with social and political concerns and her insightful assessment of shifts in our relationship to our communities, not least mediated by technology, are dealt with primarily on their own merit. I anticipate, however, that the reader will identify an array of concerns emerging in subsequent chapters and particularly noticeably within the work of specific playwrights as having been repeatedly highlighted by Churchill, whose influence on contemporary theatre traditions has been remarkable. Chapter 2 follows on with a consideration of Mike Bartlett's work, concentrating on large-scale plays that have taken on a complex combination of major issues. It proposes that in Bartlett's suitably ambitious playwriting scope these issues have ranged from the recession and the environment to dubious governments, fraught policies and the anti-capitalism movement. This section also examines how Bartlett's theatre has negotiated matters of protest and faith in social change, as well as its viability. The book then moves on to work whose form might be more minimalist, but whose thematic focus is no less expansive. If capitalism is presented as the primary issue to contend with in Bartlett's work, it is so also in the work of Dennis Kelly, as Chapter 3 discusses. This section argues that in Kelly's theatre capitalism is depicted as a corrosive force in both familial and social frameworks. It particularly concentrates on how parameters relating to class, consumerism and materialist transgressions are depicted in Kelly's theatre as the strongest determinants of behaviours, relationships and ethics.

Ethics is a primary consideration in the work of Duncan Macmillan and Nick Payne, as discussed in Chapter 4. This concerns, once more, relationships, one's place in the world, the private and social impact, or lack thereof, of our choices, as well as the ways in which individual lifestyles have direct bearing on others' quality of life, particularly on environmental terms. At the same time, as Chapter 4 argues, concerns of austerity and civic responsibility have had such influence on the emerging generation of playwrights that this is evident both in the content and structure of the texts. Chapter 5 takes on some of Martin Crimp's most formally ambitious work to date. As this section contends, obsessive self-isolation and the internalized treatment of oneself as a singular entity, predicated on asserting one's own importance while approaching every problem as entirely personal, unrelated to the social realm, is revealed in Crimp's recent theatre as the definitive human condition of our time. The consideration of how we embody and perform our environments, especially in the context of capitalism, mobility and identity, persists in Chapter 6, which focuses on the work of Simon Stephens. As this section shows, Stephens has produced his most experimental and affective theatre when attempting to locate the individual within society both by probing their self-imposed distance and by exploring to what extent the separation – a neoliberalist symptom leading to continuous malfunctions – might still be salvageable.

Chapter 7 continues with pursuing concerns of insularity and self-isolation in recent plays by debbie tucker green. This time these issues are visited as a product of trauma, of a state failing to protect the individual and of the accepted condition that the individual alone must confront any ailments, fend for themselves and, if they fail, then fail on the basis of own weaknesses. With a strong focus on mental health as well as on institutionalized political systems and their problematics, tucker green's theatre, like that of the other playwrights discussed in this book, makes a clear overture to the social sciences, as well as to science more specifically defined in terms of mental health and afflicted states. This is the primary focal point of Chapter 8, which concentrates on Lucy Prebble's work to begin with a consideration of megalomania and transition to an engagement with depression, showing both as states directly linked to capitalist prerogatives. The former, because it serves neoliberalist agenda-setting and entrepreneurial growth; the latter, because it is both a sign of the times, emerging from our troubled relationships to our societies, and a condition that becomes the product for mega-industry. Ultimately, this section argues, both mental states, however different they might appear, are equally ripe for monetization.

The entire book, then, argues that the different conditions of crisis depicted in these diverse plays are symptomatic of capitalist and particularly late-neoliberalist systemic failures as we have experienced them in the British context of the early twenty-first century. A further interconnecting thread relates to the way in which the work the book concentrates on criticizes the perception of crisis symptoms as individual, when they are, in fact, revealing a broader malaise, endemic in the system. In her still seminal study of the representation of mental ailments in Anglophone theatre, Christina Wald rightly identifies mental health, which recurs as both a theme in the plays themselves and a consideration for the critical field, as a property that is always and essentially social (2007: 2). As Wald proposes, 'the increasing employment of trauma as a cultural trope is concomitant with its rising importance in psychiatry and psychology' (2007: 2). Significantly, Wald adds that 'The cultural fascination with trauma is interlocked with the contemporary interest in melancholia' and traces its historical development as interlinked with 'the contemporary disorientation and indifference caused by the dissolution of grand narratives as a melancholic phenomenon' (2007: 3–4; Wald also references Ludger Heidbrink and René Derveaux).

It is understandable, then, why so many of the plays that this book deals with and that we have seen on our stages recently more broadly have invested deeply in capturing the often troubled mental states of their protagonists and the extent to which these are tropes of capitalism. As Kate Mattheys notes, 'Life under austerity is growing increasingly tough for the vast majority of people, and mental health is one of the casualties of this era' (2015: 475). At the same time, others argue that austerity as a concept equals anxiety, as 'an expression of fear, put in the form of a policy that seems unafraid, that developed society does not know what it is doing or why' (Appelbaum 2014: 93). It is fascinating that even the term 'austerity', associated in our time mostly with financial measures and modes of governance, originates in the domain of emotions. Linked, among other roots, to the Greek term αὐστηρότης [*afstirōtis*], it denotes sternness and exercising control over feeling, both one's own and that of others (*Oxford English Dictionary* 2016a). Although the concern is specifically highlighted in Chapter 4, it is worth noting that in different ways the work engaged with in this book offers its own response to austerity: from *staccato*, formally 'stern' plays where emotion bubbles under the surface, struggling to be contained as a way of demonstrating the futility of inflexible, externally imposed measures, to other modes of more overt resistance such as maximalist playwriting sprawling on stages while taking on the themes of austerity that claim to return us to neoliberalist well-being. This is the theatre's astute way of emphasizing that person and politics are always embedded in each other and the individual and social simply cannot be construed as binaries.

It is also not surprising that in most of the work examined in this book, cities, whether named or not, feature prominently, indispensable parts of the protagonists' mental, emotional and physical constitutions, becoming the *de facto* locale of crisis. This bears direct interrelation to the significance of urban centres to processes of austerity, as outlined, for example, by Jamie Peck:

> the nexus of deep neoliberalization and entrenched austerity is likely to be an especially challenging one for cities. [...T]he staple neoliberal maneuver of refracting crisis pressures back onto the state raises the prospect of self-discipline descending into auto-evisceration or incapacitation. The projection downward of these pressures establishes a socially regressive form of scalar politics—with cities positioned at the sharp end [... this is] an urbanization of neoliberal austerity (2012: 631)

Peck's future projection stems from the fact that the article focuses on the US context, building a hypothesis on the basis of the European austerity model as it developed post-recession. The surrounding mood of this impact is captured in the perceptions that the individuals depicted in the theatre that this book discusses have of their spaces, both private and public, as the locus of entrepreneurialism and enterprise, and also in these individuals' assertion of self-value as measure of worth. This book is concerned with the individuals inhabiting the space of crisis, attempting, awkwardly, to rediscover a sense of belonging. If it is true that, as Paul Crosthwaite argues, 'for its participants and spectators alike, the crash is not simply an object of fear or anxiety, or even of mere fascination, but also of an inchoate but urgent desire' (2010: 4), it becomes even more intriguing to ascertain the attitudes and morals we can gauge from plays such as those discussed here. It also becomes crucial to probe the theatre's need to take on the topic, the observations it produces, and the modes of engagement that it encourages in audiences.

This is a book about the theatre of our recent past and our present. It cannot be exhaustive, because theatre is a living force that evolves and adapts and does not shy away from confronting new crises as they emerge. I have, however, made the effort of concentrating on the work of playwrights who, through sustained engagement with specific topics of relevance to this book, have proven a long-term preoccupation with what it is that makes us social beings, what our challenges are in our specific political, financial and historical juncture and what the implications of these are for our identities. The following chapters, therefore, capture the need to account for the intricacies in the new forms, new topics and new combinations of the two in contemporary British theatre. They are motivated by the imperative of accounting for a transition that has occurred in our time, whereby playwriting that might once have been thought of as difficult, abstract or the Other to the British social-realist stage has proliferated in the distinctive work of a growing number of writers claiming central positions in repertoires and stages across the country, as well as, of course, in Europe, where this brand of unconventional British theatre has traditionally found supportive audiences. More than anything, the book is underpinned by the desire to show that the novel kinds of theatre produced by the fruitful collaboration of playwrights, directors and companies in the post-2000 period has provided us, as spectators and citizens, with a means and a space for locating our individual and collective concerns and reflecting on our future as communities and societies.

1

Too Much Information: Caryl Churchill and Millennial Angst

Caryl Churchill is one of the most accomplished contemporary playwrights and her work has been written about extensively. As Christine Dymkowski noted in an article written in the aftermath of *Far Away* (2000), with Churchill 'there is no playing safe, no return to familiar patterns, but constant reinvention' (2003: 55). She added that in Churchill's work intelligent, experimental and often comical writing co-exists with the political, without, however, imposing on spectators a message, or instruction (Dymkowski 2003: 55). Given that much of Churchill's early 2000s theatre has received substantial critical attention, this chapter will reference this important work but will primarily focus on Churchill's most recent plays and especially *Love and Information*, which opened at the Royal Court Theatre (RCT) in 2012.

In the fluid social and political twenty-first-century landscape Churchill has continued to produce compelling theatre, unique in its dramatic imagination, astuteness and dystopia. Her textscapes are elliptical, allowing space for spectatorial interpretation and critical initiative. This is even reflected in the playtexts, which appear sparse compared to prevailing publishing standards and more generously laid out, as though to signify to the reader/spectator that there is space for them to enter the text and engage with it critically (see also Lawson 2012). Churchill's playwriting never prescribes and never confines. Setting the tone for the analysis of Churchill's recent work that follows in this chapter, but also for the ensuing sections of this book, Zygmunt

Bauman's summation of the present critical, philosophical and social field is particularly helpful, meriting the long quote:

> The title of a paper given in December 1997 by one of the most perceptive social analysts of our times, Pierre Bourdieu, [...] told it all: precariousness – instability, vulnerability – is a widespread (as well as the most painfully felt) feature of contemporary life conditions. The French theorists speak of *précarité*, the German of *Unsicherheit* or *Risikogesellschaft*, the Italians of *incertezza* and the English of *insecurity*. [...T]he phenomenon they try to grasp is the combined experience of *insecurity* of position, entitlements and livelihood, of *uncertainty* as to their continuation and future stability, and of *lack of safety* of one's body, one's self and their extensions – possessions, neighbourhood, community. [...] Nowadays, precariousness is not a matter of choice; it is fate. (2001: 154; emphasis original; Bauman refers to Bourdieu's *La précarité est aujourd'hui partout*)

As this and the following sections set out to discuss, the vast crisis with which we are confronted and the continuous debate on our degree of agency are a guiding enquiry in the work of Churchill as well as in that of many of the most innovative and influential contemporary playwrights.

Far Away, Escaped Alone, A Number, Drunk Enough to Say I Love You?, Seven Jewish Children and *Ding Dong the Wicked*: Radical crises, new forms

As Elin Diamond suggests, 'what interests Caryl Churchill is the relatively large writ small – the indirect atmospherics of terror, the way it leaches into the psyches of ordinary citizens and ordinary lives. Ordinary lives are always dialectical for Churchill, individually marked yet ensnared, obscurely or directly, in political and historical force fields' (2009: 126). The minimalism in Churchill's later work, which became starker still from *Love and Information* onwards, far from implies ideological retreat. Churchill marked the new millennium with the play destined to become one of the most frequently cited dramatic texts of our time, exemplary of how new writing could do politics minus the social realism or the fixed historical attribution while remaining powerful and resonant: *Far Away* (2000, RCT Upstairs, director Stephen Daldry) makes a stand against political persecution, military violence, the exploitation of labour and the human cost of war in a rich palette of other topics. The play was pivotal for the representation of public and private, and the political and personal as non-binaries. It involves three characters: Harper, her niece, Joan and Joan's co-worker and later husband, Todd. As a child, Joan witnesses scenes of violence perpetrated by her uncle. When she recounts these to Harper, she is told that events did not unfold quite in the way Joan interpreted them. Some years later, adult Joan works as a hatmaker with Todd. The hats they create are meant to be worn by prisoners sentenced to death in their final procession. The play's most monumental scene is only signposted by Churchill with the following stage direction:

> *Next day. A procession of ragged, beaten, chained prisoners, each wearing a hat, on their way to execution. The finished hats are even more enormous and preposterous than in the previous scene* [at the factory, featuring Joan and Todd]. (2000: 30)

In the first pages of the playtext, Churchill comments on options for the scene:

> The Parade (Scene 2.5): five is too few and twenty better than ten. A hundred? (2000: 8)

This playfully defiant note was groundbreaking for new writing and politics. It follows that in Churchill's work as in that of other playwrights resistant to prescribing the visual world of their plays, several of whom this book is concerned with, stage directions became sharp and minimal, sometimes preposterous and always weary of realism. This challenged theatres to explore novel visual languages that would match the boldness of that spoken. The final scene of *Far Away*, for which action has once more leapt into the future, is no less iconic. The verbal matter deployed by characters is potent, bursting with images and signification and ranging from the paradoxical to the lyrical, as the three protagonists discuss the war raging outside. Joan's final monologue heightens the intensity of the piece as it nears its finale:

> **Joan** [...] There were thunderstorms all through the mountains, I went through towns I hadn't been before. [...] It was tiring because everything's been recruited, there were piles of bodies and if you stopped to find out there was one killed by coffee or one killed by pins, they were killed by heroin, petrol, chainsaws, hairspray, bleach, foxgloves, the smell of smoke was where we were burning the grass that wouldn't serve. [...] Who's going to mobilise darkness and silence? That's what I wondered in the night. (Churchill 2000: 43–44)

Writing about *Far Away*, Diamond argues that Churchill carries us 'through the looking glass that once reflected a recognizable, if crumbling, social structure [...to] enter a war of all against all with no sign of resistance or memory of an ethical alternative' (2009: 139). These concerns returned strongly in *Escaped Alone* (2016, RCT Downstairs, director James Macdonald), which we need to think about with reference to *Far Away*. As this chapter discusses, Churchill's playwriting in the 2000s and 2010s overbrims with political potency in the face of growing crisis (an idea for which the image of the bubbling tea spilling out of the teacup used for the promotion of *Escaped Alone* acted as imaginative metaphor). Of all this work, *Escaped Alone* most strongly emerges as a political act to match *Far Away*, without suggesting that the later play is derivative of the earlier one. *Escaped Alone* continues where *Far Away* left off, except the social and political landscape that it has inherited is one of such extensive confusion and uncertainty that the play both speaks to its dramatic antecedent and surpasses it in terms of dystopian extremity. As in *Far Away*, so in *Escaped Alone* the ordinary is interrupted by the apocalyptic. With the latter Churchill has delivered a response to the events that we have been witnessing and experiencing as local and global citizens, from the dominance of social media interactivity to the large-scale violent acts disrupting everyday life in ways unprecedented.

Escaped Alone deals with two worlds and two experiences: the ordinary and the extraordinary. The character linking the two is Mrs Jarrett (or Mrs J). In Miriam Buether's set she literally steps outside the frame of conspicuous normality to offer, with sombre recognition and pragmatism, grim tales of a world that is now past the threshold of destruction and at a new stage in its history. The frame itself is the average-looking garden of a house, where three women, Lena, Sally (whose backyard this is) and Vi, all seventy or older, as Churchill indicates (2016: 4), are having tea. The difference in the naming indicates the familiarity of the three women who are old friends, and Mrs Jarrett's status as the outsider in the group, but also in the play: the person who 'escaped alone' or lived to tell us the story of the apocalypse, narrated in the past tense and therefore suggesting that the events have already taken place. The play's title also suggests this time transition and is taken from the Book of Job with the line 'I only am escaped alone to tell thee' acting as the play's epigraph (2016: 3).

Still, Churchill does not mark time straightforwardly. There are two major disruptions to the interpretation of the time sequence: one is Mrs Jarrett's existence on both levels – the garden conversation and the metanarrative that forms as she delivers the news of the catastrophe to the audience in direct address; the other is the beginning and end of the play, which realistically depict Mrs Jarrett's self-narrated entrance and exit from the garden, implying that everything that unravels in the interim is an interlude. We are therefore left wondering whether Mrs Jarrett's final, anti-climactic line 'And then I said thanks for the tea and I went home' (Churchill 2016: 42) suggests that she steps back into the past, or that this is the present catching up. The latter would mean that Mrs Jarrett's accounts of the apocalypse belong to the past and therefore the women in the garden, fenced up in the beginning and ending of the play to indicate a disconnection from the outside world, have been oblivious to the crisis, ensconced, as they were, in their insularity. In that case, the play's title would indicate Mrs

Jarrett's status as the only one, the outsider to the group, to function as an individual and a citizen at the same time, stepping outside of her comfort and everyday habits of individuated neoliberalism to engage with the crumbling world around her. Churchill has specifically stated that the preoccupation with time is a consistent point of reference in her work (Churchill 1988: 4). In *Escaped Alone* she takes temporal fluidity to a new level by denying her audience any firm indicators of time transitions.

When Mrs Jarrett steps outside the frame, the stage is immersed in darkness and a rectangular frame resembling a live, burning cable is the only visual image, other than Mrs Jarrett recounting crisis while standing in close proximity to the audience. There is an almost, yet not quite 'normal' feeling of neo-absurdist verbal playfulness running through the women's conversation as events of their past are slowly revisited to reveal trauma and phobias that are still raw. Then, unexpectedly, each character enters a monologue, the duration of which is marked by a dimming of the lights – indicating perhaps a passing cloud over Buether's sunny garden. At the end of each monologue, normal lighting resumes. The monologues reveal each woman's melancholia at being bound to a situation that has defined them against their will: a phobia (Sally), an illness (Lena) or a violent past (Vi). And while it is tempting to suggest that Churchill makes the case against institutionalized transgressions affecting women and the chronic trauma they endure as a result, Mrs Jarrett's intervention once more disrupts expectations, adding yet more dimensions. Her own monologue is unlike the other characters', but also unlike anything we have seen on the contemporary stage. It revolves around only two words: 'terrible rage' (Churchill 2016: 42). As the words are repeated, gathering momentum, they become, beyond a confession, a political statement, an indictment, even a chant. As the outsider, Mrs Jarrett is not bound to the same intimate confessionals that the group of friends are accustomed to. The phrase 'terrible rage' is her succinct way of expressing her personal and social indignation without conforming to contemporary oversharing rituals.

The three women's extensive revelationary monologues focus on themselves, their histories and their experiences. However insightfully written by Churchill, and even though we may take them as paradigmatic, in one way or another, for the lives of more women, ultimately these sections are stories of individual lives, spoken singularly in decontextualized moments. Mrs Jarrett, however, does not engage in this. In a group of characters involved in their own personal narratives, she is the only sensitized citizen who imagines herself a participant and not a detached observer. Therefore, Mrs Jarrett does not indulge in the narrative of the self, but vocalizes the narrative of society. Her own extensive monologues (spoken to the audience) deal with the world outside the house, rather than with the private experience behind the fence. While we spend time rehearsing our individualisms, through the device of Mrs Jarrett, Churchill suggests that the crisis has caught up with us. It is important that the agency of women is highlighted, regardless of interpretation – and that their experience is shown as at the same time poetic and mundane, astute and withdrawn. In other words, all-encompassing in a society that has not yet worked through its ongoing gender bias crisis, let alone its ageism. For a play that was mostly met with critical acclaim, particularly in terms of its foregrounding of four older women's experience, it was Susannah Clapp's five-star review that offered the most nuances. From recognizing that the play 'is fantasy intricately wired into current politics. It is intimate and vast. Domestic and wild', Clapp also observed that 'The effect is revolutionary' (2016). In the fluid social context of 2016, Churchill's *Escaped Alone* offered knowing political commentary for audiences weary of realism, unambiguous messages and deceptive linearity claiming fidelity to the unpredictability of contemporary experience.

Having delivered stinging criticism of neoliberalism throughout her career, not least in plays such as *Top Girls* (1982) and *Serious Money* (1987), in the recent period Churchill also broached the issue from a science angle. *A Number* (2002, RCT Downstairs, director Stephen Daldry) features a minimal cast of two male actors. Without moralizing oversimplification, Churchill takes on human cloning, where the father figure is the fixed point of reference and the son figure fluctuates by taking the physical shape of one man, but the lives and identities of three. The Nuffield/Young Vic co-production (2014–2015, director Michael Longhurst) set the tone even before spectators entered the auditorium, as tickets were exchanged for numbers corresponding to each audience member. Once inside, Tom Scutt's design featured strategically placed mirrors and intelligent lighting (by Lee Curran) amplifying the performance terrain and creating a multitudinous effect for what was an otherwise sparsely decorated space providing an arena of spoken and physical action. When, between scene transitions, the lighting would change to turn the glass panel in front of us, behind which the stage was located, into a mirror, the audience were reflected unto ourselves, doubly feeling our presence as yet another body, or a mere number. Our suspicions that we were one of multiple audiences were confirmed when, at the end of the performance, the actors took bows in four different directions, acknowledging their different audiences.

A Number is significant because it probes whether we can ever be certain of our uniqueness, accomplishments and entitlements, but also because it was an early indication of how new writing would address some of the more delicate and ethically challenging aspects of science, fostering ambitious multidisciplinary intersections. Martina Donkers and Lindy A. Orthia arrive at an observation on *A Number* which rings true for many contemporary plays pursuing a scientific thread: 'It is not a pedagogic tool for increasing [...] scientific knowledge; rather it may prompt consideration of the ethical implications of technological advances. It exists primarily as part of the wider body of popular drama while also carrying the potential to engage audience members with [... specific] issues' (2014: 27). As this book shows through its engagement with theatre and science (including of course social science) as natural partners, the early symptoms as to how this partnership might work evolved into plays that became yet more laborious in their engagement with scientific fact at the same time that the popularity of such forms grew. As Donkers and Orthia note, the key benefit of such work is 'introduc[ing] new ways of thinking about [...scientific issues], putting science in a social and emotional context [...] prompting some people to state that they felt that they ought to form an opinion about it, and changing or reinforcing the opinions of others' (2014: 43). Heavy scientific fact may not be Churchill's brand, as her approach is driven by scientific knowledge instilled into the final result in ways that are defined by poetry and ambiguity rather than realism and data. This far from reduces the affective power of her writing as interventionist strategy.

In 2006, Churchill's *Drunk Enough to Say I Love You*? (RCT Downstairs, director James Macdonald) added to her critique of the binary between personal and political, or individual and society. Here, Jack and Sam are in a relationship, but things are more complex than that. Beyond the negotiation of their co-dependence, Jack and Sam's relationship explodes on the global spectrum of modern history, spanning events that have occurred, and that might occur, because of this very connection. No less minimalist than *Far Away* or *A Number*, the play signals a turn towards the more explicitly political in Churchill's recent writing. The change is understandable. *Far Away* premiered shortly before 9/11 and *A Number* shortly afterwards, both evidencing an osmosis of disorientating social context either in the sense of a looming crisis in the lead-up to the new millennium or of a radical uncertainty regarding our identity and place in the world. *Drunk Enough to Say I Love You*? was the resolute response to a protracted period of crisis leading to widespread dissent. After 9/11 the global community witnessed the War on Terror and the conflicts in Iraq and Afghanistan, extensive protesting against military action presented as inevitable, and controversy followed by discontent towards the political choices of the UK and US administrations, which were embroiled in what the term 'special relationship' succinctly described. It was a time when British theatres produced a great deal of verbatim texts and adaptations of classical repertoire in an attempt to stage war and rationalize the convoluted political experience. In what was a broadly challenging period, the theatre kept to its role as a profoundly social medium by opening avenues of communication and exchange.

Churchill's work did this quite literally: *Drunk Enough to Say I Love You?* consists of conversation and self-justification between Jack and Sam, including points of divergence, which, however, are inevitably bypassed as the two are interlocked in mutual commitment. It is, as was widely recognized at the time, a play about the 'special relationship' (Sam stands for 'Uncle Sam' and Jack for 'Union Jack'). The play takes the term at face value, exposing all it might stand for in the global political field, with references ranging from manipulating public opinion and covering up crimes to overthrowing governments and turning a blind eye to environmental catastrophe. In the interim, as part of the RCT's *A Royal Welcome* (2003), which coincided with George W. Bush's London visit, Churchill wrote *Iraq.doc*. The piece drew material from found discourse and synthesized it into a narrative featuring recent American politics and global strategy.

Yet more direct politics followed after *Drunk Enough to Say I Love You?* with *Seven Jewish Children* (2009, RCT Downstairs, director Dominic Cooke), a play made available via the RCT website and offered as response to the then recent violent developments in the Middle East. Admission was free of charge, with the theatre stating that funds would be collected post-performance in support of Medical Aid for Palestinians (MAP): Emergency Appeal for the People of Gaza (The Royal Court Theatre Presents Seven Jewish Children 2009). A recorded reading of the short play (slightly under ten minutes) was published on *The Guardian* online. 'Angry? Sad? Confused? Come and spend ten minutes with us' read the RCT's invitation (The Royal Court Theatre Presents Seven Jewish Children 2009), enhancing feelings of community at a time of crisis. *Seven Jewish Children*, running at the RCT for less than ten days in February 2009 and subtitled 'a play for Gaza' (The Royal Court Theatre Presents Seven Jewish Children 2009), was performed following Marius von Mayenburg's *The Stone*. The combination challenged the assumption that the RCT was being historically selective, as *The Stone* examined

Germany's complex relationship to its own past and, specifically, to the persecution of Jewish populations. Like *The Stone*, *Seven Jewish Children* was about family narratives, passed on between generations and adopted. In Churchill's case the family fluctuates, as one historical period fades seamlessly into the next. Still, the crux of the story, however filtered through the lens of each present time, remains essentially unaltered.

The RCT was praised for its swift response to crisis, but the play attracted admiration (see Billington 2009; Brown 2009; Gardner 2009) and criticism (see overview in Higgins 2009) in equal measure. Churchill explained that the writing was completed urgently, driven by "'feeling strongly about what's happening in Gaza – it's a way of helping the people there. Everyone knows about Gaza, everyone is upset about it, and this play is something they could come to. It's a political event, not just a theatre event'" (Brown 2009). Dominic Cooke, who at that time ran the RCT, echoed the sentiment, emphasizing the importance of moving from writing to staging swiftly so as to capture the need for dialogue and action (Brown 2009). Such was the reaction to the play that Churchill, renowned for allowing her work to speak for itself and abstaining from interviews, became compelled to produce a response: in a letter she repeated the importance that judging for oneself holds in the theatre (The Guardian 2011). As Rachel Clements notes, 'the key points of difference related to questions around the play's political and ideological balance – or lack of it – and to the question of the possibilities offered by contemporary subsidised theatre when responding to complex current events' (2013a: 359). In his otherwise reserved review, Dominic Cavendish arrived at an astute observation. The play, he noted, 'presents [...] criticism as self-criticism, as a collective internal dialogue that wrestles with the need for honesty versus the value of propagandising deception' (Cavendish 2009). Churchill's piece, however impassioned and clear on its own politics, which were, in any case, unambiguously underlined by the fundraising appeal, contains more complex layers than its deceptive simplicity might at first suggest. There is tenderness, but also steadfastness;

empathy, but also cruelty. Ultimately, the play intelligently shows that antithetical views might be harboured by one and the same person, and/or nation. All the while, the sensitivity of Churchill's writing to these tensions is unambiguous.

A short play at approximately thirty minutes, whose run partially coincided with that of *Love and Information*, *Ding Dong the Wicked* (2012, RCT Downstairs, director Dominic Cooke), is arranged into two scenes whose thematic overlap, set sharing, equally eccentric characters and role doubling render it difficult to speak of two strictly self-contained segments. The conflicts and tensions between characters transpiring in a relatively bare set depicting two living rooms (with the only change consisting of rearranging the furniture) (Churchill 2012a: 15), as well as the violence, both hinted and perpetrated, in the context of a major political development at a time of war (an important figure who remains anonymous has been killed) rendered the play confusing and dense. It created the impression of lives converging in the moment of a crisis both social and personal. The fussiness in the characters' conversations, their comical names ('A Woman Who Bites'; 'A Man Who Bites His Nails' etc.) (Churchill 2012a: 2) as well as the speed of dialogue and action infused the play with a farcical effect. Like Churchill's most recent work, this play, too, disturbed through its ellipses, deliberate in its withholding of answers and playful in its finale which seemed to imply its beginning (the play starts with a man inviting another person to enter, before shooting them; it ends with a man opening the door to a visitor). Through this tantalizing enigma, Churchill weaves a metaphor for how political developments performed on a global stage have the capacity to trigger chain reactions, but also for how violence only generates more violence.

The sense of disorientation that the play exudes also emanates from the television receiver: characters can see the screen; we can neither see nor hear it, but we understand that its presence in the room is meaningful from the characters' reactions. In both scenes, which take place in different countries, private dramas are played against political ones, and the play criticizes the interchangeability of people and places, with human casualties presented as merely par for the course. Some critics argued that Churchill depicts the similarities of two countries at war with each other (see Spencer 2012a). However, the exuberant reactions in both living rooms at the news of the unnamed political figure's death suggest it is more likely that both countries were locked in an ally arrangement, small, coerced players in the global field whose oppressor has just been eliminated. Overall, the rapid transitions in dialogue which did not allow the audience sufficient thinking and interpreting space challenged our ability to maintain focus quite intentionally. It was a technique that Churchill honed at the time, predominantly with the play on which this chapter goes on to concentrate: *Love and Information*.

Love and Information: Crisis and crises

Love and Information covers a remarkably broad spectrum, expressing the convoluted, hazing reality of our times. Its fast pace, especially as captured in James Macdonald's RCT Downstairs production, directly reflected the swift turnaround of people, feelings and situations. As Mark Lawson notes, the form of the play posed a considerable challenge, as traditional rehearsal and casting processes did not apply and so Macdonald proceeded with a workshop method, selecting sixteen actors who would share the plethora of parts (2015). Andrew Billen's review observed that the only common element for the play's numerous anonymous characters is 'an atomised hell of inconsequent information' (2012). There is indeed a strong undercurrent of fragmented, atomized lives running through the play; but the information is far from inconsequent. It is merely the case that we are not given the security of peering inside; we must fill the gaps of that which we do not see and the affect is disquieting. As Diamond notes, the play 'takes the emotional temperature of information overload and asks how we live and love among the sound bites' (2014: 463).

In one of her now rare interviews, Churchill offers insights as to her experimentation with different means of communication, discussing being 'fascinated by ways of doing things without words' (Churchill 1988: 4). There is a multitude of words in *Love and Information*, but there are also non-verbal narratives and poignant silences. But even where there are words, Churchill continues her exploration of how much can be achieved in the absence of telling and of verbal information. No sooner are we introduced to a given context and set of speakers than the play moves on, creating the impression that the narrative continues in our absence and leaving us with the lingering affect of words that need to be processed.

Overall, *Love and Information* consists of seven sections, which Churchill indicates in her opening direction must be played in the order given. Each section contains a number of short scenes of varying length, which Churchill specifies can be staged in any order within the respective section (Churchill 2012b: 2). In his recent study of Churchill's theatre, R. Darren Gobert provided a table with a breakdown of cast members appearing in each scene of the play, as well as the scene order in Macdonald's production (2014: 193–194). There is a final section titled 'RANDOM', which includes a small number of extremely short scenes, marked as 'OPTIONAL' (Churchill 2012b: 75). Most involve minimal text. In three cases ('PAINTING', 'COLD', 'SILENCE'), the last of which is indicated as potentially recurring, there is no text, but only a stage direction describing the action (Churchill 2012b: 75, 77). As Churchill notes, if performed, the 'RANDOM' scenes can occur at any point (Churchill 2012b: 74). There is, however, one segment in the 'RANDOM' section titled 'DEPRESSION', which Churchill calls '*an essential part of the play*' (2012b: 74). 'DEPRESSION' consists of ten different lines to be delivered independently in different moments (Churchill 2012b: 2, 74). Even though as a general rule characters in each of the numerous scenes must be distinct (which is not a stipulation affecting cast numbers) (Churchill 2012b: 2), 'DEPRESSION' is the one case where Churchill indicates it is possible (though not essential) to have the same silent character recur (Churchill 2012b: 74). There is also the option whereby each of the 'DEPRESSION' super-micro narratives involves entirely different characters altogether.

Other than 'RANDOM' the sections of the play are numbered rather than titled. Within these sections, each short scene carries an epigrammatic title, consisting mostly of a single word. Stage directions are sparse. Even where the text is clearly a conversation involving two or more speakers, there is no indicator as to names, or line distribution. The only cases where Churchill provides stage directions are 'RECLUSE' and 'THE CHILD WHO DIDN'T KNOW FEAR' in Section 3, and 'WEDDING VIDEO' and 'PIANO' in Section 4. In the context of a play that features fifty scenes (seven in each section, except for Section 7, which features eight, in addition to 'RANDOM' and its fourteen scenes, including a further six, listed in the 'OPTIONAL' section only as titles and lacking any text/content), the absence of direction is striking. A formal intervention in itself, this absence invites director and company to decide how best to handle the staging challenge.

Richard Sennett's discussion of crisis in *The Fall of Public Man* (2003 [1977]) provides an analytical framework for present challenges and obstacles in everyday personal and civic experience by tracing historical patterns and their contextualization. *Love and Information*, meanwhile, by exposing the awkwardness in the constant shift between private and public realms, the confusion that arises from it and the lack of time to absorb the different contexts, stands as theatrical paradigm for the complications in the individual's attempt to impose private norms to public life as Sennett also explores these (2003: 1–27). Sennett's proposition that public life must not be expected to follow the habits of private experience as it operates on different terms may be seen to produce binarism (2003: 1–27). But what is entirely accurate about this observation is that we must appreciate our roles and responsibilities outside our private lives without attempting to see the public world as an extension of these. Only then can we do justice to both domains, understanding our own duality, rather than attempting to assimilate one into the other. It follows from Sennett's discourse that appreciating the intricate balance between private and public places us at a stronger position for becoming responsible, active citizens. *Love and Information*, concerned with communication and the volume of data we collect, retrieve and process, is by default concerned with (self-)expression. The process of information exchange, however, is far from straightforward, and can be uncomfortable, prone to interruptions and interjections, as the play also demonstrates. Sennett is equally invested in disambiguating the intricacies. As he notes, to propose that there is 'an emptiness of expression' does not suffice (Sennett 2003: 6); we need to pursue its meaning and causes.

Love and Information shows that our crisis of self-perception and locating ourselves as individuals and members of our society, but also the crisis in effective, substantive communication is symptomatic of our awkward negotiation of private and public domains. The malaises that the play delves into, including dissatisfaction and betrayal, as well as the mentally and physically vulnerable and afflicted body, serve as metaphor for the ongoing discomfort in attempting to reconcile different roles in different contexts and streamline these into one uniform type of behaviour. What the episodic structure of *Love and Information* reveals is that there is no such thing as linear experience. As its title also betrays, the ultimate commitment that this play makes is to the examined life. But it is crucial to remember that there is another part to Churchill's title. The play shows that love and related concepts of compassion or empathy are precarious in our time: the more the individual retreats unto themselves, including social media which serve at once as agents of virtual communication and physical self-exclusion, the more love becomes a vague concept. Even when not tenuous, love becomes a matter of consumption and ownership, another trope of the growing dependency on virtual fact sharing (versus sharing in the sense of lived contact and community, further terms that have been usurped by the social media lexicon). Sennett notes:

> The public problem of contemporary society is two-fold: behavior and issues which are impersonal do not arouse much passion; the behavior and the issues begin to arouse passion when people treat

them, falsely, as though they were matters of personality. But because this two-fold public problem exists, it creates a problem within private life. The world of intimate feeling loses any boundaries; it is no longer restrained by a public world in which people make alternative and countervailing investment of themselves. The erosion of a strong life therefore deforms the intimate relations which seize people's wholehearted interest. No more graphic instance of this deformation has occurred in the last four generations than in the most intimate of personal experiences, physical love. (2003: 6–7)

Individualism and withdrawal into the self, which *Love and Information* emphasizes, are issues that Sennett returns to. He strikes a fascinating analogy when he transitions from the saturation of love in capitalist society to how intimacy, awkward attempts at which we are given throughout *Love and Information*, is yet another term appropriated by capitalism. Intimacy, that is, becomes a performance played out on the terms of market exchange, where individuals merely offer up a construct of themselves for consumption (Sennett 2003: 10). The swiftly changing interactions and relationships that Churchill's play depicts are entirely in line with Sennett's proposition as to the value and duration of relationships:

If people are close to each other to the extent that they know about each other, then interpersonal knowledge becomes a matter of reciprocal revelation. When two people are out of revelations, and the market exchange has come to an end, all too often the relationship comes to an end. [...] Boredom is the logical consequence of intimacy as an exchange relationship.
[...]
There is a never-ending search for gratification, and at the same time the self cannot permit gratification to occur. (2003: 10)

The effect of 'exhaustion' (Sennett 2003: 10) that this process produces is what *Love and Information* criticizes through the short attention spans that its form alludes to, in the theatre and in life more broadly. The play's argument is nuanced: it suggests not only that exhaustion arises from multiple, constant, fragmented exchanges, but also that it is the exhaustion we have sustained from the rhythms and expectations of a ruthless capitalist system that is the very cause of these fragments.

Love and Information: Politics

It could be argued that *Love and Information* is political in its entirety because of its wide-ranging engagement with humanity and society. Here, however, I am concerned with specific issues that the play raises, most directly captured in 'CENSUS' and 'TORTURE' (Section 1), 'MESSAGE' and 'GRASS' (Section 2), 'SPIES' (Section 3) and 'CENSOR' (Section 6). 'CENSUS' seems innocuous enough, concerning the routine governmental logging of human lives. The scene begins with a questioning of the purpose of a census, but the tone soon grows darker, shifting towards surveillance. Someone has defied the rules and their interlocutor warns them to expect consequences. When the first person argues 'They [the authorities] won't know' about their refusal to conform to the exercise, the other speaker retorts 'They know you exist' (Churchill 2012b: 6). The topic of the individual as mere statistic liable to legal repercussions for any act of civil disobedience emerges as a concern before the segment abruptly closes. It is later resumed, with different characters and a different storyline, in 'GRASS', which is substantially longer. Here, the conversation is more intimate, involving a couple with a family. Whereas 'CENSUS' depicts the impulse to withhold information from a system cataloguing everything, 'GRASS' deals with the spontaneous disclosure of information. If, in 'CENSUS', someone attempts to escape surveillance to maintain what they perceive as civic freedom, in 'GRASS' someone else performs what they consider to be their civic duty by participating in the state's mechanisms of surveillance. One of the speakers has informed the police as to the actions (unspecified) of a person of interest, attempting to remain anonymous by using a public phone away from any location that could easily be traced back to them. Ironically, when they reveal their actions to their interlocutor, the issue of surveillance returns – this time as a threat for the person who has volunteered information to the government. The informer's partner is not convinced that anonymity is tenable and becomes frightened. As the conversation progresses, it reveals our internalizing of profiling practices and mechanisms of surveillance translated in a state of vulnerability and fear. The two speakers consider the potential consequences of the disclosure for their lives, especially in terms of the freedom they might have to sacrifice.

From politics at the level of the individual entangled in the broader operation of a government machine, Churchill moves to how aspects of politics and military action, typical identifiers of widespread crisis, operate at the level of the individual before they become large-scale and uncontainable. War and conflict recur as points of reference, revisited from different perspectives. In the very short 'CENSOR' one person is asked to redact a document as per guidelines from 'the Ministry of Defence [that] considers it a breach of security' (Churchill 2012b: 55). It is clear that there is a difference of opinion between the two speakers as to what constitutes sensitive information; it is also evident from the extensive number of redactions that one speaker requests that there is room for neither negotiation nor flexibility. Earlier in the play, Churchill has already homed in on security, intelligence and the War on Terror quite directly. 'SPIES' focuses on the justification of the War on Terror as two speakers debate the rationale and plausibility of the action taken on the basis of the information available to British and American politicians at the time. The disagreement, which ends inconclusively when one speaker asks the other: 'Do you think you've just won an argument?' (Churchill 2012b: 25) reveals the extent to which society has wavered over the military action of the early 2000s that was presented as inevitable, with questions lingering long after the event in what became one of the most controversial political turning points in recent history.

'TORTURE' and 'MESSAGE', which are flipsides of each other, capture yet darker aspects of the War on Terror. In 'MESSAGE' at least two interlocutors debate what, if any, ideology is embedded in an act that, though again not named specifically, is clearly a reference to suicide bombing. In this moment, Churchill's text implies that the conversation involves at least one (but likely more) individual in a social group susceptible to adopting extremist practices (as a means of delivering the message that the title of the scene alludes to). This is one of the shortest scenes in the play, but also one of the most impactful for the actions it implies and the social division it captures along with the kind of ignorance and frightening oversimplification that escalates violence. 'TORTURE' has preceded it: it depicts the moment when one interrogator, who is clearly using violence as a method for extracting information, takes a break for a brief conversation with a person whom we assume to be another interrogator. In addition to the obvious moral reprehensibility of the methods used in inducing a confession, the scene brings another layer to the ethical condemnation of the process by exposing the interrogators' utter lack of humanity or principles, but also the far from guaranteed effectiveness of their extreme methods:

> He'll get to where he'll say anything.
> We're not paid extra for it to be true. (Churchill 2012b: 9)

Love and Information: Science, faith, universe

The preoccupation with science, as well as with a range of sub-topics stemming from it, recurs, evidencing the play's concern with our place in the world, as well as with points of humanity's interconnection, division and future. In Section 1 there is 'LAB'; in Section 2, 'IRRATIONAL'; in Section 3, 'GOD'S VOICE' and 'STAR'; in Section 4, 'SAVANT' and 'MEMORY HOUSE'; in Section 5, 'MATHS', 'SEX' and 'GOD'; in Section 6 'CLIMATE'; in Section 7 'FATE', 'VIRTUAL' and 'SMALL THING'. 'LAB', one of the most protracted scenes, involves a conversation between a scientist and a layperson concerning the method and value of experiments carried out on animals in order to determine brain and mental processing functions. As the scientist's description grows graphic, it becomes apparent that what scientist and layperson consider to be the accepted standard in lab research are two different propositions. Where the scientist is confident, the layperson is apprehensive. 'LAB' could make its point more economically, but its comparatively expansive length adds to visualization and our spectatorial discomfort at the procedures we hear described. The question that 'LAB' poses relates to the benefits versus the ethics of medical research. Among other things it is implied that the study focuses on memory and as yet incurable mental afflictions, therefore its essential nature becomes an effective device towards the rigorous interrogation of the limits of science. 'IRRATIONAL', much shorter than 'LAB', pursues a similar problematic, also concerned with the scientist's role and responsibilities. Despite its brevity it manages to delve into the scientist's precariousness through a combination of parable and reality (this is a recurring device, most notably in the three 'THE CHILD WHO [...]' scenes; 'THE CHILD WHO DIDN'T KNOW FEAR', Section 3, 'THE CHILD WHO DIDN'T KNOW SORRY' and 'THE CHILD WHO DIDN'T KNOW PAIN' both Section 6). Once more, we are dealing with the ethics of science, this time coming up against the question of when, or whether, specific discoveries must be publicized for fear of escalating crisis. One speaker observes: 'There was someone called Hippasus in Greek times who found out about the diagonal of a square and they drowned him because no one wanted to know about things like that' (Churchill 2012b: 16). When another speaker replies 'Maybe he should have kept quiet about it if he knew they couldn't stand it' (Churchill 2012b: 16), another person asks, at once closing the scene and revealing the status of at least one person in the scene as a scientist concerned with the outcomes of their own research: 'Is that what you do?' (Churchill 2012b: 16).

In other parts of the play, the foray into science takes an existential turn with speakers contemplating the nature of life. The length of the scenes within this cluster fluctuates significantly, and some of the segments we encounter here are amongst the shortest in the play. Scenes like these render Churchill's remarkable economy in capturing vastness of field and range of enquiry evident. In segments such as 'STAR' we experience some of the play's more life-affirming and poetic moments, open to the positive prospects of an unknown future universe, where the individual finds themselves fascinated by the unknowability rather than debilitated by it. Speakers discuss the trajectory of light across space and time, aware of their own transience, rootedness and also significance in the present moment as agents in the planet's narrative. 'SEX', which also runs for very few lines only, provides Churchill with the opportunity to expand on these concerns while creating a frame for the title of her play. A text so evidently concerned with human life from source to climax and the manifold stages in between, now returns to the moment of conception. The relationship between love and information is set up as confluence, a non-binary that serves procreation and biology:

> What sex evolved to do is get information from two sets of genes so
> so you get offspring that's not identical to you.
> […] Information and also love.
> If you're lucky. (Churchill 2012b: 49)

But Churchill's text maintains its sceptical tone; as one speaker notes, the link between love and information is not necessarily as straightforward as the other speaker imagines it to be. As the play suggests, despite best intentions, emotions are always at risk, never directly measurable qualities.

In the published script 'SEX' is immediately followed by the slightly lengthier 'GOD'. The antithesis that this order establishes, if maintained in performance, is significant. From the attempt at an explanation of life that combines feelings and biology, the play soon moves to one based purely on faith. But as with many other moments in Churchill's play, this scene, too, follows a thesis–antithesis model. Where one speaker proclaims their unyielding belief in a God that provides life with purpose, their interlocutor persistently probes the hypothesis. The mostly humorous tone of the scene, which closes as the atheist challenges their interlocutor to the point of leaving them exasperated, succeeds in making the point that conversation is always, to an extent, tentative and riddled with miscommunications. 'GOD' constitutes the play's subtle recognition of religion as a major source of contention, providing a metonymical reference for how disagreement and misunderstanding might escalate into crisis. In 'SEX' as well as in 'GOD' (at least two) speakers confidently make their case as to the purpose and meaning of life; that they are countered so readily by their interlocutors is evidence of the vast rifts in what different social groups consider self-evident. Then, further into the play, comes 'SMALL THING', the penultimate scene of Section 7, assuming textual order is retained. As the play draws to a close, the fast-paced dialogue of pithy remarks that has characterized most of the action is momentarily suspended for a scene that slows down our experience. 'SMALL THING' brings, once more, a consideration of life and of the position of the infinitesimal within the vast and universal. This time the conversation remains inconclusive and open to foregrounding the importance of life, as opposed to any concrete demystification of it. Reminiscent of Thom Gunn, this text revolves around one person's observation of a snail. As the text makes clear, the person has spent some time gazing at the same snail, without any particular intention. Rather, the person is, as they say, 'just looking at it' (Churchill 2012b: 69), in an act of due diligence to a seemingly disposable, proportionately insignificant, form of life. The point that the play, which has so far discussed several forms of personal and political crises, makes, of course, is that every life is valuable, and rightly commands attention. Even though 'GOD' is the more succinct and ultimately effective of the two in making this point, Churchill has already visited the question of religion earlier in the play, in 'GOD'S VOICE'. The conversation here involves one person justifying to their interlocutor an action they took as a result of the so-interpreted word of God. It is never suggested that this was an act of violence, although the absence of explanation leaves possibilities open. More than anything, however, what this scene emphasizes is the individual's need for faith and intervention transcending human knowledge and uncertainty. Faith, on this occasion, is presented as antidote to personal crisis. The play generally captures the individual's need to search beyond themselves and the physical world for alternatives, not only in determining their course of action, but also in finding hope. If it is not faith that provides the answer, then it will be science – and vice versa.

'VIRTUAL' represents the allure of science, which commands its own kind of faith. It is not only religion but also technology that can create acolytes, Churchill's play suggests; and exactly like fanaticism with the former, so the latter has the potential to separate individuals from their social whole, disorientating and alienating them from lived reality. 'VIRTUAL' documents the ability of the intangible to incite real emotions, in a way similar to 'GOD' or 'GOD'S VOICE'. The lines of criticism debating faith in these segments are comparable: they constitute an attempt to establish a binary between the human, or social milieu and the distant element that one person in each of these scenes is in thrall to. It is, ultimately, a process of combating love with information, exposing the lack of it and therefore the – in the speaker's view – untenable hypothesis as to the existence of God or of the virtual female that the title of 'VIRTUAL' alludes to, as the object of one speaker's affection. What the questioning speakers fail to understand, however, and what the play intelligently alludes to, is that blind devotion of any kind to that which we cannot ascertain experientially is not a cause, but a symptom. What catalyses the symptom is a crisis in humanity and society: an utter absence of certainty, confidence and community installed by a neoliberalist system that operates at the level of the individual and has, therefore, driven wedges between the person and their community, rendering them disenfranchised. Faith and science, or love and information, the play implies, may well be solutions contrived to deal with this very lack.

Finally, a cluster of scenes deals with millennial uncertainty in a world where we are constantly attacked by more information as to impending crises, further aggravating feelings of transience and inadequacy. The play suggests that these feelings manifest themselves in two main ways: as a wave of panic, or as an attempt to assert control over more than what might be considered humanly possible. As is the case with other scenes discussed above, 'SAVANT' and 'MEMORY HOUSE' can be construed as mirror images of each other, but with a different angle into the main enquiry, which is the ability to retain information as a form of power. 'SAVANT' depicts one individual's ability to remember infinite facts. The probing of the relationship between science and nature and the individual's place within it continues in 'MEMORY HOUSE', which runs atypically long and deals with one person's efforts to train their brain into storing data more effectively. The scene reveals that there is no immediate need to do this; no indication of reduced capacity. As the segment progresses, the tediousness of the exercise becomes apparent, allowing the play to make an ironic comment against the phobia of forgetting as a symptom of mental illness. In Churchill's order of scenes the irony is even more strongly felt because 'MEMORY HOUSE' is followed by the very short 'DINNER', which essentially consists of an apology over forgotten dinner plans.

The position of the singular human unit within, or even against the infinite, is also visited in the play in the context of how we fit in and impact on the cosmos, how our world might continue when we cease or how we might cease as a consequence of our environment no longer coping under pressure. *Love and Information* is intelligent in its depiction of everyday challenges, but ultimately it poses the bigger question of how significant all our conversations are if we fail in our awareness of and preventative behaviour towards environmental crisis. Even the prospect of multiverses is playfully – and briefly – engaged with in 'MATHS'. At a later part in the play, however, the mood changes: in 'CLIMATE', one person attempts to express that existence is tentative and the future uncertain. The tone of the scene captures the stark warnings and sense of imminent foreboding that conversations around the state of the environment and climate change have instigated. The short segment aptly demonstrates the disempowerment and paralysis that individuals experience towards action, riddled by uncertainty as to whether – and how – they can make a difference:

> I'm frightened for the children.
> [...]
> no, I think you're right, most scientists all agree it's a catastrophe.
> [...]
> Are you really not going to take it seriously?
> I don't know how to. (Churchill 2012b: 54)

Finally, in the play's last section we encounter 'FATE'. The scene delves into the issue from a different angle, not necessarily providing a scientific *exegesis*, but illuminating the overarching feeling of being a spectator of one's own life with no real means of intervention. One of the interlocutors believes that however problematic the hypothesis is, we must accept it; the other is profoundly uncomfortable with fatalistic logic. Ultimately, the dilemma concerns short-term versus long-term approaches and ideologies. The fatalistic viewpoint is in tandem with the neoliberalist perspective of prioritizing personal well-being with no sense of commitment to the future of a society; therefore, there is no point in attempting to change our attitudes, as we are conditioned and moulded in a certain way:

> I'm just saying you've got no choice
> [...]
> I have got a choice
> you've got a choice but you've no choice about what that choice is,
> [...]
> you do because of what you're like, [...] means that you're going to want what you want, because there's your genes and everything that's happened to you and everything else that's happening and all that stuff makes your brain be like that (Churchill 2012b: 64)

It is interesting that in the specific scene this attitude is intermeshed with the cultural materialist perspective that our environment will inevitably condition us and therefore our choices are effectively predetermined. Free will, it is suggested here, is not merely a concept

fraught with different interpretations, but one that is also highly
political.

Love and Information: Health

The debilitating effects of relinquishing control over one's life feature
extensively, not least in the recurring 'DEPRESSION' one-liners.
Concerns with health and coping mechanisms more broadly are crucial
throughout the play, especially in 'SLEEP' (Section 1), 'TERMINAL'
(Section 2), 'SCHIZOPHRENIC' (Section 3), 'FLASHBACK' (Section 4),
'CHILDREN', 'RASH' and 'SHRINK' (Section 5), 'WIFE' and
'EARTHQUAKE' (Section 6), 'MANIC' and 'GRIEF' (Section 7).
'TERMINAL' and 'CHILDREN' are in the minority as they deal with
directly physical health issues, whereas the remaining scenes are
concerned with mental health, including psychosomatic symptoms.
As its title betrays, the very brief 'TERMINAL', whose own duration nods
to fleeting lives and diminishing time, deals with a person who has just
received a terminal prognosis and attempts to establish how much time
they have left. 'CHILDREN' is relatively light-hearted, though it reveals
the main speaker's disappointment over a marriage that failed, likely on
account of the fact that he was infertile. 'RASH' depicts two speakers'
reaction to a skin irritation; they are the parents of a baby and their
comments exemplify both the over-protective tendencies that a culture
of fear towards unspecified disease and threatened crisis encourages,
and the body's vulnerability on exposure to external conditions. The
scene is equally literal and metaphorical in pointing to our varying
levels of discomfort, which are sometimes, but not always, manifested
physically.

The symptoms the play delves into range from the relatively
worrisome to the deeply serious, as Churchill considers the different
disorders that come to bear upon the individual, sometimes directly
linked to their uncertainty in a world in flux. In other cases the play
represents the apprehension towards mental health crisis accompanied

by ineffectuality of treatment. When one speaker in 'SLEEP', who appears to be a chronic insomniac, concedes that they cannot sleep and that none of the traditional solutions work because their 'head's too full of stuff', they attempt to entertain their condition by giving up and logging onto Facebook (Churchill 2012b: 12). It is telling that the automatic response to the inability to process information in a way that might allow the brain to relax is to expose it to yet more information. Churchill's play captures the instinctive turn to technology as medium of distraction, even though it is itself guilty of data overload, and, consequently, of creating additional pressure to process, understand and accept.

Whereas 'SLEEP' is concerned with the inability to contend with the day-to-day, the remaining scenes focus on more severe afflictions and repressed trauma. Such is the case in 'FLASHBACK', where, even though Churchill's laconic style divulges only the bare essentials, it is strongly implied that we are dealing with a PTSD sufferer. If we follow this interpretation, Churchill's play produces a powerful moment of anti-war commentary without any specific reference. We could take the scene to connote past abuse more broadly, of course – but the afflicted speaker's reference to what they know, and what has been embedded in their memory, does not particularly invite this reading. 'SHRINK', on the other hand, points precisely to that direction, when one person explains to another the benefits that psychoanalysis has had for them in terms of acknowledging and moving past the trauma that the transgressions of others have caused. The finale of the scene, where the patient's interlocutor challenges them as to their faith in therapy as panacea, allows Churchill to imply the indulgencies and insufficiencies of therapy culture.

Other scenes, like 'SCHIZOPHRENIC', 'EARTHQUAKE' and 'MANIC', delve into even darker aspects of trauma, depicting patients at different stages of afflictions that are certainly ongoing, and, indeed, critical. 'SCHIZOPHRENIC' deals with an individual in the grip of psychosis. In this scene the information theme of the play is construed as the warped version of reality that the afflicted person believes is being communicated to them by inanimate objects. Having questioned therapy culture, Churchill now also takes on pharmaceuticals, exposing the clashing perspectives of patient and the interlocutor who is presented as mentally healthy (it is left ambiguous whether they are a doctor, but that is certainly a possibility). For the patient, medication clouds their judgement; for their interlocutor, it is essential for the patient to maintain any kind of contact with reality. As the scene concludes, the crisis remains unresolved. This is also the case in 'MANIC', where one person reacts to minute details (the colour of a flower) with torrential, free-association speech. Even though it is never mentioned specifically, it is clear that the main speaker in this scene suffers from a form of imbalance, and it is possible that the unnatural verbal release we are witnessing is a chemical reaction, a side effect of their treatment. Certainly the scene's title implies such an interpretation. If drugs, or abstinence from these, are the triggers in 'SCHIZOPHRENIC' and 'MANIC' respectively, in 'EARTHQUAKE' we are dealing with an individual at the grip of phobia after having witnessed – remotely, on television – an earthquake that they have found disturbing. The scene visits the fine line between empathy and fear as well as grief culture, where the individual who observes feels compelled to share in the narrative of crisis, perceiving their own self as more vulnerable than they might objectively be. In itself, this is a broader symptom of the sense of exposure to an imminent catastrophe emerging from social instability and political uncertainty. The scene also presents mediated empathy as moral obligation, expressing lack of empathy as ethically reprehensible. This is achieved through the disagreement between the speakers, where one openly confesses to their devastation and emotional reaction, whereas the other concentrates on the sensationalist impact of the event's scale:

> Have you seen the earthquake? There's this building my god you think things are solid but they just break.
> Yes, I've seen it.
> [...]

But you don't care.
I can't say I feel it, no. You really feel it?
I cried. Of course I feel it. I cried. (Churchill 2012b: 60)

But it is not only mediated grief that *Love and Information*
considers. In 'WIFE' and 'GRIEF', the play delves into coping
mechanisms for individuals faced with loss. In 'WIFE', loss does not
mean death, but it does mean an undisclosed mental ailment leading
to partial disassociation and amnesia – potentially an extreme form of
depression – that prevents a husband from identifying and engaging
with his wife, treating her with hostility. Therefore, she is left to process
feelings of grief with no possibility of release or closure. It is different
in 'GRIEF' where a person's sense of self is compromised due to their
partner's death. In this case we are dealing with a loss that is finite and
terminal, though not on the same terms as the mental withdrawal in
'WIFE'. Loss, Churchill shows, can also produce numbness:

I've never had someone die.
I'm sorry, I've nothing to say. Nothing seems very interesting.
He must have meant everything to you.
Maybe. We'll see. (Churchill 2012b: 63)

It is significant that Churchill's take on grief is neither one-sided
nor simplistic: she both acknowledges its all-consuming power and
questions the extent to which it constitutes a selfish validation process.
All the while, and often with humour, she probes what courage in a
crisis means, and how we might ever confidently anticipate it.

Afterthought/Afterlife: *Here We Go*

Here We Go (2015) was a defiant act of dramatic, directing and
programming boldness. This was not only owing to the short duration
of the play at forty-five minutes, or even to the fact that a play of such
length was staged at the National Theatre's second-largest space, the
Lyttelton auditorium, but also to the play's form and content. *Here We*

Go offered a compact and affective statement on dying and the possibility of an afterlife, rendered anarchic by the decision that Dominic Cooke, the play's director, made as to the final scene – particularly when *Here We Go* is seen in the context of *Love and Information*. If *Love and Information* toys with the speedy exchange of facts and ideas, alluding to our compromised attention spans through both form and content, *Here We Go* defies these entirely.

The play opens to familiar Churchill territory as a group of different ages and personalities gather together on the occasion of an elderly man's death. Churchill leaves the number of the individuals shown in the first scene, as well as their age and gender, to the director's discretion, but specifies that three is a minimum and eight a maximum number (2015: 9). In Cooke's production, it was a group of seven, consisting of three men (one young, one in the later middle-age years, the other significantly older) and four women (one young, the partner of the young man, one slightly older and one closer to middle age, as well as an elderly woman). They interrupt each other as they speak; they reminisce. In the spare set of a house (two white walls loosely forming a room) characters come and go through doors, opting in and out of conversation; always in motion, likely to disappear suddenly. Churchill's text does not specify allocation of lines either, so the narrative that a director might create is bound to vary significantly between productions. The dialogue flows, but at unexpected times, with no major visual/aural shift or indication other than the audience direct address that Churchill stipulates (Churchill 2015: 21), characters momentarily break from the conversation to confess to spectators how much time later, and under what circumstances, they themselves come to die. The playtext includes ten possibilities of death scenarios, to be used as decided in a given production, meaning that any combination is allowed and that not all options will be used. In the performance I saw at the Lyttelton on 25th November 2015, arrangements were as follows: a young man dies after seven years (cancer); his partner dies sixty-two years later (effectively old age, but cause of death is pneumonia); a man in late middle age dies after twenty-six years (minor household accident, worsened by poor health); an elderly man dies eleven years later (heart attack); one of the two women in their thirties/forties dies thirty-eight years later (cancer); the other dies twenty-three years later (Alzheimer's); the elderly woman dies the very next day of the memorial (pedestrian involved in a road accident) (Churchill 2015: 21). In Cooke's production, the fact that the death confessions were not announced as major events, but were only slightly differentiated from the overall tone of the scene, was significant. In this way, death was presented as a part of existence; an event to acknowledge pragmatically and come to terms with. The characters' ability to narrate their own deaths, of course, also blurred the time continuum, along the lines of what *Escaped Alone* would accomplish mere months later, though under a different thematic remit.

Here We Go effectively cheats death of its impact. It depicts dying as a passage, where the individual retains all of what used to be their personality but suddenly finds themselves thrust in a new adventure. The play's second scene, 'After', captures this moment, featuring '*One person*' speaking '*Very fast*', in stark contrast with the play's final scene, 'Getting There' (a reference to the long times the same elderly person as in 'After' used to need in order to complete the mundane task of getting dressed each day with their carer's help, but also, of course, a reference to coming closer to death) (Churchill 2015: 23, 29). The character and actor were the same in both scenes in Cooke's production, which implied that the same person had been the subject of conversation in the funeral party in the first scene. Featuring no words and consisting only of stage directions in the playscript and monotonous physical activity on the stage, 'Getting There' is designed to arouse sympathy at first, then amusement, then impatience. In my experience, by the second time the elderly person, whose physical capacities were shown as severely affected, had been helped by their carer into their day clothes from their night garments and back again in near identical ways, several members of the audience were beginning to express their exasperation, non-verbally, but audibly and purposely, before the final fade-out.

The resonant point Churchill's play was articulating, albeit without the words, was that irrespective of individual circumstances the one fear and crisis of understanding that interconnects us relates to death: processing it and coming to terms. Therefore, in *Here We Go* death was displaced from its position as the ultimate tragic event by ageing. But the play also exposed the crisis in our capacity for genuine empathy towards the elderly and devoid of strength, and the popular obsession with youth culture and impatience exacerbated by the fast ways in which we live our lives. Churchill and Cooke created a slow and protracted moment within a very short play that had established the ultimately false expectations that it would run in fast pace throughout. The nervousness with which many in the audience reacted to the final part, for which Churchill does not indicate a specific duration, noting, simply, *'for as long as the scene lasts'* (Churchill 2015: 29), rendered evident that Churchill's gesture was significant, and not a mere stylistic exercise. The audience was responding; the play brought us together in a moment when we were expected to pause and reflect, and to endure repetition, in the same way that the aged person does. *Here We Go* was an exercise in coming to grips with our own humanity, tolerance, capabilities and the responsibilities of a transient life that stands to make a permanent imprint on the state of the world. That the dead person's monologue in 'After' includes a confession of middle-class contentment adds to the astuteness of the play's politics:

> and how much good did I very little because I was always loving someone or organizing something or looking at trees or having a quiet sit-down with the paper and I'm sorry I'm sorry (Churchill 2015: 25)

From these words emanates a sense that more could have been achieved with a life in which security of comfort simply did not provide an urgent enough incentive. The life had been well-lived, but more could have been done with it. In Churchill's capable hands, this emerged as an observation and call to action rather than a sermon.

Conclusion

Reflecting on *The Fall of Public Man*, Harvey G. Cox observes Sennett's ability to deliver the 'Great macrosociology' that recognizes, and necessarily relies upon 'great microsociology at the same time' (Sennett 2003: xv). As this chapter has shown, such is the task that Churchill keeps returning to and that *Love and Information* exemplifies. Diamond describes Churchill in *Love and Information* as 'Intrigued by vast data networks, [...] remind[ing] us that information percolates everywhere' (2014: 463). In the 2010s, Churchill continued her foray into science by turning to the social-scientific event that marks our contemporary experience: big data. As to how she produces her micro- and macrosociology for the stage, there is no settling for Churchill when it comes to adventurous, entertaining and astute theatre-making. One critic observed: 'Churchill now seems to reimagine theatre each time she puts on a play' (Lawson 2015). As Moira Buffini puts it, the enduring resonance of Churchill's plays, and the reason why, I add, many of them instantly become modern classics, is that 'provoking and stimulating, never reductive, [...Churchill] never patronized her audience' (2015). I appreciate Buffini's description of Churchill as the playwright 'who in the 70s and 80s was the daughter of Brecht, [and now] has become the daughter of Beckett' (2015), because it suggests the good intentions of locating Churchill within the respective artistic traditions of two major trailblazers – and certainly there are affinities. However, to think of Churchill as anyone's 'daughter' in terms of artistic genealogies risks overlooking the untamable imagination that has claimed for her the unique position she occupies in contemporary British theatre.

It seems more apt to talk about how Churchill's work has left its traces in the groundbreaking work of younger playwrights. Churchill's seventieth birthday in the autumn of 2008, whose occasion the RCT marked by asking ten prominent playwrights to direct a reading of a Churchill play of their choice, was indicative of the playwright's extensive and inter-generational influence, as well as the respect she commands.

The next chapters establish such traditions of experimentation and innovation, though it is important to note that I am not implying that the original work of any playwright discussed in the following chapters is a result of regurgitation in any form. Setting this chapter at the beginning is a way of foregrounding certain (inter)personal, social and political concerns that emerge strongly throughout this book, and which have been dealt with in Churchill's recent theatre, as well as, specifically, in the micronarratives of *Love and Information*. In its own fragmented way that corresponds to today's fractured human experience, *Love and Information* at the end emerges as a macronarrative for the trials and tribulations of humanity in the beginning of the twenty-first century. It is that same narrative that the plays examined in the following chapters go on to formulate, in their own distinctive ways, but always exploring the individual as part of the collective and vice versa. Reflecting on *Serious Money* Churchill spoke of it as operating on a 'paradox [...] that tension between it being an attractive world and a dangerous one' (1988: 16). The tension persisted in Churchill's later writing, when, as this chapter has shown, the experience of the world as paradox, but also as an alluring challenge to attempt to tackle amidst radical crises, took on entirely new dimensions. The ensuing chapters delve into a consideration of how this formal and thematic tendency, emerging from a fluid social context, has manifested itself in the work of some of the more important playwrights in twenty-first-century Britain.

2

Occupy the Audience: Mike Bartlett and the Collectivity of Resistance

There are two sides to Mike Bartlett's playwriting: the contained, minimal narratives concentrating on a small cluster of characters, and the sprawling, formally expansive theatre pieces best suited to bigger spaces. What these styles share is a thematic preoccupation with the individual's sense of insecurity and her/his constant search for identity and purpose, juxtaposed with an alienating social environment built on capitalist principles and rigid definitions of success and happiness. Bartlett's specific brand combines introspection and the quest for self-knowledge with the individual's efforts, more often than not a struggle, to locate themselves within the bigger picture. This concerns politics, the environment, the government, war, austerity, class or, more broadly even, the cosmos. Bartlett's playwriting shows a profound existential drive, and self-discovery is contingent to understanding one's civic responsibilities. The significant range of contexts and locales where Bartlett's plays unfold represents the fluctuation of individuality in different situations and environments, and his characters' attempts to cope with different roles and expectations. Occasionally Bartlett's writing is naturalistic, delving into the human psyche, mental and biological urges, triggers and predispositions. Even when Bartlett identifies cause and effect, he resists theatre with a direct message and tidy solutions. We have seen this in some of his most significant smaller-scale plays such as *Contractions* (stage version: RCT, 2008); *Cock* (RCT, 2009); *Love, Love, Love* (Drum Theatre Plymouth/ Paines Plough/RCT, 2011–2012) and *Bull* (Sheffield Crucible, 2013). These plays have dealt with workplace bullying and corporate greed (*Contractions, Bull*); class, identity and personality (*Love, Love, Love* and *Cock*); compromise and personal crisis (all of the above). But Bartlett also steers clear from the temptation of a message in his impressive larger-scale work, which this chapter will be primarily concerned with: the contemporary epic classics *Earthquakes in London* (2010) and *13* (2011), which relentlessly probe modern insecurities and capitalist limitations. Always responsive to crisis – past, present, but also future – more recently Bartlett has delivered two plays, *King Charles III* (Almeida Theatre, 2014) and *Game* (Almeida Theatre, 2015), which have taken a keen and concerned perspective on the country's, but also, humanity's more broadly transition to an uncertain future, where many of the values that have unified communities in the past have ceased to exist and individuals, as well as the structures that govern them, appear precarious. Often, uncertainty, a key interconnecting thread in Bartlett's theatre, escalates to anxiety. In 2016, Bartlett's then newest play *Wild* (Hampstead Theatre) positioned these concerns on a fearlessly international platform. Its thematic preoccupation with our civic responsibilities versus the instinct of self-protection set against a background of global politics where unpredictable developments absorb the individual like quicksand was augmented via the literally global reach of the play. This was made possible by virtue of the Hampstead Theatre's decision to live-stream the performance of 23rd July 2016. Concentrating on *Earthquakes in London* and *13*, this chapter argues that they are exemplary of the ways in which the continuous impositions and ideological failures of a bankrupt system built on profit margins have culminated in a public awareness of these shortcomings leading to actions of social interconnection and spiritual collectivity, which carry the premise of profound change and of a reinvigorated civic conscience.

Earthquakes in London and *13*: Staging communities

Earthquakes in London was a watershed moment in Bartlett's playwriting, the first of his plays to be staged at the National Theatre and to mark a collaboration with Headlong and Rupert Goold. Both text and production involved different and intersecting levels, in terms of formal structure but also performing platforms. Miriam Buether's set for the original production was an inextricable part of the intersubjective affect and sense of collectivity and community that the play created at the National's Cottesloe (now renamed the Dorfman), the most intimate space of the core building. Such was the congruence of space and set design that removing the play from this context is a challenge. As Lyn Gardner noted for the production of the play at Bath's Theatre Royal, it 'had to be substantially reimagined by director Caroline Steinbeis and designer Miriam Buether [...when] touring conventional theatres' (Gardner 2011a). Enhancing the sense of collectivity at the Cottesloe was easier because it has the architecture and aesthetics of a malleable stage and auditorium allowing for a participatory feeling. This is conducive to a heightened sense of inter-presence, of the simultaneous being there of ourselves, the actors and our fellow citizens/spectators and has the capacity to instil in the individual audience member, and by extension the audience as a whole, not only a more engaged feeling, but also an appreciation of how significant our individual contribution is to the spectacle. In other words, the theatre recreates the schema of a community.

Buether's configuration of the Cottesloe enabled spectators, depending on where they sat, to be either immersed in the action, forming part of the central performance arena themselves, or to scrutinize action, with an overview of the space from above to below. The former was accomplished by means of a 'catwalk' platform that swirled across the length of the theatre's ground level, replacing stalls with stools, benches and swivel chairs that brought spectators in close range of the action. As one journalist noted, having to constantly reposition gaze and body in order to stay apace with the action resembled the familiar act of technology-related multitasking, of juggling, for example, different open windows on a computer (Wolf 2011). The feeling of literal, physical immersion in the action was further enhanced for those spectators located at the ground level by the fact that some parts of the production were played one level above, in performance 'boxes' and screens at circle level. This latter element facilitated the sense of physical proximity to and involvement in the action that spectators seated at the higher levels of the space experienced. Rather than being physically detached, mere observers, these audience members were also enveloped in the action.

The staging of *13* was a different proposition, beginning from the fact that this production, directed by Thea Sharrock, opened at the National's largest space, the Olivier. Bartlett's significant stage direction 'The play should be performed with a circle' (2011b: 6) was largely adhered to, aided by the natural curve of the stage in the Olivier auditorium. The Olivier, however, greatly differs from the Cottesloe, in both size and shape. The pluralist and physically involved feeling of the Cottesloe production was difficult to replicate here. Equally, though, it can be argued that the Olivier's size enabled Bartlett's work to be presented to substantially larger audiences, thereby amplifying its social impact and rendering it a more inclusive and more democratic process. One handicap that cannot be overcome in a structure as rigid as that of the Olivier, however, is the distance between the stage and the furthermost seats in the theatre. Sharrock's production attempted to reduce this by extending outwards on occasion and using more parts of the auditorium for specific segments, but, ultimately, the action did create the impression of being largely confined to one part of the space.

Staging *13* in the Olivier was recognition of the success of *Earthquakes in London* and it was a bold move by the National to programme this new text that raised a range of challenging issues in a venue mostly intended for so-called canonical, or at least more standard in form and arguably more populist plays. Even though *13* and *Earthquakes in London* share a highly similar structure of multitudinous scenes interweaving and incorporating large casts while dealing with major social issues, the respective effect of the two productions was markedly different. The Olivier ultimately imposed its presence on Sharrock's production, weighing it down despite the liveliness that it retained for much of the first part. The auditorium came across as the vast space that it is, and the possibility of spectatorial disconnection arose more strongly because of the physical detachment experienced by many in the audience. Ultimately *13* became more static than it might have been under different staging conditions. Even though it gave the play a miniature of the 'polis' through its amphitheatrical layout, an important contribution given the call to partake in our *dēmos* that *13* advocates, the effect was muted compared to the energy of *Earthquakes in London*. The latter was, in fact, a more energetic 'Occupy' moment of the National's audience base, space and agenda, carrying with it the seed of change.

Earthquakes in London and *13* open up to such a range of concerns that both plays constitute stage interventions and calls to dialogue and action, driven by the same principle as Sennett's *The Uses of Disorder* (2008 [1970]). Here, Sennett explores the conditions of urban living under extant societal structures while envisaging alternatives. Such is the process that Bartlett follows too: the plays are uncompromisingly critical of the capitalist frameworks that have delivered us to our crises and unabashedly optimistic as to the prospect of change. But Bartlett, like Sennett, is a realist: change is difficult to conceptualize and it does not materialize out of nothing, but out of collective effort. Making a more poignant case, then, Bartlett draws on the opportunity to transpose the challenge into the metaphysical. He does this by displacing change from the level of everyday life to imagine it as possibly the result of divine intervention. This might strike us as removing responsibility from the human level and accepting passivity, but it is quite the opposite. By including a messianic figure in each of the two plays and showing that person as flawed, exposed to weaknesses that might ultimately render them ineffectual, Bartlett invites spectators not to anticipate divine interventions but cast themselves as the catalysts for change.

Both plays attack the culture of capitalism that encourages short-term thinking and selfish individualism. They reveal the paralysis of fear and empty aggression, weighing these against action and critical thought that might produce solutions. Bartlett's work, therefore, invites spectators to frame themselves as agents in social and political developments rather than observers. By exposing a wide range of attitudes and behaviours to common issues through his diverse tapestry of characters, Bartlett reveals that detachment can be as catastrophic as fear. But he also presents ill-conceived, ideologically empty, routine resistance by default as equally problematic. The disorientating effect of the plays evolves from Brechtian *Verfremdungseffekt*, adapting it to the modern epic. Bartlett, like Brecht in *The Good Person of Szechwan*, exposes the dangers of deflecting responsibility and urgently poses the question of how much a community can achieve today to break from capitalist insularity and address challenges that might appear individual but are actually collective.

The concerns that Bartlett takes on in *Earthquakes in London* and *13* have global reach. We could characterize *Earthquakes in London* as an environment play, but it is, also, of course, a recession play, and a play that deals with crisis in the family, society and community. *Earthquakes in London* reflects its context, capturing the widespread fatigue and anxiety of societies reeling from the major financial downturn of 2008–2009, whose ripple effects were still being felt well into 2010, despite a slowly developing recovery climate. *13* is also a product of its historical moment, capturing the atmosphere of the 'Occupy' movement, which erupted internationally in numerous urban centres in 2011, the lingering repercussions of the recession and civic disillusionment in capitalist systems, the instinctive need of societies for unification towards a common cause and the compromised faith in governments.

The dialectical approach that Bartlett takes to these issues, synthesizing aspects of the problem towards a synchronic and diachronic exposition while staying close to the core pivot for the enquiry, the individual's role within society in a historical moment of flux and transition, further establishes the link to Sennett's work. Significantly, *The Uses of Disorder* was Sennett's first book, which, a product of the rapidly changing sociopolitical landscape of the 1960s, reflects both the challenge and the opportunity that the specific period represented. It reveals uncertainty intermixed with the energy of the possibility for change. Such is also the feeling that *Earthquakes in London* and *13* produce over four decades later, as humanity finds itself at another turning point with major issues such as climate change and capitalist collapse setting the agenda and requiring urgent action. Sennett writes of the power of uncertainty as a positive force in parallel to the individual's transition from observer to participant in social developments:

> Adolescence is necessarily a time when young people have to define and judge the world they live in before having much experience of it; adolescent identities tend to be rigid, imaginary constructs. Adult experience should take these certainties apart; complexity should make human beings less categorical, less certain. Or at least this possibility beckoned to me in my own early adulthood; I found doubt to be a liberating condition. [...In] cities [...] I found [...] a site for living freely, and also for living with unsettlement and uncertainty. (Sennett 2008: xii-xiii)

Earthquakes in London and *13* reflect the awkward, sometimes simply painful and often failed attempt of individuals inhabiting cities such as the ones Sennett writes about to establish themselves as citizens with confidence and influence, transitioning from adolescence, taken literally and metaphorically, to adulthood. Considering Bartlett's work in the context of Sennett's enables us to understand why Bartlett's characters fail, and appreciate the complex factors that render their uncertainty not a positive catalyst but a debilitating agent that stumps most attempts at growth and future fulfilment.

Another major factor in Bartlett's writing, as well as in Sennett's, is the perception of the individual's positioning in an urban society and their sense of community, and of belonging. Bartlett depicts communities as fractured; as non-communities, in fact. Sennett, meanwhile, proposes that to expect homogeneity of communities is a fallacy bound to lead to disappointment; the point is, rather, to make sense – and use – of the ideological differences as creative dissonance (see Sennett 2008: 27–49). This is precisely the mistake that Bartlett's characters make, expecting to fit into a mould that is ultimately restrictive and repressive, rather than finding their own voice and turning difference into an essential parameter for action and improvement. Bartlett's characters have a tendency to self-isolate, even, as in the case of John in *13*, when they emerge as leaders in a crowd. Therefore, the possibility of change, which John embodies, essentially remains extrinsic from society and is doomed to fail when the individual that represents it is revealed to be as vulnerable as anyone else. In Bartlett's theatre as well as in Sennett's work what emerges strongly is the call for a group of individuals, who might fathom themselves as a community, to construct collectively a ground that encourages personal labour towards a common cause, rather than to give in to the kind of impotence that we witness in an array of characters in *Earthquakes in London* and *13*, who ultimately surrender themselves to what might superficially appear as a failure of their community.

Sennett argues that the awkwardness with which we respond to change, and to the uncertainty that change generates, is a result of judging social fluctuation in the present against conditions of the past that no longer apply, and creating unrealistic expectations (Sennett 2008: 10). This is not to say that the effects of capitalism and financial collapse, to borrow from Sennett's lexicon, have not been corrosive (see Sennett's *The Corrosion of Capitalism: The Personal Consequences of Work in the New Capitalism*, 1999). It is, rather, to suggest that by anticipating that the present and future will unfold on the basis of precedent is a false expectation and one that, as Sennett notes, is bound to grind to a halt not only progress, but, more importantly, our understanding of ourselves as 'free historical beings' (2008: 10). Only when we acknowledge the radical change in our conditions and the responsibility and role that we hold in shaping these are we able to take action confidently and, returning to Sennett, unimpeded by fear (2008: 10). In Bartlett's work we observe the effects of being unable to extricate oneself from the past and its assumed certainties that come to acquire an aggrandized, almost mythological status. These include, for example, job security, cohesive communities or safe societies. And so Bartlett's characters experience catastrophic crises of identity at the loss of institutions or qualities previously considered as staples (see Sennett 2008: 3–26).

But in Bartlett's plays we also observe an attitude contradictory to this, however shown as bound to its own naïveté and inadequacies: the force of change against what we might perceive as regressive social behaviours, or as the 'repression' that Sennett writes about (2008: 26). Sennett notes that the limitations imposed on life options by the obsessive attachment to the past need not only be destructive; they can also serve to instigate, in some, the 'search for a new kind of community life' (2008: 26). *Earthquakes in London* and *13* depict the feverish search for identity at the level of the individual and the collective: disparate – but ultimately interconnected – characters attempt to define themselves and their role through different means and methods. The two plays, then, capture the awkward and tentative reimagining and rebuilding of a community in a new formation, which is necessarily heterogeneous (see Sennett 2008: 27–49).

Earthquakes in London and *13*: Platforms for democracy

Earthquakes in London was warmly received, with critics calling it 'the theatrical equivalent of a thrilling roller coaster ride. It swoops and twists, rushes and soars, and provides a great shot of adrenalin-fuelled excitement' (Spencer 2010). Others noted the ambition in Bartlett's range, commending the 'gorgeously carnivalesque production' and the play's 'naturalistic detail with a sense of being part of an epic fable' (Billington 2010). Paul Taylor remarked that the set was 'powerfully evoking a society bent on distracting itself from the truth through decadent excess' (2010). One year later, many critics endorsed *13* equally strongly, calling it a 'maximalist epic' and a 'phantasmagoric fable' (Billington 2011b). Billington's praise for Bartlett's skill to capture crisis is indicative:

> Bartlett has pinned down, in a way few dramatists recently have, the unease that is currently in the air: the sensation that we are sleepwalking into some kind of disaster that may stem from economic

collapse, environmental upheaval or the logical extension of the war on terror. Bartlett has his finger on the pulse [...]. (2011b)

In the context of *Earthquakes in London*, but also given the complexity of *13*'s own palette, understandably critics also commented on the feasibility of tackling all the issues that *13* boldly takes on. It is true that despite the gloom of the crises that it addresses, and without any claim to resolving them, *Earthquakes in London* emerges as a more optimistic and, to a degree, conclusive play than *13*, which is more cautious of optimism and driven by dialectics, and, all in all, a shade darker in its tone and atmosphere.

A primary angle through which Bartlett approaches the identity crisis that Sennett also discusses, and the anxiety and inability to move on that sudden change, consistent with the unpredictability of the economy, causes to one's status, is unexpected unemployment. In *Earthquakes in London* this is represented by two very different characters, evidencing that the problem is cross-generational. The inner crux of the play forms around three adult sisters who have had to deal with the loss of both parents – a dead mother and an absentee father. The fact that two family members are affected by professional insecurity is significant and entirely proportional, considering that *Earthquakes in London* opened in the aftermath of the recession when redundancies grossly overtook employability with workforce supply outstripping demand. The play depicts the established professional's uncertainty as well as the young person's anxiety caused by an educational and professional lack of purpose.

Colin, the husband of the eldest sister, Sarah, who is in turn shown as an awkward by-default maternal figure to her sisters, struggles to re-enter the workforce post-redundancy. Even though Colin's sense of emasculation mostly stems from his unemployment, it is also clear that his already weak personality places him in an inferior position to Sarah domestically. Sarah's career has moved in a complete juxtaposition to Colin's: as he is failing, she takes on a government role as minister in the Department of Climate Change. Colin, formerly a banker, is now reduced to running the daily shop, showing neither aptitude nor desire for managing a household, and submitting endless applications for new roles. One of these moments is powerfully foregrounded:

> *A computer screen is projected.*
> *Someone is writing.*
>
> **Writing**   'I feel that I would be right for the position of senior accounts manager as I am both strong ...
>
> *He deletes.*
>
>   strong both as a team player and a leader.'
>
> *Lights up on* **Colin**, *who is typing.*
>
>   '... I have demonstrated this on many occasions, leading my team through many years of excellent service over the last ten years. Ten. Years ...' (Bartlett 2010a: 35)

Bauman writes: 'The shrinking volume of employment is not [...] the sole reason to feel insecure. Such jobs as are still to be had are no longer fortified against the unpredictable hazards of the future; work is today, one may say, a daily rehearsal of redundancy' (2001: 118). He adds that in our time flexible employment effectively means that all the familiar employee rights and employer responsibilities have been removed so anyone, at any stage, is at risk (Bauman 2001: 118). This brief yet meaningful moment in Bartlett's play exposes not only contrived modes of self-description that regurgitate market terms, but also the disposability and interchangeability of workers pursuing the same roles and eradicating any sign of individualism – ironically the very trope of neoliberalism – for the same generic aggressive persona. Bartlett confronts the utter failure of a system masked as the failure of any individual, who, like Colin, is held accountable for his inability to transition swiftly to another post. At the same time, Colin's youngest sister-in-law Jasmine also experiences the condition of operating outside the system, though she perceives this as choice rather than necessity. Jasmine and Colin intersect in different moments of the play, becoming attracted to each other and sharing their respective rejection by Sarah, who represents the establishment in the structure of the family and in society more broadly. Critics may have argued that *Earthquakes in London* and *13* take on too many issues, attempting to juggle them in ways not always successful, but Bartlett's critique is considered and nuanced. He does not provide a rejection of capitalism at large; he questions whether the individual's bombardment by a multitude of causes, which social media have exacerbated, may in some cases produce a superficial adoption of principles that is no less problematic than ignorance.

Jasmine is the prototypical example of such tendencies. Educated yet resisting the establishment almost by default, she feels compelled to lend her voice to the latest cause but her rebellion is spasmodic and lacking in conviction. Jasmine embodies disobedience in a society of attention deficit, and so she takes no issue with casually admitting that she has become bored with one cause and must move on to something new for her own titillation. As she states, her protest is primarily driven by a reaction to Sarah's questionable policies, but she disdains these more as a sister than as an indignant citizen. The angst may reach deep, but its motivation is yet another example of the neoliberalist individualism that Bartlett's work consistently attacks: Jasmine is concerned about her feelings; making a social difference is merely incidental. The protest is, therefore, a form of self-therapy, a manifestation of operating at the level of the personal under the pretext of serving a community:

> **Jasmine**   [...] I've had enough of the environment, hear about it all the fucking time, I only did it [protested] for my sister and she didn't even turn up. I'll do a Nazi one next week probably. They love Nazis. [...] (Bartlett 2010a: 33)

This attitude betrays profound disillusionment with society and the individual's agency in change and politics, which Jasmine articulates to Colin, in a moment that is as close to 'state of the nation' as Bartlett comes. Her monologue also exposes the modern individual's inability to conceptualize a future by using the tools of the present, rather than the moulds of the past. Jasmine, who perceives of herself as a rebel, essentially emerges as entirely reliant on old familiar capitalist structures, which tie her to the loop of repeated behaviours that prevent progress, much in the way that Sennett discusses. The significance of the speech, which also exposes the fallacy of a homogeneous community – physical or virtual – justifies the long quotation:

> **Jasmine**   I feel so fucking aimless Colin, I want to go where I want, do what I like, spend money, I want to shout all the time. Cos it's bullshit, just everyone, isn't it? Pushing emails around, shall we meet? […] let's pencil that in, fucking about on facebook, events, messages, profiles, pretending to have friends, […] none of it's *achieving* anything, it's one big 'general meeting', just chatter, and when it all fucks up, which it will, just statistically, historically, when it all goes pear shaped, they'll be full of regrets. […] And I never want regrets Colin so while I still can I'm gonna fuck some shit up. (Bartlett 2010a: 81)

The monologue could also be taken as a thinly veiled reference to the role of the theatre and the audience as a group of citizens, gathering together to observe a realm of possibilities that might lead to action – although it is equally probable that it might not. Such is the 'general meeting' that Jasmine talks about, whose continuation and outcome is dependent on us.

In *13*, Bartlett probes the fine line between agency and detachment further, continuing to explore social media as not only a networking but also a diversionary practice from on-the-ground action that might implement change. Unemployment plays a substantial role here too, as it is Bartlett's angle into the problem. We are introduced to the couple of Rachel and Amir early on, two young people both invested in protesting. When we first see Rachel she is in a moment of distress, on the phone, attempting to locate Amir following his arrest, the result of a fight at a demonstration. It is at that moment, in the street, that Rachel suddenly comes across John: an old friend of the couple, who had disappeared from their lives abruptly. Their reconnection coincides with the new stage in John's life as part public speaker, part proselytizer. Regarding John and the social significance of this character, Chris Megson observes:

> The central character in *13* is a Messiah-like figure [...] who upholds belief as both constitutive principle of social life and antidote to a political culture [...of] anxiety and compromise: the staging of the play in the aftermath of the August 2011 riots in English cities, and during the anti-capitalist 'Occupy' protests then encamped outside London's symbolic religious centre of St Paul's Cathedral, invested the production with arresting topicality. (Megson 2013: 41)

John's cause may not be entirely clear, but he evidently possesses the ability to attract and gather people around him, and his allure over crowds prompts trust and familiarity. Bauman writes about faith as both a tested institution in contemporary capitalist contexts and as in itself an 'investment', the one act that has the power to lift one above the limitations of a failing system (2001: 158). Even if faith does not procure an afterlife according to traditional belief systems, it can function on the basis of providing the individual with a sense of purpose and a legacy beyond a life consumed only for its own sake; therefore, it is not as abstract as one might think, but tied to the realm of the here and now (Bauman 2001: 158). And so, crowds begin to congregate around John. One example of this is Rachel's behaviour when, swiftly overcoming her anger at John's absence, she begins to treat him as a confessional vessel:

> **Rachel**   [...] So I'll start – Amir was working as a lecturer which was nice but then they lost funding, shut the department so now he's miserable as fuck and as for me, well, I was doing my PhD but gave it up cos one of us had to earn something. So now I have a job. I work for a charity. [...]
>
> **John**   Your sort of thing.
>
> **Rachel**   I sit on the phone and call people up and ask them for money.
>
> **John**   Like sales.
>
> [...]
>
> **Rachel**   [...] literally every day I get a call, an email, this person's ill, that one's depressed, I'm a walking Samaritan people

think I can deal with their problems but for some reason they never
imagine I might have some of my own [...]. (Bartlett 2011b: 21)

Following Amir's release, the rift that the financial crisis has created
between him and Rachel is further manifested. Significantly, it is not
only the lack of income, but also Amir's general inaction that Rachel
takes issue with, as she returns from work one evening. When this
conversation takes place, John's public lectures have started to attract
attention, whereas Amir is a passive observer:

Rachel [...] you've been on the internet all day reading the *Guardian*
website, watching your videos – how's John getting on?

Amir Good – people are starting to write about what he's doing –

Rachel Yeah and you've been posting and tweeting and all of that
and you've had a nice day which is good but I've got work [...]

[...]

Have you left the sofa today? (Bartlett 2011b: 58–59)

The couple's relationship and their contrasting behaviours towards the
crisis – beyond their common commitment to protesting – serve as
a focusing lens not only on unemployment, but also on social class,
the fallacy of the presumed superiority of the middle-class intellectual
and the very (un)tenability of middle-classness as a state for the
increasing in numbers educated urban intelligentsia, particularly
in cities like London. This intelligentsia, as the case of Amir and
Rachel also evidences, is a strongly represented social group in anti-
capitalist protest, which, as Bartlett's play again shows, is typically the
product of social networks operating on platforms such as Facebook
or Twitter (there are, of course, also others). By the end of the play,
Amir has reached a state of radicalization; as for Rachel, even though
Bartlett steers clear from reductively suggesting that she has become
too complacent in the promise of financial comfort to care about
principles, it is evident that she is less than willing to follow Amir into
a line of thought that views conflict and violence as necessity. Such is

Bartlett's way of exposing ideological binarism and suggesting that it constitutes far from a productive way forward.

Amir's behaviour typifies the trend of falsely equating virtual to actual intervention. As the play reveals, the danger is all too plausible and education leading to assumed intellectual superiority provides no immunity to it. In fact, the risk is amplified by easy access to different forms of social media that relegate participation in one's community to membership of an online community, whose aims, ideologies and proposed actions may well produce short-lived results and resistances whose power quickly detonates, then fades. Bartlett's critique consists in the fact that communities must not only resist, but also know what they are resisting for, interrogating their methods as much as their convictions. In both plays, then, the adoption of causes that is not necessarily followed through with committed and sustained action is not shown to be the property of the so-called manipulable masses. As in Eugène Ionesco's *Rhinoceros*, to be convinced of one's intellectual superiority might well be the safest path to complacency, and *13*, particularly, verifies the hypothesis. Like *Rhinoceros*, *13* is a political play about a community at the edge of annihilation, the result of a long-brewing crisis that eventually manifests itself suddenly, and dramatically. Both plays are parables and at their centre lies the relationship of the individual to her-/himself, as the core from where the individual's relationship to her/his community springs. Faith and mental health, therefore, are key issues – but as Rachel's confession to John, cited earlier, reveals, they can also be mere commodities. This is another creative twist by Bartlett: in a play where all characters are haunted by nightmares of insufficiency, charity, therapy and support are also framed as yet another type of business, exerting the same kind of pressure on the individual worker as any other kind of industry. Such is the case of Rachel, who feels that supporting others for a living leaves her exposed to stress and amplifies her own mental and emotional insecurity, which the fluid social context continuously fuels. The conflict between ideology and reality that Rachel represents serves as a vehicle for Bartlett to set up the key problematics of his play: the way in which social crisis, morphing into mental and emotional crisis and catapulting individuals into radical insecurity engenders, in turn, a craving for faith – and that faith, if not rigorously questioned, harbours its own danger for a society already at risk.

In *13*, crisis in mental health is shown as the product of an overarching sense of powerlessness stemming from the fact that agency is constantly deferred to a new platform. Amir's own confession to John captures his personal turmoil as well as the public feeling:

> **Amir** I've got some job applications I'm supposed to fill in, and eventually I have to sign on … I don't know …
>
> *He sits on the sofa.*
>
> Yesterday was this big moment, we all went out, an early start, we were like 'get it [university fees] back on the agenda, in the headlines' – but when you get there and the turns out's [*sic*] not as many as you think, the police are aggressive and then everything that happened [his arrest] and you come home and you just *know* you haven't made any difference at all. They just sit up there in that fucking building and they really – I really don't think they give a shit. (Bartlett 2011b: 43)

In this context, faith fills another gap in the open market of people's hearts and minds and in a political system whose proliferation of disappointment appears inevitable, despite attempts at intervention. Amir's dejection is a catalyst for John as following this conversation his own social intervention by means of public talks is fully set in motion, gradually coming to embody the people's faith and appetite for change.

Issues of psychological vulnerability recur in the play, representative of the therapy turn in a fluid sociopolitical milieu, which this book predominantly discusses in Chapter 5. In the two plays by Bartlett considered here, the common thread and narrative undercurrent of vulnerability affecting all characters in different ways is conceived as the breeding ground for a need for faith extending beyond the worldly and its limitations. Out of this need, John materializes as a spokesperson with the power to unite disparate members of a heterogeneous community into a collective. As John's discourse, a potent mix of preaching and political pontificating gains momentum, Bartlett affords him a number of speeches in which he delves into the current climate, the need for collective action, resistance and for the people's setting of a new agenda for presenting to the government. But Bartlett's play is too committed to rigorously problematizing the issues that it takes on, and too aware of their challenges to present John as a mere sermonizing vehicle. Through the play's interweaving individual storylines the question of faith emerges as a complex one. Both *Earthquakes in London* and *13* demonstrate that as faith can be a healer, it can also be divisive, both a prompt for change and a pretext for transgressions. Where faith and ideology become intermixed, treated as panacea for a collective malaise, Bartlett shows, matters become complex and deeply problematic. *13* probes faith as a one-size-fits-all fix for the characters' mental ailments. In *Earthquakes in London* Freya's pregnancy mirrors the journey towards faith, the main interconnecting storyline of the play and metaphorical extension of Freya's literal role as the middle sister and interconnector in her family structure. The problem is that when that state of faith is reached and embraced, as Bartlett's plays reveal, its effects are far from predictable. Faith might emerge from a singular collective need – spiritual and emotional support – but the actions it produces are radically divergent. Here, I concentrate on the most representative examples in two plays that are ripe with possibilities in the interpretation of ideology and the embodiment of belief.

The most extreme of these occurs in *13*, in the storyline of Dennis, an American mediator between the US and UK governments, his wife, Sarah, and their daughter, Ruby. Sarah does not work and Dennis is mostly absent due to his job, especially since America and Britain are interlocked in a potential military conflict with Iran likely to escalate at any moment. Whereas Dennis is close to Ruby, Sarah has a strained relationship with the child, whom she perceives to be cruel. Whether this is the reality or we are seeing a distorted view of the child's behaviour exacerbated by Sarah's own mental ailments remains ambiguous. Ruby, active and intellectual, is different from her mother, openly challenging her lack of a career. Ruby's questions make Sarah uncomfortable, and an odd dynamic develops between them whereby Sarah begins to perceive her daughter not merely as a bully but an evil force. This is the justification she offers after she commits Ruby's murder: that the child had to be eliminated so as to prevent the force from growing and inflicting grievous harm on others.

Bartlett sets up a fascinating binary of good and evil not only in terms of motherhood – by default seen as a selfless, noble act – but also in terms of the ethics of faith. Before Sarah resolves to kill Ruby, she has an encounter with John. John certainly does not encourage her – yet the ambiguity and global applicability of his preaching is such that Sarah applies it to her situation indiscriminately. As we see in the beginning of the play, Sarah is also one of the play's 'twelve' – with John the thirteenth who acts as a catalyst – who suffer from night terrors. Sarah's distress is accentuated by the security detail observing her every move in a domestic life that she deems the equivalent of imprisonment (Bartlett 2011b: 61). In her meeting with John, Sarah recounts their chance encounter, one of the first events we witness in the play, where an impatient Ruby avoided John because, as a homeless wanderer, he had acquired an unpleasant smell. To Sarah this evidences an automatic repulsion of evil (Ruby) by good (John) (Bartlett 2011b: 62). Once the murder has transpired, at a later stage in the play when John, representing the community, is in negotiations with Prime Minister Ruth to prevent a military intervention in Iran, Bartlett further emphasizes how mental health and faith might become reduced to mere business – negotiating ploys between opposite political forces. A recording of Sarah in police custody offers an account of how she felt in thrall to John, interpreting his call to take matters into one's own hands and act righteously (the same principle he has applied to his call to the community) as a *carte blanche* for violence (Bartlett 2011b: 124–125). Ruth states that she is uninterested in binaries of good and evil, but believes in the role of ambiguity in any problem – and so she devises an entirely plausible indictment of John as an instigator of crime given the evidence from the testimony (Bartlett 2011b: 122). Government spin aside, the story of Sarah casts the ambiguity of faith and political rhetoric under new light: essentially, as Bartlett shows, both can operate on dogmas that might prove detrimental. And so, noble causes – the people's protest against increased university fees, the anti-war lobby – are lost in partisan narratives (of either persuasion) and personal shortcomings. Ruth, once a mother herself, is after all haunted by the loss of another child, this time her own son Simon, whose behaviour, as she recounts, changed dramatically from the moment he became close friends with John. Ruth may have been unable to indict John for the events leading to her son's death in the past, but she is able to deprive him of his credibility in the present.

Earthquakes in London presents a similar hypothesis with the bigger issue – climate change – becoming buried under personal histories of familial dysfunction. This extends beyond the domestic, stretching over centuries to depict and imagine different stages in social crisis, community intolerance and debilitating insecurity for the future as natural disaster looms. In this context, when Freya confides in her estranged, scientist father regarding her pregnancy, he advises her to terminate, convinced that any child Freya carries to term will 'Hate her mother for forcing her into a terrible world' (Bartlett 2010a: 96). For a play that can also be bright and outward-facing, in its core *Earthquakes in London* is characterized by profound disquiet, and its anti-climactic finale far from promises salvation, although it does offer a warning against fatalistic surrender to despair. Once more, motherhood is at the centre of events as we are witnessing a woman's slow progression towards it through Freya's storyline. The problematic of future generations inheriting a world in crisis is embodied in Freya's burgeoning pregnancy anxiety. Although Freya's solitary quest for answers produces numerous poignant moments in her encounters with strangers throughout the play, two moments, in particular, highlight the failure of empathy. It is after these episodes that Freya's mental and emotional state is thrown into further disarray.

In the first of these, Freya has a chance meeting with a group of carbon-copy mothers, uniformly dressed, taking their babies to the park in prams. They all answer Freya's questions concerning their children's future in the same dismissive tone that reveals ignorance and disregard as to the state of the world. Therefore, they utterly fail to provide any kind of solace to Freya (Bartlett 2010a: 63–65). The other poignant moment follows soon after, when a distraught Freya begins to experience symptoms psychosomatically and seeks medical support, concerned about the foetus. Tellingly, the scene is titled 'Mad Bitch' (Bartlett 2010a: 69), a verbatim quotation from the doctor who examines Freya, spoken to a colleague when they believe Freya is not listening (Bartlett 2010a: 98). Freya indeed cannot hear, but she can lip-read as she is trained in teaching deaf children. The treatment that Freya receives at the hospital, where she is effectively dismissed as paranoid when none of her exams reveal any issues with the pregnancy, both accelerates the climax of her crisis and evidences a society of individuals so subsumed in their own respective crises that empathy becomes the first casualty of neoliberalist insularity. Freya's hospital stay climaxes in one of the most striking visual and aural segments of the production, as she has a vision of her unborn baby calling her from inside the womb during an ultrasound. At that moment, Freya believes that her baby's lips move, and that she is speaking to her. In Bartlett's playtext, lines are specifically allocated to a Foetus:

Foetus   Mummy?

Mummy?

Help.

Help me.

Sound of the womb getting louder and louder.

Sounds like an earthquake.

Mummy?

Shaking.

The foetus turns its head to face us and screams.

Blackout. (Bartlett 2010a: 99–100)

It is not only the visual impact of the amplified foetus image as the singular point of focus in a dark auditorium that makes for a show-stopping moment. It is also the fact that the show literally pauses for an interval following this segment. Therefore, the sound and image of an unborn child pleading for help, unexpected and haunting, linger even more intensely as we are given time to absorb the moment and reflect before the performance resumes.

The scene achieves more that aestheticized shock and awe. It communicates the dramatic extent of Freya's mental and emotional turmoil, and her struggle in sustaining some degree of faith for a future beyond the apocalyptic scenarios propagated by some, including, of course, her own father. But the problematic that Bartlett weaves around responsibility is manifold: Freya is concerned about the well-being of her child, and the ethics of in any way terminating a pregnancy, and especially one this advanced; she is also concerned about bringing her child, assuming she carries it to term, into a world facing inevitable catastrophe, environmental, social and political; and, of course, she is concerned about the extent of a transgression that bringing a child into an already exhausted and overpopulated world constitutes. The image of Freya's baby serves to hold us, in a way, accountable for transgressions against our environment that has, like Freya's womb, become inhospitable, but also for failing to see the turmoil and terminal crisis of our fellow human beings at risk. A surreal image bringing together past and future allows Bartlett a moment of radical mixed-media alienation without pointing an accusatory finger.

Complicating matters further, the metaphysical turn in *Earthquakes in London* then begins to materialize as it turns out that Emily, Freya's child, is a messianic figure. Then again, we have the option of interpreting the status of this child as a manifestation of Freya's fragile mental state accentuated by the delicate state of her body. If in *13* the ultimate problematic binary is good versus evil, in *Earthquakes in London* it is science versus religion. This is summed up succinctly in one of the later conversations between Freya and Peter, a teenaged boy who visits her while she is off work:

Freya My dad says, in a few years, they'll look back, on the ruins of London, when the city's underwater, and the old people will say, do you remember walking down Oxford Street? The view from St Pauls [*sic*]? By that time there'll be heat waves, storms, even this earthquake might be caused by us they think. Something to do with ice sheets crashing into the sea. Decreasing amounts of sediment between the tectonic plates.

Peter I think it's God.

Freya What?

Peter Don't you think if there is a God, he's pissed off? Like when you have a mug in your room too long and it grows into this rank horrible green pus. You throw it away when that happens don't you? You get a new one. Start again. (Bartlett 2010a: 123–124)

It is towards the end of this exchange that Peter's transformation into a teenaged Emily occurs, giving Freya a moment of confrontation with her daughter in the future. Once more, Bartlett moves us forward in time, or we might prefer to interpret this as Freya's intermixing of Peter with Emily on the grounds of her view of them both as vulnerable, at risk, angry children. Future Emily, in particular, puts further strain unto any nascent faith that Freya might have; her report of a post-apocalyptic London confirms Freya's worst fears (Bartlett 2010a: 131). And so, transported back into the present, Freya and Emily, together, travel to Waterloo Bridge for Freya's suicide; at that moment, Emily is no longer her future self, but the foetus in Freya's womb. Then, suddenly, while Freya wavers, nature makes her choice for her, as the long-anticipated earthquake finally happens, causing her to lose balance and fall into the river. Fate and faith as slippery concepts merge into a potent moment of crisis to make the point that postponing action only increases the likelihood of eventually losing choice. Anxiety, in both Bartlett and Sennett, is depicted as a numbing force, and deferred action transposed onto faith is equally problematic. As Bartlett puts it, this is the moment when we must begin to face up to our own responsibilities, taking charge of developments, rather than merely anticipating action by others (see Bartlett 2010b; Bartlett 2010d).

The play, however, resists didacticism until the end: by transporting us to 2525, where we witness an encounter between Freya and her mother, both long dead and presumably cryogenically preserved, or metaphysically meeting in an unspecified afterlife, we come to discover that Freya's death catalysed positive change. It appears that when she died the new messiah, a woman called Solomon, materialized upon earth and rescued the city, and the planet. It could be – in the likeliest interpretation – that she is a version of Emily, who was delivered safely, or indeed that she is a version of Freya. This promising vision of the future/past and an interventionist new messiah bears the traces of, as Dan Rebellato notes, a '"radical naivety" […] an experiment in authorship that has some political value' and 'a key area […] that offers the potential to ask questions about who we are and who we might be' (2013: 17–18, 28). When, at the end of the play, we encounter future Emily, at the same age as in her earlier conversation with Freya, she is dramatically different: a figure that transcends her human constitution and consumed, like John in *13*, by an otherworldly conviction for a brighter future. As she leaves home to deliver her message to the world, the play ends in indeterminacy. Amidst the darkness Bartlett allows a glimmer of hope.

Conclusion

In both *Earthquakes in London* and *13* faith emerges as a tenuous concept and insufficient solution. The answer, both plays suggest, lies at the level of the human; it is s/he who must strive to implement social change. As this chapter has shown, Bartlett not only takes on the big issues of humanity, undaunted by their scale, but he also dismantles binaries, and, if the process of thematic exposition and audience immersion involves a certain degree of structural and thematic messiness, this is par for the course. Bartlett notes that a play does not necessarily need to be 'tidied […] up, because the gesture of the play was always "too much"' (Bartlett 2011a). Even though this chapter has concentrated on the most pivotal storylines that best serve to showcase Bartlett's educated, serious, but also lively and playful study on morality, faith and their applications in the human and metaphysical field, it is important to note that even in the sub-plots, where we are dealing with other crises, not necessarily more easily containable but certainly less terminal in the grand scheme of things (mid-life; marriage; ageing; relationships; loyalty, to name but a representative few), what Bartlett's plays suggest is that the blind adoption of any ideology, and the belief that grand narratives function in real life, is utterly problematic.

Bartlett's work is pragmatist, it is idealist, and it does not shy away from the role of the instigator. The first and foremost challenge it takes on, I argue, proceeding from Sennett, is the rigorous questioning of our *doxa* as to what constitutes a community, and how it is meant to move forward. The plays discussed in this chapter evidence Bartlett's ability to capture the spirit of changing communities, and the energies, drives, hopes and fears of the individuals that constitute them. At the same time, these individuals must conceptualize themselves as more than singular units functioning under the neoliberalist model. Bartlett's mosaics of urban life depict an adolescent appetite for change that bears the potential of reaching adulthood in the shape of a new state of being together in our world, if it is followed through. This is what Sennett describes here:

> To make good use of affluence, we must create a set of social situations that will weaken, as a man matures, the desire for controlled, purified experience. [...] For there is a *possible* adulthood that lies beyond this adolescence. If that adulthood were brought into being, [...] the slaveries to which affluent community life is now subject could end, and the abundance used to enrich man's freedom [...] a life with other people in which men learn to tolerate painful ambiguity and uncertainty. [...M]en must subsequently grow to need the unknown, to feel incomplete without a certain anarchy in their lives, to learn, as Dennis de Rougemont says, to love the 'otherness' around them. (2008: 107–108)

Sennett's social view, like Bartlett's, is neither fatalistic nor utopian. Sennett's proposition shares affinities with Bartlett's work not only because of the crux of the argument, but also because they both conceptualize the city as the key hub for activity and possibility, even though it is a space that might be seen as disorientating, alienating, even a hindrance. For Bartlett and Sennett, the essential course of action is such that will maximize potential and persevere over the readily available individualistic patterns that we might fall into in our cities. We may be different, and diverse, but working together in a new, more inter-aware version of our communities, will be crucial. A significant shift in how we view ourselves and our communities, *Earthquakes in London* and *13* demonstrate, will not only take appetite for change, but also the zeal for its sustained implementation: changes in the micronarratives of lives that will manifest themselves in the future macronarrative. And so Bartlett's texts may occasionally feel awkward in their scale, but they are purposefully hyper-inclusive in their depiction of different lives, because this formal expansiveness points to the realities of disparate everyday experiences in modern urban conditions. The plays may not be political manifestos as such, but they are certainly hypotheses for the future that we might choose to have, and, to an extent, blueprints for action.

Defined by Debt: Dennis Kelly
and Capitalist Dependencies

Dennis Kelly's career reflects the wide-ranging activity of many contemporary writers producing work that spans different genres and media. Kelly has written plays for audiences of different ages and theatres of different budgets and specifications, including the major commercial vehicle *Matilda the Musical* (2010); he has authored or co-authored television shows as diverse as BBC's *Pulling* (2006) and Channel Four's *Utopia* (2013). Though not as prolific in theatrical output as some of his contemporaries, Kelly commands attention: his artistic voice is as distinctive as his theatre is eclectic. This is largely owing to a sense of haunting emanating from his plays – the feeling that the structure of the text is inhabited by the unseen, or unspoken. Characters' lives forever revolve around a missing element, the stabilizing ingredient that might give them a moral compass were it not slightly out of reach. Kelly's personas strike us as disorientated, misguided by their own intentions, always vulnerable in the extremity of their experience. They are not naïve but aware of the options available to them and yet they gravitate away from these, seduced by danger and transgression, drawn to the darker side of humanity, bringing to Kelly's theatre an element of the dystopian.

Writing about Kelly's *DNA* (2008), which centres on a group of youths who brutally victimize one of their peers, Lyn Gardner described Kelly's style as 'sharp' and 'reflective' (2012a). The description is accurate: Kelly paints a vivid image through language that cuts to the bone. Gardner's review also pinpoints one of the main concerns of the specific play, which, I would add, characterizes Kelly's oeuvre in general: 'an inability to really connect and empathise with others' (2012a). In recent years we have seen an increasing number of playwrights paying attention to this phenomenon of social desensitization but Kelly was certainly one of the frontrunners, along with Mike Bartlett and Simon Stephens, to pay attention to this form of cruelty. Beyond *DNA* and the co-dependent group of violent adolescents, Kelly's work offers an abundance of examples. Behind each transgression – and in Kelly's plays transgressions are only ever constituted on a large scale; there is nothing discrete about them – lurks an overwhelming desire to prove oneself worthy and powerful. Therefore, imposing one's will and might over other human beings is conceptualized as an initiation, and a rite of passage.

Love and Money: An aesthetic in formation

There is an archetypal element running through Kelly's theatre, as it takes on humanity's big questions and primal emotions. His radical adaptation of *King Lear*, *The Gods Weep* (2010), offers an anti-capitalist extravaganza of a performance exposing its protagonists' crimes in full view, and leading to a form of catharsis – a method that it shares with Lucy Prebble's *Enron* (2009). Both plays are tragedies of humanity, which is different from describing them as human tragedies, as we can never be entirely convinced that the perpetrators experienced any sense of empathy, let alone remorse. The playwright, rather, represents their characters' sociopathy as a profit-driven malaise and conscious self-isolation from a society and community. *The Gods Weep* was a symptom of an ongoing thematic preoccupation of Kelly's, which began with an exploration of how capitalist dependencies can lead to the abuse and even sacrifice of human life in his play *Love and Money* (2006; in Kelly 2007). Like other contemporary playwrights, notable amongst them Martin Crimp, Duncan Macmillan and Nick Payne, Kelly imagined the couple as the core unit from which all action springs. Also like the work of these playwrights, *Love and Money* combines naturalism with expressionism, moving from an exposition of choices made on the basis of family, society and predisposition to the abstract representation of the individual's sensory experience at the moment of crisis.

Love and Money remains Kelly's most experimental play, adopting an unconventional narrative arc for the story of the young married couple Jess and David. Through it Kelly avails himself of the opportunity to also tell the stories of others, sometimes directly related to his protagonists, while others less so. Kelly's play confuses spectators, introducing us to the turmoil of characters that in some cases we only encounter for a fleeting scene. His critical distance is poignant; this is Kelly's *Verfremdungseffekt*, a foray into a Brechtian path that he would continue to explore with moral fables such as *The Ritual Slaughter of Gorge Mastromas* (2012). In *Love and Money*, the terminal crisis that characters experience might strike us as decontextualized, as we are attacked with information which demands fast processing immediately. The key narrative twist is that the play begins at the end, after the main characters have experienced trauma too major to recover from, and closes with the hope of the beginning in the couple's shared life. The reverse chronology means that the play begins on a climax as David admits to facilitating his wife's untimely death, and ends on an anti-climax, depicting Jess contemplating her future. This device accentuates the emotional poignancy of the play, focusing our attention on the events that we know have unfolded all the more intently. We are aware that crimes have taken place in the name of neoliberalist entitlement, that the victims had a degree of complicity as their obsession became a physical condition, that there are multiple perpetrators extending from a small circle of people to society more broadly. The reverse order makes *Love and Money* into a 'whodunit', as we are informed of a crime – Jess's overdose, made terminal by David – in relation to which various moral transgressions are gradually unveiled. This is a running theme in Kelly's work more broadly; in *The Ritual Slaughter of Gorge Mastromas* the procedural aspect of dissecting a crime is even foregrounded to the play's title.

In his review Alastair Macaulay compared *Love and Money* to Harold Pinter's *Betrayal* (1978; in Pinter 2011) due to the reverse chronology and romantic relationship around which both plays revolve (2006). What the plays have in common other than their storytelling is razor-sharp language and a richness of imagery beyond what unfolds on stage, but *Love and Money*, despite its own title, is much less evenly divided between the two. The analogy can only work so far, because whereas Pinter's play explores intimacy found and lost, in the case of *Betrayal* the dependencies are carnal and emotional, and the debts are moral. In Kelly's play, however, the debts are emotional but mostly financial; therefore, when they become impossible to manage, consequences extend well beyond the domestic sphere.

Productions of *Love and Money* have generally responded to its polished formal minimalism and edgy contemporary language with equally stark and stylish visual language. In the case of the Young Vic production directed by Matthew Dunster, Macaulay specifically credits the set designer, Anna Fleischle, for her aesthetic intervention capturing 'the suspense and slickness of the play, with many smart revelations hidden within [...] blank-looking walls' (2006). The set design astutely emulated consumer tastes in the first years of the twenty-first century, before the recession, when the promise of credit and glossy lifestyles seemed infinite. Clapp also alludes to this, arguing that Fleischle's set engendered the play's 'consumerist point', the image of 'a multi-purpose bit of furniture, with each change marking a shift in location. Its white walls are made of cubes that pull out to show a desk or café table, down to provide a hospital bed, or back to reveal an aquarium or a window. It's like something you'd buy from IKEA' (2006). The verbal and visual slickness of the play, taken together with its bold approach to relationships, might make the case for *Love and Money* as the *Closer* (1997) of the '00s, except Kelly's play reaches deeper inside the human condition. Whereas *Closer* tapped into the indulgent *thlipsis* at the abundance yet ultimate emptiness of possibilities for transgressive behaviour, *Love and Money* captured the excessive post-indulgence state when desire reaches the point of saturation and *catathlipsis*. The latter is a more complex term than depression signifying the innermost depths of sorrow and resignation, the kind of emptiness that Kelly's characters experience. Fleischle's design represents any imaginable aspect of everyday life – at its most poignant, it might depict corporate file cabinets where the data of lives are stored and forgotten, or even drawers storing bodies in the morgue. The swift changes and transitions from one stage of life to another are emblematic of the avalanche pace in which debt culture developed, rendering us observers and affected, albeit by our own hand – a fact felt particularly strongly in the case of Jess.

Love and Money is a collection of people and things, evoking the lack of commitment to relationships that continuously gravitate around the central force of capital and profit. Macaulay mentions that the characters – as well as the audience – inhabit 'a world where financial pressures keep our private emotions at bay' (2006). Such observations are merited; however, I would argue that Kelly's play shows that much as one might attempt to develop a shock-resistant exterior, the crisis that mind and body sustain under capitalist pressures is always verging on the unmanageable. Kelly's play is filled with such hints, presented when his characters are given the opportunity of interaction, at moments when time slows down and they find themselves in confined contexts with others. This is also where Kelly's greatest similarity to Pinter lies. In a play that boldly explores the concept of addiction not to substances but to possessions through Jess's shopaholic behaviour, all characters are shown to nurture quiet addictions that prevent them from being empathic to others. They are addicted to self-destructive behaviours, social status, power, authority, jobs and, of course, to anything within their material ownership – even when the latter, in a culture of debt, is an ambiguous concept. Their pathology is not shared but inwardly experienced, underlined by profound dissatisfaction and emotional deprivation in stark contrast to any financial or professional achievements. Eroded by performing their capitalist selves, Kelly's characters therefore forget how to communicate meaningfully, and so their interactions lead to unmitigated verbal aggression.

Kelly also exposes another topical conundrum: in a world in flux, which offers ample choice of 'crises', which specific crisis is most worth investing in for the playwright, if the aim is to encourage change in community attitudes? (2012). Kelly wrote, as he notes, plays like *Osama the Hero* (2005; in Kelly 2007) and *After the End* (2005; in Kelly 2007) to offer a clear line of counterargument to the overwhelming political rhetoric on the War on Terror at the time (2012). Meanwhile, with *Love and Money* he delivered what one German reviewer described as 'capitalist critique crisis-drama' ('kapitalismuskritische Krisendrama', Ullmann 2009), a direction that his writing would continue to pursue through different forms in the following years. The same reviewer describes the state that Kelly's characters in *Love and Money* experience as '*Sehnsucht*', a strong term indicating a corporeal and emotional mix of desire and yearning, albeit, in this case, merely directed at everyday objects (Ullmann 2009). The feeling permeates the entire play, with characters experiencing a physical and emotional craving, a hunger, even, for connection. We observe this in the play's third scene, the increasingly disturbing interaction between Val and David – at this stage desperate to deal with the debt Jess has amassed – in the context of a job interview made all the more uncomfortable by Val and David's past romantic relationship. Val perceives of a debt between her and David, one that he must now repay at the cost of his dignity, as she offers him a post at low pay. Eventually, Val's verbal subdual of David culminates in physical transgression:

> **Val**   [...Y]es, there are quick ways you can make money, but in general you have to do it the hard way. In fact it's all the hard way. If it wasn't you wouldn't get money for it. Did you ever get that mole checked out?
>
> [...]
>
> Can I see it?
>
> *Beat. He roles [sic] up his sleeve. She gets up, comes over and inspects the mole on his forearm. [...] She reaches out and touches it with her finger. Pushes it. Beat. Licks it. Beat. Goes back to her seat. He rolls his sleeve back down.*

Keep your head down, get on with stuff. I'll look after you. (Kelly 2007: 240)

The segment signifies David's impending consumption by the profit-driven system that he will now serve, embodied in Val's physical devouring of his body. It is a typical Kelly moment in exemplifying the characters' flirtation with and eventual trespassing of boundaries for the sake of asserting their power. There is an almost ritualistic element in the slow execution of the scene and its physical choreography builds momentum: this is David's initiation in the corporate world, of whose greed he will now partake. He will learn to feed off of others, even facilitating Jess's suicide so that he may be absolved of her debt.

Therefore, even in relationships where we expect to find genuine intimacy, such as that of David and Jess, or Jess's bereaved parents, Kelly's text refuses to meet expectations and console us that there might be a feeling deeper than resentment, which is the only unifying thread in *Love and Money*. In the case of Mother and Father, as Kelly's text introduces them, everything is defined by its monetary value, including the cost of their daughter's burial; the loss is not processed emotionally but calculated financially, like any other expense (see also Angelaki 2013: 57–78). Their successes and failures as parents are similarly judged on the basis of how comfortable a living they were able to provide for Jess, as their deep-seated neoliberalism seeps through. This scene also demonstrates that entrenched ideologies withstand even major personal crises, evidencing how capitalist dependencies shape consciences and supersede emotions. We witness a different manifestation of this in the play's fifth scene, depicting an encounter between a young woman, Debbie, and an older man, Duncan, at a pub. Duncan, aiming to exploit Debbie for her sexuality in one form or another, promises her a show-business career, and aggressively over-shares under the influence of alcohol. It is a form of self-medicating for what is an obvious mental health ailment caused by unhappiness and personal trauma. For Debbie, who reveals her own transgressive actions in the office the deeper she is drawn into her conversation with Duncan, the antidote to everyday ennui is a fetish of borderline anti-social behaviour against co-workers, spurred on by the thrill of getting caught. Both characters are as irretrievably sunken into their lifestyles as they are made repugnant by their own actions – it is a distinctively Kelly way to be.

Describing Kelly's technique as Brechtian would be consistent with the play's form and methods. The opening scene that involves an e-mail exchange between David and colleague/love interest Sandrine, where he reveals his involvement in his wife's death, can be configured into a part physical/part technologically mediated set (again reminiscent of Marber's infamous chat room scene in *Closer*). The converging point of the play backwards and forwards, the fourth scene, provides an even more open, fluid exchange of voices. These are only identified by numbers, and each speaker shares their own experience of debt culture. Kelly's mixed dramaturgical references are evident, moving from Brecht to ancient tragedy: the voices at first appear superimposed onto the remainder of the play, but they gradually assume a narrator's role. They might be a Greek Chorus, even, summing up the events of this contemporary tragedy and inviting the interjection of the main protagonist, Jess, who interacts with them by recounting the story as she has experienced it, building a bridge between past and present:

> **Jess**   I'm staring at these forks, just standing there in this shop staring at these forks in my hands and praying for a sign like one set of forks, […] are going to suddenly get heavier as a sign that I should put back the […] more traditional Terence Malone forks, but then I thought would the forks getting heavier be a sign that I should put them back or that I should keep them and a sweat broke out on my forehead, I felt prickles in my armpits and suddenly I felt the cold that sat around my heart like a blanket of oil creep out and begin to expand into the rest of my body and I thought 'Here we go. This is it. Here we fucking go' and I don't remember the rest.
>
> *Beat.*
>
> **1.** And you might see her on a ward.
> **3.** Gone crazy in a shop, of all things

1. crying, screaming
2. panicking, actually, real terror
4. and she's taken to a ward
2. Sectioned. (Kelly 2007: 249–250)

The deep pathos of human emotion and physical reaction in extreme crisis, and even the appeals to the supernatural, are reduced to musings on earning and debt. Consumerist *Sehnsucht* is the ultimate modern ailment. It is a concern that Kelly went on to explore further, most notably in *Orphans* and *The Ritual Slaughter of Gorge Mastromas*. If we are treating them as tragic, then what interconnects Kelly's characters is their hubris against the world; the insularity that they committed themselves to comes at a dramatic price.

Orphans: Dependencies of family and class in post-recession Britain

Orphans (Traverse, Edinburgh, 2009; director Roxana Silbert) is decidedly elliptical, both in its gradual and economical disclosure of the pivotal event that triggers the action of the play and in the characters' laconic speech. The play presents a perilous negotiation of present, past and future, all of which hang in the balance one fateful evening, when Liam interrupts Danny and Helen's celebratory home dinner. Our first contact with the play startles and unsettles: it opens in stillness, with Liam already standing in the couple's living room, his clothes blood-stained. He is Helen's brother, and even though Kelly provides no indication of Danny being much older, it is clear that in the absence of a fatherly figure Liam has projected unto Danny feelings of authority and respect. The title of the play refers to Liam and Helen: orphans since childhood, Helen is a hybrid of sister and mother in Liam's eyes. Essentially, when we encounter Liam in the couple's home, we are witnessing the moment of inevitable confession of a transgressive child to his parents, at the stage when his actions have left him irretrievably exposed and he can no longer cope with the weight of their repercussions.

Liam's confession, though, is selective in its disclosure, while he attempts to remove blame from himself by concocting a justification for his violent actions. Upon hearing Liam's early version of events, Danny and Helen adopt prototypical parent attitudes, playing to gender stereotypes: he is concerned but more withdrawn, she is fiercely protective despite suspicions. The dynamics of the play revolves around Helen and Liam's relationship, though Danny emerges as catalyst for the watershed revelations towards the finale. *Orphans* may at first strike us as a simple structure, but it allows for vast crevices of emotion. The issues that the play delves into are manifold and intricate: social aggression, urban violence, community segregation, class divides, racist tensions, capitalist deficiencies and repressed emotions blend into one potent combination. 'The poor are today the collective "Other" of the frightened consumers', writes Bauman (2001: 116). Kelly's play shows the liminal Other as being both inside and outside; Liam is Helen's brother and at the same time close to and far away from the life she inhabits with Danny. Even his oscillation as he makes his stage entrance, not quite entering the couple's living room, marks this state (Kelly 2009: 17).

To do justice to the facets of Kelly's play we must reflect on these characters' personal challenges and responses to stimuli, while locating them within their immediate community. Anticipating the interdisciplinary scholarship of the later 2000s that currently characterizes performance analysis and literary/sociology studies, Simon J. Charlesworth's *A Phenomenology of Working Class Experience* (2000) offers a convincing attempt at blending phenomenology, primarily that of Maurice Merleau-Ponty, with sociology, through frequent references, among others, to Pierre Bourdieu. The embodiment and performance of class is the main concern of Charlesworth's work, from its physical manifestations to its spoken expression. It is a helpful point of reference when dealing with the subject as a thinking and corporeal entity, especially in terms of the way s/he perceives and articulates her-/himself. Moreover, cases like Liam's must necessarily also be understood on the terms that Mattheys sets out in arguing that 'There are well-established and known consequences to people's mental health from living in poverty, unemployment and underemployment, and from living in areas with high levels of deprivation' (2015: 477).

Much of the tension in *Orphans* originates from the class divide that Liam experiences. It manifests itself as personal deficiency, envy towards those in his immediate environment and even racial intolerance. Where Liam has struggled to formulate a life narrative, Danny and Helen appear to have theirs neatly established. Even the dinner that Liam has interrupted is in celebration of an impending addition to the family, as Helen is in the early pregnancy stages with her second child. As appearances go, Danny and Helen, whose professions are never stated clearly, have found relative success, from humble beginnings to accomplishments that elevate them socially against many in their local community. On closer inspection, however, things are not quite as settled. Danny is out of a job – presumably by choice as he is contemplating a change – while he has also recently sustained an attack by local youths. This random violence is causing Helen both insecurity and anger and Kelly's play makes it clear that the couple are entirely disconnected from a community at the early stages of gentrification: a racially mixed, underprivileged local population where many are unemployed and at risk. Through Danny and Helen's depiction *Orphans* emanates what Suzanne Moore calls the 'distress' of 'The diminishing middle class', which, as she rightly identifies, is far from a Britain-specific phenomenon (2013). Moore observes that 'if the middle classes cannot invest even imaginatively in a better future, democracy falters' (2013). The comment extends beyond issues of class, access and morale. It suggests that with the prospect of mobility accomplished not on the basis of neoliberalism but hard-earned reward at stake, tensions mount. Kelly's play demonstrates that in our mostly multicultural societies the Other can easily morph into the target of one's aggression and anger. Even though the first transgressive act in the play is committed by Liam, less educated and integrated into society than his sister, it is clear that Helen's behaviour is also motivated by racist angst, magnified by neoliberalist ambition 'orphaned' by a system that no longer plays by the rules it created for the upwardly aspirational middle classes:

> **Helen** Because I tell you one thing, I am sick of this place. I am sick of the people I love, my people being subordinate to the people out there, people who basically do what they want, run around, calling me a cunt, yes, Danny, because that happens Danny, when I'm with Shane [their son], Danny, bitch this, and bitch that and you just want to close your eyes? (Kelly 2009: 46)

Immigration, integration, identity, access and rights to social benefits become hotly contested and the Other becomes vilified. Then, there is also that social group personifying the middle-class Other regardless of race: the unemployed lower working-class person who, as Moore also suggests, is represented as under-motivated and yet ready to collect any available financial aid (2013). What is easy to miss of course, where such ideologies become entrenched, is that any attachment that the poor display to lavish luxury items ultimately stems from a misguided sense of how to establish self-worth by conforming to the rules of a capitalist consumption frenzy. The play's title offers a poignant reminder of the complete separation between generations, with today's young and/or those within the working age bracket experiencing the consequences of the financial crisis more severely, left to fend for themselves in an uncertain world. At the same time, a crisis in ideology is leaving us further bereft of guiding principles, making us more vulnerable as institutional structures are failing. We appear to be abandoned, acting *in loco parentis*. It is striking that, as relevant studies reveal, in our current climate 'as many people in working families as in unemployed ones [...] live in poverty', with labour losing its capital as living standards guarantee while salaries fail to match the rising cost of life (Milmo 2014).

Through a small number of characters and strong imagery which allows us to visualize their context, Kelly represents both the disillusioned, chronically unemployed individual and the dissatisfied workers whose labour has gone unrewarded. *Orphans* could be misinterpreted as focusing singularly on a racially motivated hate crime, but Kelly's method of inviting the audience into the play *in media res* shows us the symptom and invites us to uncover the cause. The parallel schema of family and community within which Kelly locates the crisis is significant. As Charlesworth argues,

> [as] work has become more atomised and more precarious, insecurity has become the condition of too many. Elementary solidarities of family, work and place, once consolidated by the culture of the trade union and tertiary education, have been washed away by the corrosive cleansing of *laissez-faire* economic practice [...i]n place of the dignities embedded in these elementary solidarities we can see a fractured anomie [...]. (2000: 5)

Affected by the economy, lives such as those Kelly depicts are at best lived under tentative conditions and at worst under heightened anxiety. The accomplishment of *Orphans* is that it stages two worlds within the same family that are seemingly connected but in reality entirely disparate. Helen performs a balancing act between the kind of society represented by her brother, one of exclusion and lack of opportunity, and that represented by her husband, who has played by the rules of the neoliberalist game. Helen might be motivated by her own social ambition in seeking to keep Liam's transgression hidden, but she is primarily driven by the need to ratify her own past sacrifice. When Helen missed out on an adoptive family that would have provided her with security as a child, the trauma she sustained was translated into fierce protectiveness over Liam. Keeping her brother safe from prosecution is, therefore, an act of self-preservation for Helen on two fronts.

Helen has learned to handle her domestic and social insecurity by means of overcompensating with an impenetrable front that often manifests itself as mental and emotional cruelty. She makes no secret of her resolve to terminate her pregnancy should Danny fail to prove himself the family protector by covering for Liam, even if this action might require violence. Helen's pregnancy is rendered doubly precarious as a threat lingers over the entire play, relating to the viability of delivering another child not in terms of biology but economy, as it would add financial pressure onto the household budget, not to mention impose limitations on the couple's social mobility. Charlesworth provides a wide-ranging discussion of how environment and individual are locked in a relationship of mutual impact, a concern that recurs in *Orphans*, where the outside is as much an indispensable part of the characters' life narratives as it is hostile and threatening (2000; the concern recurs throughout the book). Such issues expressed within the context of phenomenological discourse stretch back to Gaston Bachelard's seminal study of the profoundly reciprocal relationship between humans and their surroundings in *The Poetics of Space* (1994 [1958]). The intricacies deepen when class is introduced as necessary factor: such is Helen and Danny's experience as their hard-earned middle-classness clashes with the deprived area in which they live. For Liam, on the other hand, his immediate social environment is what fully conditions his experience – as Charlesworth adds, 'To be working class […] is to be part of a socially realized category' (2000: 7) and this is the only life that Liam has had access to, unable to adjust to institutional structures that might have enabled him to continue in education. It is problematic, then, that in Liam's environment, the work that might have furnished him with a sense of identity has been unattainable, producing a sense of loss and disorientation, a failure to see oneself as an active, accepted member of society and experience 'an intersubjective realm of mutually constituted empathic self-involvement' (Charlesworth 2000: 8). This ultimately produces the kind of sociopathy that Charlesworth's text identifies as a manifestation of the inability to locate oneself within one's own society through labour and reward, and also the misdirected rage that leads to the act Helen and Danny spend most of the play attempting to manage: Liam's brutal, unprovoked assault against an Asian man.

While Liam is impacted by the crisis in terms of the economy, welfare and state provision of viable options, Helen and Danny experience the failure of work to provide a fulfilling narrative that delivers anything other than limited financial gain. Helen's comments about her work are passing, denoting detachment and lack of pride or commitment: the performance of the everyday is merely perfunctory. For Danny, on the other hand, work is a frustrating process, resisting the yield of any meaningful outcomes such as a better life or a rewarding experience; these are, we assume, the reasons for which he has decided to move on to a new role. Helen and Danny represent the social group commonly described as the 'new poor': in theory they should have enough to be comfortable, but in reality they are deprived. If in the past 'the poor were defined by geographical location', today's state of play, of which Helen and Danny are exemplary, is far more intricate (Editorial 2014). In 2014, research by the Rowntree Foundation revealed that 'those meeting the definition of poor – a fluid concept – are increasingly young, in work and living in private accommodation' (Editorial 2014). That this state of being is 'invidious' is of particular value to understanding Kelly's play (Editorial 2014). Through Danny and Helen's exchanges, which range from passive-aggressive to poisonous, Kelly communicates their deep-rooted resentment for their social stagnation, a debt to capitalist rules that engulf them without rewarding them. Their relationship has been broken by the economy long before Liam's crime delivers the final blow – but it is particularly meaningful that Helen deploys her unborn child as a negotiating device, aiming to hurt Danny where he is most vulnerable while attempting to convince him to cover for Liam: in his vision of a wholesome middle-class family. We have seen Helen's accusations against Danny for failing to protect his family – and although the trigger might be the immediate situation arising from Liam's actions, the underlying attack relates to his inability to provide financially to the extent that would implement a dramatic lifestyle change. An orphan who has based her life's expectations on the model of the idealized adoptive family she never had, Helen cannot help but notice the shortcomings of the life she has created with her partner:

> **Helen** When I look at this, our life, or lives, here, I'm not, if I'm honest, one hundred per cent that it is entirely working or working out to, or in such a way, as, as, as well as we might have
>
> been led to believe
>
> expectations … allow.
>
> […]
>
> and on balance, looking at everything, and are we comfortable bringing another [child], and it's just a question, I'm not accusing and it's me, us, both, Danny, but the question is still there. (Kelly 2009: 60)

It is indicative that Helen uses the phrase 'on balance', adding up the facts of her life as though they were figures on a spreadsheet. Helen's misdirected anger at Danny for not quite measuring up to the middle-class dream reveals her conviction of being victimized by the system which has failed to provide for her, first as a child and then as an adult; the life she craves forever slipping out of reach.

Helen and Danny are not an exception, but entirely average, exemplifying the conditions identified by Rowntree:

> In 2012/13, 6.6 million people in working families were living in poverty. This was almost identical to the figure living in workless or retired families, meaning that half of all poverty is found in working families. This has been the case for the last five years – since 2008/09, more than 45 per cent of poverty has been in working families. (MacInnes et al., 2014: 30)

The squeeze on the middle classes as a wider phenomenon has typically been discussed on the basis of income versus quality of life, particularly in terms of home ownership and everyday lifestyle. In *Falling Behind: How Rising Inequality Harms the Middle Class* (2013 [2007]), Robert H. Frank traces the phenomenon's different manifestations. Even though Frank is primarily concerned with American paradigms, his conclusions are highly relevant to the present discussion. The crisis experienced by Helen and Danny relating to the opportunities that their child (or children) will have in life against the fear of this being restricted within their local environment rings true in the context of Frank's statement that real estate in combination with education is one of the main sources of pressure on families (2013: xii, 43–45). The observation is directly translatable into British living conditions, where local school data are now a recognized factor for home buying, pushing prices upwards and adding to the competitive experience of performing one's middle-class self. To ensure equal opportunities for one's child, one needs, if not to outspend others, then certainly to match the offer and failure to do so, as Frank's work also explores, leads to a real social handicap. Arguing that neoliberalism has rendered family life and education highly expensive commodities, separating them from their core human values, is only to acknowledge part of the problem. What we must also recognize is that to describe education as a commodity is not only to point to the increasingly extortionate fees it commands; it is also to appreciate the neighbouring costs of placing oneself in the position to be educationally competitive – meaning the cost of securing a home in the right area. Kelly shows us that for Helen and Danny the problem is insurmountable, leading to a profound sense of inadequacy for both, which will likely contribute to the termination of a pregnancy and which is, also, a driving factor for Helen's aggressive protection of Liam as an extreme reverse defence mechanism: unable to control what will provide a better life for the family she has created, she at least strives to protect the family she has inherited.

Frank discusses lifestyle envy as 'a corrosive emotion' (2013: 29) and in *Orphans* we witness first-hand how it has influenced Helen's decision to support Liam, as she is fuelled by anger at feeling socially marginalized. The increasing financial inaccessibility of major urban centres by median income families is a key issue adversely impacting Helen and her family, and one of the major thematic nuances of *Orphans*. Frank notes that in the American model a way of resolving the unaffordability of housing within a desirable school catchment area is to substitute the convenience of location by adding to one's commuting time but at least securing desirable schooling standards (2013: 80). For Helen and Danny, whose situation is emblematic of the UK system, however, the compromise of living in an undesirable area does not at least come with the bonus of a positive educational environment for their son – it is merely an act of drastic compromise for the sake of survival, of managing to uphold basic middle-class standards. Even though *Orphans* is a different and more overtly political play than *Love and Money* or *The Ritual Slaughter of Gorge Mastromas*, the texts share common ground in how they explore feelings of lack and envy. Envy, Frank rightly argues, is a complex emotion to account for, as it does not manifest itself directly, but rather emerges as an after-effect of absorbing facts in a way that comes to impact on behavioural choices (2013: 5). As he notes, 'most of the income gains [...] during the past several decades have gone to people at the top of the income distribution [...] [leading] these people to build larger houses' and even though 'There is little evidence that middle-class families envy the good fortune of the wealthy [...] the larger houses at the top have led families in the middle to spend sharply higher fractions of their incomes on housing, in the process forcing them to curtail other important categories of spending' (Frank 2013: 5). As the texts examined in this chapter reveal, the false sense of attainability of a more luxurious lifestyle, the product of a neocapitalist bubble, eventually leads to private and collective financial crises. Ultimately, the symptoms of these crises adversely impact well-being even though they were in the first place caused by a misguided drive to improve it. Kelly's writing demonstrates a commitment to understanding how aspects of envy and material desire might manifest themselves corrosively whether self-directed or targeted at others. Frank's observation that 'it's often hard to separate psychological consequences of low rank from other forms of consequences' (2013: 50) mirrors the experience of Kelly's characters, who undergo their own transformation the more they make their way through the processing machine of capitalism. Therefore we witness these characters manifest ailments; inflict these upon others; and in the case of Gorge Mastromas, experience all symptoms at once and transition to a radical form of inhumanity.

The Ritual Slaughter of Gorge Mastromas: A capitalist fable

The Ritual Slaughter of Gorge Mastromas (premiering as *Die Opferung von Gorge Mastromas*, Ruhrfestspiele Recklinghausen; Schauspiel Frankfurt 2012, director Christoph Mehler) was Kelly's first play at the RCT (2013, Theatre Downstairs, director Vicky Featherstone), and, at almost three hours, it was also one of Kelly's longest plays. Critics were divided over it. Some thought the play was a triumph (see Billington 2013), while others declared it utterly disappointing (see Spencer 2013). Starting off deceptively as an abstract text presented on a near – empty stage with speakers recounting major events in Gorge's early life, the play soon takes the shape of a predominantly naturalistic drama which goes on to delve into the protagonist's defining moments as he grows older. From the cool distanciation of the beginning we transition to the intimate detail, the tediousness, even, of a life. More than anything, Gorge is presented as an Everyman in a morality tale which combines the metaphysical – the beginning of the script marks him as a singular entity in a tangled universe, a solitary light in a constellation of stars, as the set points to – with the utterly mundane, and the morally blank with the psychologically complex to echo the question that we encounter throughout: 'goodness or cowardice'? (Kelly 2013b, recurring).

The way in which *The Ritual Slaughter of Gorge Mastromas* tackles the definitive question of how much of oneself must be sacrificed at the altar of success shows that with this play, too, Kelly remained highly attuned to the crisis of individualism at the face of radical financial challenge. This is where the value of the text lies – in the contribution it made to the debate on the international stages of major EU economies, rather than in how it pushed forms further. Compared to some of

Kelly's earlier work, including the plays discussed in this chapter, *The Ritual Slaughter of Gorge Mastromas* is structurally and aesthetically regressive. Particularly in Featherstone's production, designed by Tom Scutt, the text never quite encouraged interpretative or visual complexity, staying rather two-dimensional and mostly coming across as safe and predictable. In Frankfurt, Mehler's production, designed by Jochen Schmitt, had taken more risk, draining the pictorial element of the play off of its inherent naturalism through blacked out backgrounds that rendered the text more haunting and less directly referential compared to the mostly faithful to reality set that we saw at the RCT. If *The Ritual Slaughter of Gorge Mastromas* merits our attention, this is because it invests in the anonymous individual, who, ironically, is given a distinctive name and surname that are even foregrounded to the play's title. This technique emphasizes the individual's role in maintaining or questioning capitalist structures, not a name or a face in a crowd, but an active agent. Responsibility, then, becomes less readily renounceable. Once Kelly has focused on the individual, he then concentrates on their tragedy leading to inevitable collapse. The individual's surrender to capitalism is shown as a ritual slaughter indeed.

In fact Gorge (pronounced 'George' in performance) is the only character given a full name in an array of characters who are only elliptically introduced by means of a first name or merely an initial. The titular character's name could be interpreted in many ways – the misspelling might be an accident, implying the near-accidental coming into being of Gorge, whose conception was not entirely planned (Kelly 2013b: 7). If the protagonist's name were pronounced as it is spelled [gôrj], it would underline what it implies: the hidden depths and inner workings of the human body. In Gorge's case, how others perceive him differs greatly to how he experiences his profound dilemmas and catastrophic choices. The surname points to another misspelling – it is almost, but not quite right. The same sensation accompanies Gorge his entire life as he attempts to build his narrative of success. The 'Mastro-' prefix implies a man who creates, a leader, even. These are the qualities that Gorge strives for, except his labour is ultimately fruitless, irrespective of his wealth, because he does not attain moral contentment.

Everything about Gorge imbues the play with the style of a fable and even a parable, from the dialectical introduction to his story, to the definitive moment of choice between good and evil and the dire consequences that follow. Where Kelly's play is challenged is in accomplishing a nuanced portrayal of Gorge: even though it invests in depicting his turmoil, it does not blur the boundaries between 'good' and 'evil' substantially to capture the complexity of wavering as sacrifices are made. This lack ultimately renders the play more descriptive than inquisitive, making it more difficult to grasp why Gorge is a character worth spending time or attention on. But that is also the play's main device: the unremarkable nature of Gorge renders him the potential double of anyone at all – he is a blank canvas unto which our worst fears over humanity might be projected.

Gorge's Vice or Virtue choice arrives relatively early, when he is presented with the business option of an ethical failure or an immoral success. Gorge's crucial moment occurs when 'A', a woman in a position of power against Gorge's employer, whose company is failing, tempts Gorge with a life-changing offer:

> **A**   [...] Existence is not what you have up until this moment thought it is. It is not fair, it is not kind, it is not just – the majority of the universe is in fact so cold that it would freeze the water in your eyes in an instant. [...] Most of the world are ignorant of this, they believe in god, or daddy or Marx or the unseen hand of the market or honesty or goodness. They swim through life, eyes closed, taking it on the chin and getting fucked. [...] You're like that.
> But a tiny, tiny handful of us, a small fraction, [...] know the real nature of life. And to those people is given the world. They are rich and powerful because they have everything and they will do anything. The rest of the world will always be meat to them, cattle, animals to be herded and sometimes hunted. We are a secret society [...]. (Kelly 2013b: 46–47)

All Gorge needs to do to join this 'secret society' is advise his employer that selling the company is the only viable option, as he proceeds to do. From that point onwards Gorge achieves success, building his career and life on the same principle of emotionless, relentless deceit. We hear from the intervening narration interrupting the otherwise linear plot (a technique of stepping outside the frame which allows a 'breaking the fourth wall' moment) that Gorge essentially developed an empire reigning over rivals, absorbing others' businesses and expanding into every conceivable outlet, including, of course, the media, from where his influence became immense (Kelly 2013b: 51). Gorge's godlike presence, constituting hubris of the highest degree as a human believes he has the authority to manipulate the lives of other humans, further adds to the play's parabolic slant. As Kelly's text puts it, 'Without wanting to get too biblical it was as if he [Gorge] had been given the keys to the kingdom' (Kelly 2013b: 50).

In terms of Gorge's relationships, there is never a separation between professional interest, manipulation and personal matters. From the conquest of a reluctant Louisa through the construction of a false life narrative of abuse, recovery and success that saw him win her sympathy and love to deploying this same narrative as a popularity mechanism, Gorge creates a persona for himself that draws admiration and acceptance, becoming paradigmatic of the triumph of overcoming and humanity. In this way, Kelly's play adds a metaphysical twist to the modern-day experience of wealth equalling power and celebrity, pointing to anyone's ability to concoct a life narrative and establish it as fact in the era of a digitally mediatized experience, whose outlets are as intangible as their impact is immediate. As 'Gorge went Global', a brand bigger than the person, it appeared that nothing was out of reach – and that he had complete control over life or death (Kelly 2013b: 82). This becomes abundantly evident when Gorge murders his brother Gel, who threatens to expose his deceit, and suffers no consequences. As he says in their final confrontation:

> **Mastromas** You idiot, you moron, you stupid moron. You don't know the world, are you telling me about this world, you don't know it! I know it, I make it, Gel, I fucking make the world, people like me, we own it. (Kelly 2013b: 97)

What is more interesting than this somewhat expected transgression is Kelly's treatment of time and dramatic action and how he works to create the impression that Gorge's time has extended beyond our real time, as we transition into an uncertain future with him. The scene between Gorge and Gel takes place, as the text tells us, in September 2013 – the time when the play opened at the Royal Court (Kelly 2013b: 85). It follows, then, that everything that occurs after this moment happens in the indeterminate future, near or otherwise. This includes the scene when Louisa leaves Gorge and his encounter with the grandson he never knew he had, a son of the daughter he fathered with a woman, who Gorge thought had terminated her pregnancy. That we leave Gorge in flux is symptomatic of the wider feeling of fluidity characterizing a world in crisis, a crisis brought on by the same driving force that gave Gorge his godlike power: money. In that moment, Kelly's play engenders the sense of an uncertain future as shared experience. When Gorge encounters his grandson Pete, he is dumfounded by Pete's resistance to the allure of his world. And even though, mere moments ago, we have witnessed a delirious-sounding Gorge say to Louisa,

> **Mastromas** [...] The things I am capable of. I have changed the inevitable, I have super powers, super abilities, I can stop time and I have the power of prophecy. (Kelly 2013b: 105)

now Gorge's fate seems to be not entirely within his grasp, as we have transitioned to someone else's time, as fluid and self-determined as Gorge's was; and it is a universe of possibilities that does not appear to include him. Pete leaves Gorge in a state of uncertainty as to whether he will return to see him, suggesting, however, that it is unlikely. Thus, he deprives otherwise childless Gorge of an heir – of someone to whom he could bequeath his so-called kingdom. And even though Gorge gives Pete the same spiel he received from A in the beginning as he says 'I'm offering you everything. You can do with it [...] whatever you think is right', Pete resists (Kelly 2013b: 116). Leading up to what is likely his final goodbye to Gorge, Pete employs metaphysical rhetoric to deny Gorge what he desires:

Pete This moment, this... choice – it hasn't happened before. Never. So it could go either way...

[...]

What you've said [the offer of money and power] is of no interest to me whatsoever.

[...]

There's a whole world out there, Gorge. It's not all just about you, you know. (Kelly 2013b: 117)

As Pete succinctly reduces Gorge's assumed cosmic significance, the play exposes the limitless grandeur-, god-delusion of capitalism in a manner bearing consideration. The metaphysical manoeuvre in new writing has been discussed by Megson, who has traced the development of this phenomenon in the work of some of the most experimental contemporary playwrights, particularly with reference to how they have conceptualized experience and time – for example in suspended moments and non-realist, non-linear depictions (Megson 2013: 32–56). The relevance to the specific text is clear when we consider how time is conceptualized in the form as well as content of the play as subjective and flexible. Megson's consideration of faith in the context of the post-secular in contemporary experience is also significant. The affirmation of the supernatural power of wealth as described by A in the above-cited quotation, particularly when she mentions the omnipotence of those who 'know the real nature of life', the same group who are 'given the world', is striking. The parallels to the myth of Hercules and the choice of Vice or Virtue persist when we consider this description alongside the fact that Hercules was a demigod on earth – the same status that Gorge is essentially invited to assume. Kelly's play is turning the myth on its head, exploring the other path, that of Vice, in a world where morals are derided as weakness – a lesson that Gorge learns early in life. What follows is a process of labours, though far from driven by a noble goal: demanding strategy and careful execution, these are the moments in which Mastromas must repeatedly conquer his humanity and eradicate others in his path towards corporate domination.

We have previously seen Kelly's fascination with paradigms of the theatre canon involving the trials of iconic male characters in *The Gods Weep*; in *The Ritual Slaughter of Gorge Mastromas* he reaches further back into humanity's storybook to continue his quest into the primal instincts that rate power and survival above all. In his analysis of the metaphysical turn in contemporary drama, Megson specifically refers to *The Gods Weep*, framing it in a way that is directly relevant to *The Ritual Slaughter of Gorge Mastromas*. As he notes, *The Gods Weep* 'is set in a world of corporate infighting where economic competition and physical brutality have become indivisible, and where capitalist exchange has colonized the deepest levels of subjectivity' (Megson 2013: 48). Megson's analysis of how Kelly structures time and experience, his 'dramatic trajectory [...] recalibrat[ing] the experience of what "now" might mean outside of the temporal matrix of capitalist production' (Megson 2013: 49), will remind us of the way in which, in *The Ritual Slaughter of Gorge Mastromas*, the entire experience of humanity is recalibrated through the viewpoint of one man and his forever suspended experience. Mastromas inhabits a present that is rooted in capitalist insularity and yet transcends 'here and now' limitations to render him both of this world and superstructural to it through his overtowering control. Proceeding from Megson, I argue that as we observe Gorge's interactions with others we witness constant manifestations of A's trick of pausing time so she and Gorge could step outside of the office 'here and now' in the definitive moment in the play for him to experience his reckoning with the universe as he makes the decision of which cosmic path to follow and thereby subscribe to his fate. Megson concludes that the '"metaphysical turn" in theatre' is responsive to 'a time when public confidence in ideological and religious belief-systems has become increasingly embattled' (Megson 2013: 52). Writing about Kelly's earlier work, Rebellato notes that 'Kelly's characters occasionally demonstrate an imaginative landscape of cosmological scale [...] reaching for some foundational beliefs (even, at times, a kind of religion)' (2007: 605–606).

Today, when we examine Kelly's playwriting following the major crises of the late 2000s and early 2010s, we can contextualize such views more fully. After subscribing to the transformative power of money and deifying capitalism has failed, leading to the collapse of a major institution – the economy, which, unlike religious belief systems, transcends cultural and geographical boundaries with great ease, humanity found itself at a crisis so extensive and unfathomable that no familiar storytelling devices could suffice to capture this capitalist apocalypse. The metaphysical manoeuvre provides a schema within which the unfathomable might be represented, its cosmic open-endedness offering an outlet for the frustration and wonderment we are experiencing in our present day. It is unsurprising that Kelly has found it difficult to identify 'capitalism', 'corruption' or the process of learning to be deceitful as the defining theme of the play (Kelly 2013a). *The Ritual Slaughter of Gorge Mastromas* may incorporate these themes, but it also extends beyond them, asking large-scale existential questions about experience, perception and our place in a world that we share with others – and how that tension might be negotiated, or, otherwise, become catastrophic.

Conclusion

This chapter began with a reference to Pinter and it seems suitable to conclude in the same way. The hovering sense of menace, claustrophobia within the confined spaces of oneself and one's surroundings and dark humour alongside a gradual revelation of the truth after multiple digressions, as well as the investment in politics and formal experimentation in Kelly's theatre locate his writing sensibilities close to Pinter's. In his oft-quoted Nobel acceptance speech, 'Art, Truth and Politics', Pinter begins:

> In 1958 I wrote the following:
> 'There are no hard distinctions between what is real and what is unreal, nor between what is true and what is false. A thing is not necessarily either true or false. It can be both true and false.'

I believe that these assertions still make sense and do still apply to the exploration of reality through art. So as a writer I stand by them but as a citizen I cannot. As a citizen I must ask: What is true? What is false? (2005)

Kelly's quest for truth emerges strongly (see also Rebellato 2007); when *The Ritual Slaughter of Gorge Mastromas* opened in Germany, one critic commented on Kelly's ongoing preoccupation with the topic, noting that Kelly's audience and his characters experience equal difficulty in the search for truth, which never yields a straightforward answer (Heppekausen 2012). Kelly, like Pinter, probes the intricate relationship between truth and falsity and in his frequently referenced Theatertreffen/Stückermarkt speech, we can detect both commitment and frustration (Kelly 2012). The question that lies at the heart of Kelly's work is how we might account for the truth of our frustrating experience as humanity finds itself at a crossroads, having to account for the transgressions it has committed in the name of so-called progress and prosperity. Kelly's plays have the forensic focus of police crime scene investigations: once the inevitable crime has taken place, what we need to embark upon is an understanding of what brought us here in the first place. The puzzle needs to be pieced together by the spectators and our own inactions and culpabilities might render us part of it. Given the remit of this book, this chapter has concentrated on work by Kelly that has been directly responsive to issues of financial crisis and social class, but it is fair to say that Kelly's theatre has never wandered far from politics. Against the progress that was promised, the surrender to capitalism has returned humanity to its pre-civilized beginnings and survival of the fittest mode and Kelly's playwriting is committed to depicting the implications of the fact. The very title of Kelly's recent play, referencing a 'ritual slaughter', points directly to this return to primeval behaviours in the twenty-first century, suggesting a theme that persists throughout his work.

4

Austerity vs Prosperity: Duncan Macmillan, Nick Payne and the Ecology of Emotion

From the 2000s onwards civic responsibility towards the environment became heightened and accountability foregrounded. If we were the generations at risk of bequeathing only debt to those who came after us, a by-product of over-consumption and the subsequent austerity crisis, the latter manifested itself in intriguing ways, in both the form and content of new work for the stage. Other than the grand media narratives of an impending natural catastrophe from the 1990s, presented with a sense of urgency and preventability that appealed to basic human decency, an almost romantic call to action for Greenpeace or WWF at a time when environmentally friendly brands were still a novelty, the generation of writers that came of age in the 2010s also inherited another major narrative: that of austerity. It is not surprising that much of the most memorable work of the twenty-first-century British stage, especially from the 2010s onwards, has asked questions about our relationship to a universe growing weary of our self-indulgence. At the same time, the key principle of austerity, the omnipresent moral call to repay and economize, began to affect the texts themselves, from themes and content to structure and length. What the writers had absorbed in terms of social climate generated an artistic response that drew us deeper into dramatic minimalism. The plays were shorter, the dialogue snappier, the feeling one of alienation. But at least the need to discuss our alienations – from each other, from our world, from ourselves – was starting to bring us together in the theatre.

At the heart of the texts discussed in this chapter lies the need of appreciating our debt, broadly conceived on financial, social as well as preservational terms, to the world. The plays on which this chapter concentrates, Duncan Macmillan's *Lungs* (2011) and Nick Payne's *Constellations* (2012), highlight the issue in different ways, while sharing key representational devices. The texts are economical, their form an instinctive response to the financial crisis. In dispensing with excess and being notably sparing in the staging resources they require, the plays are also very attractive for international productions. Still, even in their own kind of austerity, the plays are also defiant. As this chapter will discuss, the texts open up expansive avenues for the imagination, resisting any possible restrictions that may have been imposed by their own forms from within and undermining spectatorial expectations.

The economical text as antidote: Tackling mega-crises against the austerity of feeling

It is telling that two of the most notable examples of how nature and our universe became a pivot for new writing, *Ten Billion* and *2071*, took on the economic form of the performance lecture. As these works examined how the planet has been led to a combustion point with mathematical precision, the directness of the titles was reflected in their style and content: now was the time for the audience to pay urgent attention. The director Katie Mitchell was the link between the two productions, a driving force for their commissioning. Both performances opened at the RCT, though in different spaces: *Ten Billion* (2012) at the Theatre Upstairs and *2071* (2014/15) at the Theatre Downstairs.

Stephen Emmott, Mitchell's academic partner in the making of *Ten Billion*, subsequently published the text in a style and format that made it accessible and attractive to a wide readership (2013). One can imagine the challenge of the task, which *2071* also had to contend with in terms of digesting arguably the largest-scale crisis facing humanity in a way that would engage audiences, and subsequently readers, encouraging change. The fact that the text of *2071* was initially made available as a free download from the RCT website following its premiere production emphasized the importance of its social message and the fact that it was imperative for it to have a wide reach. In the recent period, the crises that humanity has experienced on a global scale had primarily been constituted on capitalist terms – most notably the banking crisis of the previous decade. *Ten Billion* and *2071* were also about the economy, but broached from the angle of its mutual reciprocity with the environment. Ultimately, both shows asked, it was a matter of whether we would continue foregrounding a failing capitalist system at the expense of the natural world and of humanity's very survival.

That texts like these were not 'heavily theatrical', as Mitchell observes, is an understatement (Merritt 2014). Finding the right form was crucial and the major concern was how to create the impression of a story with a climax that would be the call to collective action coinciding with our realization for its imminent necessity (Merritt 2014). The fact that Emmott and Rapley had on-stage rather than merely consultant roles served the affective engagement of the audience, cultivating the urgent attention to data that the expert could command, as opposed to an actor, whose presence, working within the frames of theatrical convention, might enable a 'switching-off' for the audience, a surrender to the belief that there is an element of fiction involved (Emmott and Mitchell 2012). Emmott and Rapley's respective data, then, presented in a theatre auditorium for the audience to ponder on, immediately acquired amplified reach.

The greatest difference in two otherwise similar shows, driven by the same impetus of incentivizing audiences towards understanding and action, is their perspective and the message they leave us with. In *Ten Billion*, this was the brutal revelation of how much has been irretrievably compromised and how accountable we are. In *2071*, it was taking responsibility for what happened next. It is a difference identified by the theatre-makers themselves as well as by critics, mostly stemming from the final lines of Emmott's text:

> We urgently need to do – and I mean actually do – something radical to avert a global catastrophe. But I don't think we will.
> I think we're fucked.
> I asked one of the most rational, brightest scientists I know [...] if there was just one thing he had to do about the situation we face, what would it be?
> His reply?
> 'Teach my son how to use a gun.' (2013: 196–198)

Drastically deviating from Emmott's climactic and indignant finale, Rapley and Macmillan's closing statements on what Emmott calls 'an unprecedented emergency' (2013: 195) took a conversational tone:

> There will be carbon atoms that were generated by this event [the performance] that will still be in the air in 2071 [...].
> That's our legacy.
> [...]
> Do we care about the world's poor? Do we care about future generations?
> Do we see the environment as part of the economy, or the economy as part of the environment?
> The whole point about climate change is that, despite having been revealed by science, it is not really an issue about science, it is an issue about what sort of world we want to live in.
> What kind of future do we want to create? (Macmillan and Rapley 2015)

An engagement with the texts in performance, but also in their published versions, renders another difference clear: the playwright's presence. Although both shows created powerful stage moments, *2071* stood out in how it reached audiences. It delivered the next act in the theatre's effort to merge the private with the public as the path towards collective action. Macmillan's dramaturgical intervention was crucial in that the piece did not only appeal to our intellect, but also to our sensitivity towards humanity and our own human condition. Then again, *2071* also emulated and honed a formula that Macmillan had used previously: the exhaustive discursive analysis of data, removed from the daunting sphere of scientific research and applied to the everyday level of lived experience.

Lungs: From the personal to the universal

No work by Macmillan provides a more apt depiction of the non-binary between personal and universal than *Lungs*, a two-hander about a couple debating whether they should have a baby. The concept of crisis is twofold: it relates to the couple's relationship, namely to the internal questioning processes and trauma that the decision instigates, but also to society, as the couple deploy numerous arguments against having a baby relating to the impact one more human would make on an overburdened environment. Until *Lungs* British theatre had been circling the topic of the environment, but results were sometimes lukewarm. There was still some way to go towards making an urgent, knowing statement that adequately reflected the complexity of the contemporary experience, as individuals are confronted by the dual challenge of the environment and the economy. The question of what form would adequately represent this wavering and uncertainty was pivotal. The early indications of what Billington called 'the new growth industry' (Billington 2011a), that is plays dealing with climate change, included attempts taking different shape and form.

In terms of the most impactful moments, the Bush Theatre's *The Contingency Plan* (2009), consisting of the plays *On the Beach* and *Resilience* by Steve Waters, took a naturalistic approach to the exploration of an impending earth disaster in Britain, locating questions of scientific responsibility firstly within a family and then within a government context, with partially recurring characters and the action unfolding in '*The near future*' (Waters 2009: 8, 86). Later that year in the same theatre Nick Payne's *If There Is I Haven't Found*

It Yet dealt with the environmental crisis through the lens of familial crisis. In Chapter 2 of this book I discuss one of the definitive plays of the period, Mike Bartlett's *Earthquakes in London* (2010), which combined climate change with a host of other social and existential concerns. Meanwhile, in 2011, the RCT staged Richard Bean's *The Heretic*, which once more followed a naturalistic style combined with satire and a somewhat far-fetched plot. The protagonist was Dr Dianne Cassell, an academic specializing on Palaeogeophysics and Geodynamics. As the central metaphor of the play suggested, Dr Cassell committed the sin of negating the dominant narrative in her field: the existence of climate change as an objectively provable phenomenon. The idea of the environment becoming a new religion, creating fervent believers and deniers of climate change, was also identified as a new thematic strand by critics in other work staged at the time, most notably the National Theatre's *Greenland*, expansive in its coverage yet more economic in duration. The piece saw collective effort by Moira Buffini, Matt Charman, Penelope Skinner and Jack Thorne attempt to tackle environmental crisis through diverging personal stories converging in the same universal problem in an elaborate staging at the Lyttelton. Meanwhile, at the Tricycle Theatre and running concurrently with *The Heretic* and *Greenland*, *Water*, a piece by the company Filter and director David Farr found an evocative expressionist way of intermeshing facts, fears and experiences into performance. *Water* managed to conceptualize the impact of climate change on an international yet individualized scale without following the path of the large-scale, resource-heavy spectacle. Interestingly, this piece was not actually new: the Tricycle run was its second one, as *Water* had previously been staged at the Lyric Hammersmith as early as 2007. The theatre, then, was redefining its methods of staging major political issues through personal stories, recalibrating them to adjust to the fluid atmosphere of our present with varying degrees of success.

It was in this context that *Lungs* premiered at the Studio Theatre in Washington D.C. in a production directed by Aaron Posner, followed by the British premiere at Sheffield's Crucible Studio Theatre (Paines

Plough Roundabout Season) directed by Richard Wilson. Early reviews of *Lungs* were indicative of the attention the play attracted. Gardner found *Lungs* to be 'distinctive [...], brutally honest, funny, edgy and current', adding that 'It gives voice to a generation for whom uncertainty is a way of life' and describing its protagonists as 'flawed, but deeply human, people who you don't always like but start to feel you might love' (2011b). The play takes an honest, peering look at human transience in a world where we have already made an imprint for future generations, not only in terms of our debt and overconsumption of material goods, but also in terms of natural resources and, of course, energy. The hesitation of Macmillan's characters, therefore, is a defence mechanism in a social climate that encourages self-restraint. It is both our permanence and our impermanence that the play deals with and Macmillan's intelligent dialogue is neither optimistic nor pessimistic, neither hopeful nor fearful, but decidedly in the space in-between, as characters attempt to negotiate their individual lives and collective future.

The dialectical structure of the play communicates the characters' self- and social discovery through conversation and debate. The couple are not given names, their generic nature rendering them comparable to anyone belonging to a broadly conceived Western middle class, educated group in their late twenties or early thirties. Macmillan simply calls his characters 'M' and 'W', presumably for 'Man' and 'Woman', hinting at their adaptability and universality. The characters' dialogue reflects with eerie accuracy the hazing experience of working-age generations at the grip of a crisis that, like a post-capitalist Hydra, is rearing heads in too many directions simultaneously. Other than economy and the environment, the play presents us with issues including employment and labour versus intellectual and creative reward, social expectations and norms, compromise, illness, failing families, trust, loyalty and sexuality. That these concerns are debated by the couple in a breathless verbal pace with no changes in set, costume, light, sound or time (an interval, for example) that might indicate shifts in action serves the exhausting feeling of modern lives, where transitions are speedy, tensions multiple and problem processing time little to none.

This feeling of chronic uncertainty rampant in working-age individuals, especially those who have not experienced the stability and permanence that was at least a possibility for previous generations, is amongst the concerns that Zygmunt Bauman and Carlo Bordoni discuss in *State of Crisis* (2014). Bordoni provides a historical overview of the transition in humanity's relationship to the natural world upon the realization that man was not at the mercy of nature, but had an element of control, which came with the acquisition of greater scientific knowledge. This is where, he notes, a shift was recorded, meaning that what were formerly thought of as natural disasters changed to moral ones due to the unquestionable factor of human agency (Bauman and Bordoni 2014: 55–56). As Bordoni observes, this has involved the understanding that all events occurring within the natural world are explicable and humans are accountable, since there are 'always breeches, carelessness, incompetence, omissions' on the basis of which a natural disaster changes from preventable to inevitable (Bauman and Bordoni 2014: 55). In Bordoni's discourse nature is given as paradigm, our control over it and the failures to which our (in)actions have resulted illustrating that with more means comes more power. It is part of the same process of arrogance and ignorance that also led to the identification of well-being with financial prosperity, eventually forcing the realization that resources are finite and over-consumption produces dire consequences (Bauman and Bordoni 2014: 55). Therefore, any certainties that were built on the belief of a 'permanent' flow of resources were bound to be destroyed. In the recent period, treating the environment in a utilitarian way without a consideration for consequences has been metonymic for every other neoliberalist act that has served personal goals over public welfare. And so we have arrived at the present juncture of resource exhaustion (natural, financial, moral), which has delivered society into a situation where all previous certainties are collapsing. As Bordoni observes, 'behind this philosophy of uncertainty, [...] which not only affects Europe but is rampant [...] at a global level, lies the neoliberal belief that everyone should provide for themselves [...]' (Bauman and Bordoni 2014: 57). Of course it is not merely a question of compromised empathy having a domino effect on community, but of a callous disregard for how one's choices might adversely impact on others' quality of life. Proceeding from Bordoni and with specific reference to the Anthropocene, Bauman asserts that what is ailing society is the enduring misconception that we have either the authority or the knowledge/ability for the 'human management of humans, nature and their mutual interaction' (Bauman and Bordoni 2014: 76).

Macmillan's protagonists attempt to reconcile the known and unknown variables impacting their lives, seeking to take some moral responsibility in a neoliberalist climate where the sense of moral responsibility has become redundant. This process of trying to synthesize the little they can control towards a viable solution for their future, as well as for that of society, is the epicentre of their dialectics. We are dealing with two individuals who have been indoctrinated in the world of neoliberalism but have also seen it collapse, therefore having been given the tools to question it – as they do, repeatedly in the course of the play. In the process they interrogate their own rights, desires, impulses and duties and attempt to trace their way back to functioning not as part of an individualist vacuum, but of a social unit. They are trying, therefore, to shed the past narrative which was, as Bordoni adds, driven by the urge to deplete the environment as one more act of selfish procurement for oneself, with one's fellow humans seen not as such but as extrinsic to our own goals (Bauman and Bordoni 2014: 81). The way in which this concept is delivered formally means that *Lungs* is also shedding the narrative structures of the past. Staged in isolation, the couple may be shown as separate from the world, but only insofar as they are struggling to resituate themselves within it, to find a narrative for themselves as individuals and citizens whereby one does not annihilate the other. There is a primal and paradigmatic feel emanating from this 'Everycouple', debating one of the oldest topics in human history: life and procreation. Even the generic names 'M' and

'W' point to the fact that these characters are a metaphor, big and small at the same time: from them stems the creation of life, the future of the planet. The text might be tight and economical, but through such a device Macmillan allows space for the metaphysical. 'M' and 'W' are a kind of contemporary Adam and Eve.

Lungs has the capability to take the spectator on a journey on the basis of its intelligent language alone. Macmillan does not call for anything radical in his stage directions, noting that 'The play is written to be performed on a bare stage. There is no scenery, no furniture, no props and no mime' (2011: 9). Such a guideline, however limiting it might appear – especially as it is accompanied by the note that no other performance effects should be used to alter the natural flow of dialogue – still allows space for interpretation and intervention. This was accomplished particularly poignantly in Mitchell's production at the Schaubühne Berlin (2013), which responded intuitively to the rhythm of the play, from the physical effort of speech to the somatic and metaphorical breathlessness involved in keeping up pace with the world, as Macmillan's characters are attempting to do. The two actors were each placed on a substantial podium/capacitor, separate from each other and facing forward, towards the audience, for the duration of the seventy-five minute performance. As spectators waited to enter the auditorium, an explanatory note was distributed to us, offering a diagram of the space as well as the core facts behind what each member of the company contributed in terms of energy production and keeping the show running.

Specifically, the two actors on standard, stationary bicycles (centre stage) and four additional cyclists on A-Frame standing bicycles (visible to the audience but on the edge of the set, two cyclists placed front left and two front right, following the curvature of the auditorium) produced the energy resources for the show in real time. Upstage centre spectators could see the sound operator's desk. The show was built in such a way that it enabled actors and cyclists to produce a combined result of 623.5 watt-hours, as the accompanying material for the production explained. Every aspect of the production, including lighting, sound, microphones, speakers and projector was powered through this. Therefore, the performance was the undertaking and product of collective labour, with cyclists also being credited in accompanying materials. This directly reflected the level of collective work and responsibility to power and preserve the world that the play alludes to. In the two actors' case, the task was twofold: on the one hand delivering their lines and maintaining the realm of the play and on the other pedalling as required to maintain the necessary energy levels for the show. This was a metaphor for the kind of constant, even relentless multitasking that individuals such as those that Macmillan portrays are expected to perform on an everyday basis. Overall, Mitchell's staging offered a visual representation of the fact that the world does not stop for us, but nor can we take a passive stance; rather, we need to imagine ourselves as part of the developments that we are shaping ourselves, through our very presence on the planet, and simply keep going. Mitchell's method was, therefore, highly responsive to the content of this environmentally conscious text.

The play has barely started when we encounter the first reference to effort to cope with and process facts, physically exemplified: 'Breathe', says M to W (Macmillan 2011: 11). He has just introduced the idea of having a baby, and she is panicking. The irony strikes us immediately: the environment for their conversation is a megastore (IKEA), dominant and alluring for global middle classes, typifying easy access to goods, encouraging consumption and uniformity, over-production and our enabling of it, by promoting a desirable life image. The pace and mood for the entire piece are set from that point onwards; references to breathing and discussion of consumption and languishing resources come at torrential speed. Throughout the play characters describe struggling to breathe: from 'hyperventilating' (Macmillan 2011: 12), to 'Catch[ing] [...one's] breath' (Macmillan 2011: 13) to 'oxygenating' (Macmillan 2011: 21) to 'tak[ing] a deep breath and giv[ing] a huge sigh' (Macmillan 2011: 61) to being unable to find comfort from dyspnoea even by opening a window because it might be 'stuffy' inside but 'it's just as bad out there' (Macmillan 2011: 75). Like the experience of being in constant motion, intuitively captured in Mitchell's staging, characters – and we, alongside them, working to process what we are seeing and hearing – feel that 'This is all just going at a hundred miles an hour and I need a second to breathe' (Macmillan 2011: 83). The ultimate breathless moment of the play comes as it climaxes, captured in the rhythm of labour contractions, when M and W finally have their baby after a miscarriage, a separation and an unexpected reunion (Macmillan 2011: 85). If the play has leapt from one episode in the characters' lives to another at fast pace, from here on it speeds through life events at a dizzying speed of extreme fast-forward. In the final moments of the play, we encounter a monologue by W. She is ageing, at the early stages of a mental ailment, about to be placed in a care home by her son. Speaking at her husband's graveside, she is unsure whether she will be able to return. In an atypically quiet moment, the play suggests that only when we have taken ourselves out of the everyday race can we experience a sense of relief and pause. There is one final breathing reference that communicates this. Now in a future that has become present, in a world even more burdened by pollution and emergencies, W observes: 'It's a nice cool day today, like we used to have. Fresh air. No sirens. No noise. Nothing' (Macmillan 2011: 87).

In Mitchell's production M's death was communicated silently by the light fading into darkness on his podium, as the actor stopped pedalling. W spoke her final lines as a large part of the 'stage' was now immersed in darkness. The soft yet stark image of loss coinciding with the finale of the play captured powerfully the significance of Macmillan's final '*Lights out*' stage direction (2011: 87). In this production the note acquired rich poignancy, as lives expire, having performed their inevitable circle, for which the bicycle as object but also the very act of cycling, a course towards a destination, served as metaphor. The absence of light and electric power at the end of *Lungs/Atmen* implied the extinguishing of humanity and its energy through time; the struggling planet gasping and expiring as its resources dwindle; the cessation of constant movement as the need to re-evaluate our choices hits home. Of course it also hinted at the power of humans to intervene, interrogating how our collective efforts might be put to good use. If the labour of a theatre company powered a night out in the theatre for a community of spectators, the question of what we might accomplish for our community on a larger scale, when we actively try to put our resourcefulness to the test, lingers.

The very title of Macmillan's play points to the human anatomy, our biology and the pulsations of breathing, emphasizing physical effort. Its rendition as *Atmen* [to breathe/breathing] for the Schaubühne production may have sacrificed some of the visceral implication, the idea of bodies inhabiting the planet, absorbing its resources, but it served Mitchell's concept well. The act of increasingly laboured breathing by the performers, as well as our spectatorial experience of physically sharing in the same space that they worked to keep viable in terms of energy, likewise working with them to stay in the incessant pace of the narrative, was reflected in the title. The overarching meaning of the title, of course, which remains in both cases, relates to the act of requiring oxygen to stay alive. The images of being out of breath, pointing to a sense of metaphorical and/or physical suffocation are therefore supported by the text through continuous references to the transgressions against the environment that our mere act of living – let alone procreating – delivers daily. As Gardner observed, the play offers 'a sharp and contemporary look at love at the age of anxiety' (Cook and Gardner 2013) – and that anxiety permeates every aspect of being, from the microcosm of the house to the role we play in our universe. This is about decisions as they are made dialectically and debating the cost of actions in real time, echoing Macmillan's note that he is 'interested in characters struggling with decisions in the present tense [...] characters attempting to come to a consensus and the impossibility of this when every individual experiences the world differently' (Macmillan 2013: 451).

Macmillan's characters, striving to extricate themselves from the neoliberalisms of the past, returning to Bauman and Bordoni, are burdened by narratives of civic guilt, trying to be responsible at an age of uncertainty. They live with the fear that their goals and achievements might ultimately appear pointless in a world that is not accommodating of the individual, despite the facile doctrines of neoliberalism. The play reveals how capitalist structures have been inherited by post-recession generations who recognize their vacuum, yet are not able to extricate themselves completely. *Lungs* is entirely aware of the shackles and keeps returning to questions of economy, austerity and how the financial systems presented as inevitable, alongside the transgressions they enabled, have conditioned our current experience. What makes this, and other plays that share the sensibilities of *Lungs* (one of which is, certainly, *Constellations*), distinctive is that their angle of vision is the environment and our cosmos more broadly, returning to the question Macmillan and Rapley later posed in *2071*: 'Do we see the environment as part of the economy, or the economy as part of the environment?' (2015). *Lungs* is therefore a cultural product of its time; its stark structural lines reflect the present austerity doctrine of both being contained, disallowing excess, and containing our experience within set parameters to prevent further crises.

Macmillan has been open about his reservations towards dialogue that flows seamlessly, without manifesting the infelicities of everyday speech and experience. What redrafting affords him, he notes, is the ability to strip the text from anything redundant and arrive at a form and content that are 'the most economical', a 'cutting' process that continues in rehearsals (Macmillan 2013: 451–452). It helps that Macmillan brings the dual perspective of playwright and director to the process, the ability to sense the rhythm of the text and how it might physically translate on the stage. It is indicative that a play Macmillan chose to direct in 2013, in the same theatre where *Lungs* premiered, was Bartlett's two-hander *Contractions*. This intelligent and abrasive text depicts successive stages in the bullying and eventual submission of a female office executive by her female line manager, where the extreme violence of the plot is contained within language. It is a starkly economical play, painfully honest in how capitalism has the power to erode all layers of basic human decency. What Macmillan reveals as attractive elements in choosing a directing project, namely 'a compelling central dynamic between the characters [...] under pressure to make decisions' (2013: 452), links to his own playwright sensibilities. There is a sense of urgency, of cosmic significance in decisions made by individuals, contributing a metaphysical element to the plays alongside a social critique. It is a concern also captured in *Constellations*, where the implications of our decisions take a much broader significance. The central structural device of *Constellations* offers a way of transcending the limitations and confines of the theatrical here and now. *Lungs* achieves this through the feeling of sailing through time, so that experience flows rather than being tied to the realistic reproduction of the everyday.

As Macmillan's characters struggle to keep breathing through choices and changes, they experience moral asphyxiation and spiritual apnoea: this constitutes a major part of their private crises, triggered by the capitalist narratives continuing to shape the public realm. We observe this, for example, when M, an artist, concedes defeat and agrees to a corporate job in order to legitimize his transition into adulthood and the decision to have a child. M's body experiences symptoms of rejection of the old value system within which he awkwardly attempts to situate himself. When W compliments his smart suit, M replies 'I feel sick' (Macmillan 2011: 37). When W's first pregnancy ends in a miscarriage, she declares: 'Feel like I've had my skin peeled off' (Macmillan 2011: 65). M and W are both going through their own stages of abjection: his conformity makes him feel that he has sacrificed his integrity; her inability to reproduce imposes a stamp of social failure experienced corporeally. Their environmental concerns, then, become impossibly intermeshed with their personal insecurities and social anxieties. At the heart of their crisis lies the fact that they are acutely aware of the value judgements they are receiving both as a couple and as citizens. Failing to start a family will hurt them on the front of social expectations; failing to abolish their desire for a child and persuasively indoctrinate themselves in the environment narrative renders them less effective as responsible, political subjects.

Balancing their agency seems unlikely and reconciling the tensions is, for all of M and W's dialectics, ultimately doomed. Therefore, their relationship eventually succumbs to gravity. The reason emerging is what the text astutely describes as 'the last real taboo' (Macmillan 2011: 38): man versus humanity. When M and W meet again after their separation, they are both, to an extent, disenfranchised; time has weakened their defences. Their bodies have also been weighed down by a world whose atmosphere feels increasingly heavier – other than the laboured breathing, we now hear references to bodies sweating and uncomfortably attempting to adapt (Macmillan 2011: 71). At the same time, M admits that he has surrendered the effort of critical thinking over facts he cannot alter – in mental inertia he has discovered a way of feeling lighter (Macmillan 2011: 72–73). But rather than conscious inaction, he seems to have been affected by over-information paralysis: as we see in *Ten Billion* and *2071*, having the knowledge at our disposal does not necessarily mean that we can bring ourselves to the position of implementing change. The task seems too enormous, and the spectrum of choices seems as much infinite as it does predetermined, a concern that *Constellations* elevates to its primary thematic concern.

Constellations: From the individual to the multiversal

As in *Lungs*, the stage economy of *Constellations* is striking, the entire plot revolving strictly around a couple, and, also as in *Lungs*, the thematic spectrum of the play widens its frame of reference considerably: the text conjures up its journey to the cosmic via the personal, bringing a metaphysical hue to major existential questions. This time, however, the economy of the narrative does not only concern travelling speedily through time, as in *Lungs*, but also contained micronarratives. These miniature segments of life comprise the bigger picture of the play – one that transcends the spatial and staging minimalism of the production to speak of a human experience spanning different universes. Like *Lungs*, then, *Constellations* also achieves a perceptually maximalist effect.

Finally, there is the ultimate interconnecting thread between the two plays: the fact that they both capture, with heart and imagination, the nervous uncertainty regarding the modern-day individual's place, path and future in a world that seems entirely transient. Mortality becomes a major concern, stacked up against a universe that seems unpredictable, slipping from our control. It is an amplified sort of double anxiety.

Lungs has had a successful UK and international trajectory, but *Constellations* has exploded on a different sphere altogether, starting off from the RCT Upstairs in early 2012, directed by Michael Longhurst, to transfer to the West End, at the Duke of York's theatre later that year. In early 2015, having received a number of international productions, *Constellations* opened on Broadway at the Samuel J. Friedman Theatre, directed, once more, by Payne's regular collaborator Longhurst. Macmillan and Payne belong to the same generation of playwrights and *Lungs* was shown alongside Payne's *One Day When We Were Young* during the early Paines Plough Roundabout season. There is an inevitable bundle of social changes and political narratives that playwrights of this generation have inherited: from the War on Terror to the recession and from the dominance of technology to sophisticated methods of surveillance. Certainly, the global crisis impacting our habitat, our environment, was chief amongst these major events. Gardner's description of Macmillan and Payne's work as aware that 'Love is hard and the future uncertain' is entirely accurate (Gardner 2012b). The challenge of dealing with the rapidly changing human narrative coincided with some British new writing resisting the prevalence of social realism. *Lungs* and *Constellations*, therefore, are the product of their time socially, politically, but also artistically – and one play illuminates the other when discussed together.

In *Constellations*, Roland and Marianne have their twenty-first-century version of a 'meet cute' when they encounter each other at a barbecue. It does not go any further because one of them is not single. They form a relationship and move in together. He cheats. She cheats. They go their separate ways. They meet again by chance. He proposes. She is diagnosed with brain cancer. The tumour is treatable. The cancer is terminal. Roland adapts to the new reality, supporting Marianne as she contemplates assisted suicide. They meet again by chance after their break up and entertain the idea of giving their relationship one more chance. These, and numerous more, are all shown as plausible scenarios in Payne's text.

Despite enough plot twists and turns to fill not one but many plays, *Constellations* still manages to feel elliptical, open, far from saturated by events despite the impression of infinite interweaving of storytelling. The primary reason for this is Payne's main narrative device. His opening stage direction indicates: 'An indented rule indicates a change in universe' (Payne 2012a: 2). This bold note makes it rather difficult for a director to depict this infinite cosmos. Any staging of the play begins with the challenge of identifying a way of serving and complementing this visually and aurally. The play is necessarily built on the two protagonists' verbal and physical behaviour, but the stagescape, contrary to Macmillan's note against any such interference, punctuates the transitions and the different universes. Productions of the play have so far avoided extravagance, ranging from a sparsely decorated set, often featuring balloons alluding to the suspended nature of the characters' experience, but also to a multitude of possibilities, where existence is light, transient and contingent, to an entirely bare stage. It is lighting and sound design that predominantly carry the weight of communicating changes and transitions, along with the actors' shift in tone, which alters from romantic to comedic to heavily dramatic within mere minutes, or, indeed in some cases, split seconds. The London production of the play benefitted substantially from the nuanced performances of Sally Hawkins and Rafe Spall, who were able to navigate this very broad range with confidence and authority, rendering every emotion from romantic giddiness to terminal resignation credible. Even though *Lungs* could hardly be accused of sentimentalism, except for W's final monologue, *Constellations* strikes a yet more austere tone. For all the different scenarios between Marianne and Roland, the depth of possibilities is never matched by a sense of intimacy in their relationship akin to that of M and W. The superficiality imposed by the temporal constraints on each segment causes fractures to the overall feeling. But then again, these are very much individuals of their time, whose romanticism has been curbed by limitations – it is infinite love in the era of constant cuts and adaptability. Attachment and permanence are irrelevant notions.

Due to the nature of the play that involves repetitions of events and/or dialogue with different outcomes, we are confronted by the idea of how social context irrevocably impacts on lives. It is an intelligent device that enables Payne not only to offer poignant commentary on human relationships, fragility and mortality, but also criticism on upward mobility and class inequality. The play is built on the fusion of conflicts and the obliteration of binaries, captured in the way that Roland and Marianne bring – or perhaps have their lives brought – together in a way that heightens how dissimilar they are, an impression that, again, is forced through repeatedly as we revisit the same moments in their lives. She is an academic scientist with expertise in quantum cosmology; he is a beekeeper committed to producing his own honey, having moved from Wiltshire to Tower Hamlets partly for a relationship (now failed) and partly to start his own business. The point is made ironically to highlight the disjointedness between goal and realization, aspiration and reality, both personally and professionally. Despite differences in social status and education, as well as, presumably, in income, Marianne and Roland share the same uncertainties. Payne's play reveals that even though success in the profession might make us feel less vulnerable to unexpected change, what ultimately dictates life and happiness extends far beyond financial rules and constraints. This is pivotal to Payne's attempt at opening the existentialism question far wider than materialism and into the cosmos, the origins and cycle of life.

Payne uses the specifics of Marianne's profession as a framework on which to set up the world of the play. As she explains to Roland, at the same time as he attempts to seduce her in a successful outcome version of their early meeting, there is a 'possibility that we're part of a multiverse' (Payne 2012a: 16):

Marianne   In the quantum multiverse, every choice, every decision you've ever and never made exists in an unimaginably vast ensemble of parallel universes.

[...]

Let's say that ours is the only universe that exists. There's only one unique me and one unique you. If that were true, then there could only ever really be one choice. But if every possible future exists, then the decisions we do and don't make will determine which of the futures we actually end up experiencing. Imagine rolling a dice six thousand times.

[...]

In none of our equations do we see any sign whatsoever of any evidence of free will.

[...]

We're just particles governed by a series of very particular laws being knocked the fuck around all over the place. (Payne 2012a: 17–18)

Marianne's brutal yet scientifically robust statement that 'We're just particles' points to the transience and disposability that the entire play feels like an attempt to rationalize. Marianne's comment that 'In none of our equations do we see any sign whatsoever of any evidence of free will' is particularly significant. Its resonance extends beyond the scope of a character explaining her work to a lover and of the complex scientific implications of the statement. Marianne's words carry powerful social and political allusion, pointing to the very feeling of our contemporary human condition in a post-recession, mid-austerity world of tired capitalism, extreme conflict and global crisis.

In their discussion of the crisis of modernity and of society's fraught transitions from one state of being to another that vows to deal with the crises of the past only to promise what it cannot deliver, Bauman and Bordoni probe the constant precarity of the individual in a way that helps us better understand *Constellations*. As Bauman characteristically notes, 'Our settlements are temporary, transient, supplied with the clause "until further notice"' (Bauman and Bordoni 2014: 86). As he adds, any effort towards firming up the variables of our lives and exerting control is subject to unforeseen circumstances, which he characteristically describes as 'kaleidoscopically changing' (Bauman and Bordoni 2014: 86). The statement captures the feeling of *Constellations*, where we are confronted by kaleidoscopic fractions of lives, mere passing fragments unto which characters are unable to assert sustainability, let alone permanence. The form and subject of the play are therefore wholly responsive to the kind of social, political and historical climate that Bauman describes. He writes about contemporary lifestyles as amenable to liquidity by default, where the understanding that stability is a thing of the past is implicit – and the necessary qualities are, rather, adaptability and being able to move on swiftly (Bauman and Bordoni 2014: 86). The entire structure and premise of Payne's play mirrors this. Accepting our temporariness and disposability is a necessary part of the scientific equation of our existence.

Throughout *Constellations*, we see Marianne and Roland come to terms with this in different ways. They treat their encounter as fleeting, their relationship as having run its course, and they even accept her life as having come to an inevitable, untimely end. With each new start or step in their relationship there is always the hint of knowing that time will be called on it very soon. Through cross-reference to Sennett, Bauman exposes the notion of 'flexibility' for the perils it conceals as opposed to the positive adaptation and progress attributes it might be seen to imply (Bauman and Bordoni 2014: 86). This notion of acknowledged transience, as it is depicted in Payne's play, is not only to be understood on the basis of the characters' relationship, or the rules that the multiverse imposes and science is cognizant of. Rather, flexibility as the root of the inability to attach to relationships and contexts and to make some claim to permanence, is an elusive concept emerging from the neoliberalist context of modern lives. Payne's play takes on the very notion of being '"set adrift"' by the rules of a volatile world that keeps moving forward at the expense of the individual's needs for stability, simply because economies dictate the standards of living (Bauman and Bordoni 2014: 86). For Bauman, it is flexibility, presented as false friend, a kind of desire, we might add, that is the most effective device for propagating 'servitude and impotence', the individual in constant flux, in a relentless surge for an externally imposed 'Mobility' (Bauman and Bordoni 2014: 86–87). It is the very concept that Mitchell's production of *Lungs* captures through its staging and that *Constellations* depicts in its own dizzying speed, as characters adapt to new circumstances and new fractions of their never entirely complete personalities, while the whims of the world – and of the economy – deprive them of their agency.

Having played on this motif for the duration of the play, *Constellations* then appears defiant by means of its open-ended finale. When Marianne and Roland run into each other at a dance class (an encounter of which we have already witnessed multiple possibilities), he invites her to a drink. The last words we hear from Roland are: 'if you change your mind and you wanna call it a day, then we'll just call it a day. We'll just call it a day and you'll never have to see me again' (Payne 2012a: 70). 'Call[ing] it a day', as *Constellations* has already shown us, of course, is ultimately an impossibility, as 'again' can never be defined by a 'never', because it is not a limitable quantity but an infinite notion. We can never, perhaps, ultimately define our chances but the open (in) conclusion of *Constellations* allows a multiversal margin for optimism and hope; a brief window of decision-making where happiness might be a genuinely plausible outcome.

Payne has revealed that the process of researching and writing *Constellations* altered his notion of limitless possibilities as "'terrifying and really romantic'" (2012b), positioning the play under the cold light of human accountability and responsibility, as opposed to the alluring idea of infinite escapism. The comment offers a social statement not entirely corroborated by a play that, in contrast to Payne's imperative, does not end on death (Payne 2012b), but, rather, on optimism, on the hint of continuation. The question of whether uncertainty and impermanence render us less socially accountable comes with its own immensity, as does the possibility that a play exploring the idea of parallel lives and alternative selves to shed light on our existential crises might not be socially engaged but morally dubious. As Payne reveals, his consultation with an academic expert on the play's topic led to pondering the conundrum of how the concept of the multiverse might be 'dangerous', eliminating the '"idea of consequence"' (2012b). In a universe reeling from ill-conceived, consequence-free neoliberalist individualism and overindulgence it is not difficult to imagine where the scientist's, but also the playwright's crisis of conscience might stem from. If anything, it would be entirely ironic for a play that delves into the inner workings of the human brain (ultimately literally represented in Marianne's brain tumour) to give its audience an ethical *carte blanche*. It is true that *Constellations* runs the risk of being seen as dubious if we linger on Payne's impressive dramatic device of universe transition or on the romantic relationship as the play's main pivot. However, even though the couple is at the centre of the play, it is not accurate to suggest that the romantic relationship is the only focal point. Rather, it shares this attribute with Payne's exposition of the broader social context, of whose rules Payne presents the transience of Marianne and Roland's relationship as a symptom.

Payne's range of topics, combining the personal with the political through forays into the science of human experience and the potential imprint of our presence on the world proves his social astuteness. He has also, like Mitchell (2014), made an impassioned case for the necessity for offsetting at least part of our environmental transgressions through other choices, speaking, for example, of his choice to become vegetarian, when he grew uncomfortable with the amount of flying that his work began to require (Payne 2012b). Even though *Constellations* does not pontificate its ideology, it would be problematic to consider it bereft from a social and political position. The concept of free will that the play throws into question is pivotal to its politics. The ever elusive free will, captured in the way the play bounces its characters from one situation and outcome to the next, is shown as one more unattainable good, one more product that we cannot afford because of our insecure position – a perfect mirror or metaphor for the constant sense of slipping control that individuals have over their lives at the time of austerity and emergency solutions. It is apt that Payne installs social difference at the centre of the couple: Marianne is, for much of the play, presented as more professionally accomplished than Roland, not only in terms of material capital but also social one – a highly educated scientist employed in a public institution. Her precariousness is delivered by her illness, one of many possible random twists outside of one's control; Roland's precariousness, on the other hand, is courtesy of his status as self-employed in a system that valorizes professional ambition over menial labour and workmanship, driving a wedge between the two. This is partly the reason why Marianne and Roland's union seems so untenable: a constellation of social factors acts against them, rendering them a binary. As Bauman observes, 'Bringing back social differences, restoring priorities, allows the system to acquire and maintain social control' (Bauman and Bordoni 2014: 146). He expands, unequivocally linking the compromise of economic freedom to the way in which we perceive and act out our entire lives: 'deprive them of freedom, [...and] The victims of the economic crisis are isolated, fearful, depressed and alone in facing an uncertain future' (Bauman and Bordoni 2014: 146). Marianne's illness and Roland's struggles to establish his professional credibility constitute evidence for how the feeling is experienced socially but also psychosomatically. Happiness is never guaranteed, not even when all the social determinants of success are aligned. As Bauman concludes

> Impermanence and instability are reflected in every aspect of daily life, from work to romantic relationships, [...] in a more and more frenetic race against time. Liquid society is a fast-flowing society that [...] erodes everything increasingly rapidly [...] in a state of continuous evolution: the state of transition is its state of stability. (Bauman and Bordoni 2014: 146)

Hence the story of Marianne and Roland can only ever be fractured and episodic, as extended temporal sequences and macronarratives of experience are no longer possible. In its own way, using a personal relationship both as a vehicle and a deflector, *Constellations* goes some way towards capturing the contemporary human condition and the awkwardness of this experience as described by Bauman.

Conclusion

What makes plays like *Lungs* and *Constellations* particularly interesting is the tension they expose in the relationship between responsibility and governmentality. On the one hand, characters in these plays strive to be better people, to become more mindful of the needs of others and of the world enveloping them. On the other hand, they resist the external directive conditioning their lives, most acutely represented in their reaction against conformity and neoliberalism, which the central device of Payne's play, the allusion to the fractured temporariness of life and loss of free will astutely captures. It is a schema within which to situate the futility of neoliberalism as any kind of plausible belief system banking on our obsession with individuality in a universe (or in multiverses) where individuality is scientifically a non-factor. At the same time, the plays tease another paradox: the extent to which the emerging orthodoxy of accepting responsibility for the environment and adjusting one's lifestyle accordingly may be yet another directive, a narrative as externally conditioned as neoliberalism, another form of governmentality, however noble the cause it might serve.

Paul Alberts has recently explored such intricacies, pursuing the syllogism Bauman and Bordoni later developed as to the unsustainability of the imperatives of modernity, the problematics inherent in human control over the natural environment and the uncertainty embedded in contemporary actions and decisions (2011). Alberts rightly speaks about 'the particular emergent conditions of the Anthropocene, which constrain and delimit in new intensities' (2011: 8). The kind of paralysing uncertainty that Macmillan's characters especially feel is summed up by Alberts in the impossibility of conceptualizing the magnitude of our consequences on future generations so far removed that we are unable to fathom the realities of their lives (2011: 8). This is the key factor, I would add, that renders our re-sensitization towards the environment tenuous. And so, at the heart of *Lungs*, as in *Constellations*, where Payne passionately pursues the different possibilities for how lives might be realized, lies what, proceeding from Alberts, we might call an 'aporia [...not] readily solved or even easily reconfigured' (2011: 8). With this aporia, this radical uncertainty, that, given the current environmental crisis leads humanity to an unprecedented monumentality in the weight of our actions, comes, as Alberts notes, the postponement of action (2011: 9). Plays like *Lungs* and *Constellations* are alert to the significance and incomparability of the present historical moment in which we are agents and catalysts. It is understandable, then, that both plays frame their plots on dialogue and debate, postponement of action, failure to decide, interrupted and fractured moments and, ultimately, paths taken irrespective of one's volition, when external factors intervene. The paradox embedded in the transience of lives which, however, stand to leave a permanent mark on the future life conditions of others, at the same time when individuals are confronted by the limitations of their own mortality, not necessarily able to project the value of their social intervention unto the future is captured by Alberts. He notes the additional concern, showcased in these plays, of how neoliberalism is an ultimately corrupt system that fails to account for the uncertainties experienced by societies in the twenty-first century:

> Governmentality is confronted with the fact that guaranteeing the well-being of human populations is becoming difficult using the established liberal formulae of encouraging ever-more economic growth at the expense of non-human life and environmental stability. (Alberts 2011: 13)

In this context, Martijn Konings's suggestion that 'austerity [...has often been portrayed] as an ideological programme imposed on populations from above' (2016: 87) allows us to better understand how it has become the invisible and resistant adversary that adds to the aporia, which becomes doubly debilitating in the context of the environmental crisis. The overall doctrine of containing oneself and one's actions, this hyper-governmentality of our time, leads to convoluted and confusing experience, whereby limitations and control become a way of life. *Lungs* and *Constellations* have absorbed this; their form and content mirror the fact.

Even though these are plays that do not proclaim to serve a specific ideology, their socialist perspective emerges strongly, especially in terms of their anti-classist approach and critique of neoliberalist middle-class entitlement. This is the reason why it is particularly fascinating to observe how in taking on major existential and environmental crises that lead to the obfuscation of identity and agency *Lungs* and *Constellations* appear to have internalized the spirit of their time, almost as a defence mechanism: their form is resilient because it is tightly woven, avoiding excess; their economy embeds their stageability, regardless of resources. They may not be austere ideologically, but formally these plays perform their era. At a time when, as Konings notes, 'the operation of economy' must be understood 'in terms of the redemptive promise of austerity' (2016: 89), these texts purge themselves of formal indulgences. Yet, through their key formal device the plays prove that despite the social climate they have absorbed what remains is the core that defies constant cuts: humanity defined by its language; speech, and the bare essentials of human communication, forever attempting to rationalize, and to connect disparate lives, despite the odds. The maximalism in the plays' thematic scope, working against their form, offers further evidence for their defiance. Against the inflicted 'neoliberal promise of purification through austerity' (Konings 2016: 95), or perhaps because of it, as a radical response, the two plays show that imagination endures and resists. Konings writes:

> The event of the crisis made abundantly clear that money was nothing but a hugely complex constellation of promises and obligations that

> had been shaped and manipulated by special interests. And it was
> precisely this sudden awareness of the corruption of money that
> produced a clamour for austerity [...]. (2016: 95)

The fact that, after a crisis so extensive, playwrights like Macmillan and Payne turn their attention to the cosmic, to the world that envelops us without promising permanence, exposes the flawed logic of capitalism. If there is a crisis to be managed, these plays show, this concerns the individual's relationship to their fellow humans, and to the planet that has been so violently transgressed upon for financial profit. And so the minimalist form of the plays flirts with austerity so as to evidence that this contained mode of life we have inherited, the tension in the 'complex constellation of promises and obligations' must not, in fact be conceptualized on the basis of the economy. Rather, it must be understood on the basis of how it has affected our relationship to our world and our expectations of it, so that we have become only able to perceive of it in fragments making up a continuous, relentless, uncertain course.

5

Utopia to Dystopia: Martin Crimp and the Illusion of Insularity

The critique of middle-class life and its attachment to consumption and materialism have always been at the forefront of Martin Crimp's theatre. I have previously discussed such concerns in Crimp's work at length (Angelaki 2012); therefore, in this chapter I will concentrate on Crimp's writing in the post-2010 period. During this time Crimp produced work that proved, once more, his capacity to re-envision and redefine his theatre, breaking with previous forms and avoiding stagnation on set norms. Crimp's monumental play *In the Republic of Happiness* (2012), accommodating three distinctly different types of narrative in the three acts of one and the same text, provided a novel vehicle for experimentation. In so doing, it broke with any cliché as to what text-based theatre might look like in the early twenty-first century, or any lingering hypothesizing as to the potential confines of playwriting. With *In the Republic of Happiness*, fifteen years after his opus on consumerism, art, life and spectatorship, *Attempts on Her Life* (1997), Crimp delivered another major text that allowed companies that same, vast amount of freedom on new and original formal grounds. *In the Republic of Happiness* revisits some of Crimp's recurring themes while infusing his palette with a multitude of nuances proliferating as the play unfolds. Without aiming to diminish the importance of *Attempts on Her Life* to Crimp's body of work, I would go so far as to argue that *In the Republic of Happiness* brings us Crimp's formally boldest and thematically most philosophical moment to date. At the same time, it is a profoundly funny and highly entertaining play, which still manages to slide into abstraction and ellipsis for its finale without seeming incongruous. *In the Republic of Happiness* is also Crimp's most distinctively expressionist moment, filled with ruptures, clashes and disjunctions and revealing, through its hazing affect, a horizon of possibility for humanity; an invitation for the re-examination of our motives, intentions and behavioural loops. Happiness exists, Crimp's play proposes, but it is elsewhere: to be found neither within the popular rhetoric of consumerism, nor within material and moral entitlement, which the play exposes as equally dubious. Ultimately, the play demonstrates, to tie happiness to individualist neoliberalism is a utopia, from which not only isolation, but also dystopias spring.

Crimp's twenty-first century

Crimp ventured into the 2000s with a play about a doctor's wife, who has followed her husband to an unnamed, remote countryside, where the landscape feels as cruel as her marriage, in a relationship compromised by his addiction and adultery. For this play, *The Country* (2000), Crimp created two highly articulate female characters, Corinne and Rebecca, the wife and lover respectively, who negotiated the realities of life and failure – and a male figure who represented everything that might be rotten inside the affluent middle classes' projections of success and happiness. In 2004, *Cruel and Tender*, Crimp's radical adaptation of the Sophoclean *Trachiniae*, enabled him to concentrate on the profound cynicism and unhappiness saturating the lives of those in the political and military elites, in private and public realms alike. Crimp transformed the ancient tragedy to produce a cast of modern-day protagonists in a military operation whose moral ambivalence rendered it catastrophic. A year later (2005), Crimp revisited his earlier pieces *Face to the Wall* and *Fewer Emergencies* (2002), adding the new text *Whole Blue Sky*, and creating, through these playlets, a triptych staged under the title *Fewer Emergencies*. Through their open form and lack of representational devices, other than speech and the conceptual imagery it enables, these texts immersed spectators into the constant everyday rehearsal of middle-class unhappiness as experienced by characters whose lives were also mediated, narrated by anonymous speakers. The device evidenced the contemporary individual's loss of agency and disenfranchisement in their own life. The unhappiness, meanwhile, was shown as a product of the submission to the imagined rules of a life that was seen to guarantee prosperity – but the deep dissatisfaction that this led to propelled a chain reaction of private and public crises, from mental health afflictions to violent explosions against the community such as a school shooting and urban riots.

Crimp's next new play, *The City* (2008), followed the profound melancholia of *Fewer Emergencies* and cut more deeply still, delving into the world of a couple confronted with the husband's sudden redundancy, which prompts questions of self-worth and leads to a domestic crisis emblematic of a social one. Chris, who is unexpectedly thrust into unemployment, typified one of the many, once more, disenfranchised individuals whose identity was thrown in disarray at the aftermath of the late 2000s recession. Fascinatingly, Crimp's play predated the worst of the financial crisis, evidencing his astute social perspective and perceptiveness as a writer. In *The City*, the central protagonist is Clair. She is Chris's wife, an intellectual who works as a translator. Clair's effort to furnish her life with meaning is the primary formal device and thematic focus of the play. The challenge for Clair is that the structure of her narrative keeps collapsing in its hollowness; there is no reality behind the façade, no substance beneath the surface. A Girl, whom we initially assume to be the couple's daughter, and who is gradually revealed as merely another character draft in Clair's life story, delivers the play's most disquieting moments. Her non-innocent, austere and quietly aggressive, even cruel nature, exposes the moral and physical victimization of children and compromise of childhood in fast-moving, transgressive consumerist societies where individualism prevails and vulnerability beckons. In addition, a further character, the couple's neighbour, Jenny, brings even more discomfort. Her odd appearance in her nurse's costume as well as her incongruous verbal and physical behaviour are manifestations of the social alienation and disjunction that impact private lives. By the end of the play, Jenny and the Girl are revealed to be attempts on the formation of a character in Clair's story that ultimately fails to materialize. Therefore, through a small set of characters with intermixing crises, Crimp delivered a play questioning the degree of control that we are ever in a position to exercise over our own lives, leading to the ultimate question of whether our lives even belong to us at all in a context of capitalism and governmentality.

In 2012, Crimp directed his new short piece *Play House* alongside one of his earliest texts, *Definitely the Bahamas* (1987). *Play House* follows the young couple of Simon and Katrina as they awkwardly attempt to find their road to fulfilment, not only domestically, but also as individuals navigating the new economy. From their smaller everyday conflicts events gradually escalate to an exposition of the profound crisis in their relationship, with joy forever eluding them. As the play ends, the future of the couple's relationship is inconclusive. Yet, despite the insufficiencies of their draining everyday life, despite their alienation from each other and the fact that Katrina's mental health has become compromised, Crimp allows a glimpse at the defiant optimism that the relationship might, after all, survive. Simon and Katrina's emotional bond might ultimately sustain them, against the dissatisfactions and the pervasive logic of the market that constantly intrudes in attempted happiness.

In the Republic of Happiness: States of disquiet

Within a brief period following its RCT Downstairs premiere, productions of *In the Republic of Happiness* opened in major theatres including Berlin's Deutsches Theater (November 2013), Hamburg's Thalia Theater (Thalia in der Gaußstrasse, January 2014) and the Parisian Théâtre National de Chaillot (November 2014). European audiences, who have always been particularly receptive to Crimp's work, had eagerly awaited a new play since *The City* and the impact of

In the Republic of Happiness was strongly felt. Hamburg, in particular, was a frontrunner with Crimp's *Alles Weitere kennen Sie aus dem Kino* (*The Rest Will Be Familiar to You from Cinema*), his new, radical adaptation of *Phoenissae* by Euripides, also playing in repertoire at the city's Schauspielhaus (from November 2013), a commission of that same theatre, for which Crimp worked with his frequent collaborator Katie Mitchell.

Back in Britain, critics in mainstream press mostly greeted *In the Republic of Happiness* with bemusement, concentrating on the fact that the RCT had scheduled it as a subversive Christmas spectacle and neglecting the significant broader sociopolitical commentary that the play provided. Theatre bloggers, on the other hand, reacted to the work in substantially more nuanced and enthusiastic ways. Another trend in criticism relating to the play was the contextualization of *In the Republic of Happiness* with reference to *Attempts on Her Life*. In one of the most insightful reviews, Paul Taylor described *In the Republic of Happiness* as a thoughtful exposition of 'The self-serving delusion that you can lead an apolitical life, the individualism that's just a type of paranoid narcissistic conformity; the culture of victimhood and therapy-speak' (2012). These are also the concerns that this chapter concentrates on in addressing the intricate weave of Crimp's play.

Two of the characters that we see in Part One of the text return in Part Three; the middle part, although played by the same actors, relinquishes them from any attachment to character. The fact that Crimp presents this as one consecutive – though non-cohesive – play is significant: the suspension of identity in Part Two, which is also the fastest moving section in terms of action and verbal exchanges, is indicative of the rapidly changing, confusing nature of a life experienced in flux and shaped by information and normative behaviours that are easier adopted than questioned. Meanwhile, the action of the play is frequently interrupted by song, which serves to flag up, summarize and satirize some of the play's most important touchstones of social critique. Roald van Oosten, who had already been familiar with Crimp's work through a 2007 production of *Attempts on Her Life* in Leiden by

De Veenfabriek, wrote the music for *In the Republic of Happiness*. As he suggests, 'The songs functioned as a kind of continuation, maybe even a summary of the previous act' and they were 'dark, but not too dark' (Van Oosten 2014: 412). It is true that the music perfectly complemented Crimp's text; beneath the playfulness and glee, pain and aggression lingered. The songs may have been entertaining in their irony, but they were also deeply uncomfortable.

Part One of the play is titled 'Destruction of the Family'. The darkness of the title is not immediately justifiable by the events that we see unfold, as Crimp opens his play with an extended Christmas dinner sequence, which, for the most part, is both funny and entertaining. On closer inspection, however, all is not what it might seem as it becomes evident that characters are profoundly unhappy and their semblance of superficial contentment is built on misguided principles contradicting any sense of community. Each character in this scene is the construct of hardened neoliberalist individualism. The family consists of the parents ('Mum' and 'Dad'), the paternal grandparents ('Granny' and 'Grandad') and two teenage sisters (Debbie and Hazel). Their conversation drifts into topics including Debbie's unplanned pregnancy, Grandad's pornography habit, the younger generations' bitter financial sacrifices as by-product of a troubled economy, Granny's obsession with the staples of middle-class life and Mum's dissatisfaction with feeling undervalued. Then, Crimp injects some further discomfort: Grandad, who is visibly senile and oblivious to the fact, has his own dubious past; the young sisters, meanwhile, are entirely poised to embrace patriarchal structures and misogynist, self-hating clichés. At the same time, the family is in constant disagreement, and the threat of a rift looms. The tension is heightened when Uncle Bob suddenly enters the frame. He announces that he has come to bid farewell, as he and his wife, Madeleine, are preparing to board a flight to an undisclosed, remote destination. Even though emotions between Bob and the rest of the family are strained, it soon becomes evident that Madeleine's feelings towards Bob's family are outright hostile. As Madeleine unleashes a vitriolic rant against the family, she even implies that Bob might have had sexual relations with at least one of the teenage girls. The scene ends with Madeleine singing the play's second song (the first, 'Marry a Man' had been sung by the sisters earlier as a Christmas treat, disturbing in its loaded references to objectified femininity), titled 'I Don't Go Deep'. Here, Madeleine expresses her feelings of violence towards the family and her desire to escape them.

Part Two of the play is dramatically different. With the Christmas dinner set dismantled and the naturalistic façade destroyed, we transition to an unruly section of text demanding even more rigorous verbal and physical work of the company, as well as swiftly established collaborative methods. Part Two carries the overall title 'The Five Essential Freedoms of the Individual', consisting of 'The Freedom to Write the Script of My Own Life', 'The Freedom to Separate My Legs (It's Nothing Political)', 'The Freedom to Experience Horrid Trauma', 'The Freedom to Put It All behind Me and Move On' and 'The Freedom to Look Good & Live for Ever'. As the set dissolves, so does character: for this part of the play, Crimp does not use names or any other descriptors as to which company member will speak each given line, transitioning to a fluid narrative and dialogical mode that blurs boundaries between different voices. This is a device that Crimp has used previously, in some of his more openly experimental work, such as *Attempts on Her Life* and *Fewer Emergencies*. He has also used it in the more formally conventional *The Country*, to indicate the diminishing boundaries between individuals in tense relationships (from lovers to adversaries), and the shared practices of dishonesty, self-preservation and aggression. Where *In the Republic of Happiness* differs from those plays is in its emphasis on the individual who speaks as an 'I', reflecting on themselves, as opposed to narrators describing another's experience in the third person (*Attempts on Her Life*; *Fewer Emergencies*), or named characters interacting in a dialogue where names are not provide on the playtext (*The Country*). This is Crimp's ironic way of heightening the antithesis: those speaking the doctrines of contemporary individualism in first-person singular may think of themselves as unique, but what the play draws attention to is the extent to which they have merely adopted popular narratives as to how lives are meant to be lived and challenges dealt with. To add to the effect, in a nod to *Attempts on Her Life* and *Fewer Emergencies*, where the script of so-called individual lives is shown as yet another part in the process of manufacturing and selling narratives, Crimp starts off this part of the play by having one of the speakers deliver the line 'I write the script of my own life. I make myself what I am' (2012b: 41). This part of the play, too, features songs, which break the speakers' relentless confessional to serve Crimp's satire through a different form.

The final part of the play, titled 'In the Republic of Happiness', is entirely anti-climactic; as, in *The Country*, the married couple of Richard and Corinne find themselves together after strong moments of conflict between Richard and his lover Rebecca, but also Corinne and Rebecca, and certainly Corinne and Richard, and attempt to re-stage their dismantled marriage, so in *In the Republic of Happiness* we encounter the centripetal force of the couple once more, as Bob and Madeleine come to terms with their new situation. The new situation, however, is unlike anything they have experienced before, and indeed unlike any of Crimp's previous work. As in *The City*, it is a woman – Madeleine – who controls the action and manages a man's – in this case Bob – expectations. But in contrast with *The City*, the traces of empathy that Clair and Chris shared for being part of the same social conundrum, a life that they had no ability to exert any control over, have now disappeared. The reality of Madeleine and Bob is suspended and their utopian image of happiness has metamorphosed into an uncomfortable dystopia. Surrounded by a serene, yet empty and sterile vast landscape, Bob and Madeleine have been given the opportunity to rule their own world (unlike Clair and Chris), but he is paralysed when it comes to taking action. The play ends with the '100% Happy Song', which Bob and Madeleine awkwardly attempt to sing together, and, once more, their projection of happiness desperately clashes with their reality of emotional hollowness and isolation. Not unlike the elderly couple in Ionesco's *The Chairs*, Bob and Madeleine, who are, of course, much younger, find themselves in conditions of stark alienation and isolation from society. They clearly take it upon themselves, like the couple in *The Chairs*, to deliver a political message – but whereas in *The Chairs* the couple set up the scene for the arrival of an Orator, in Crimp's play it is Bob himself who has been tasked with the responsibility of delivering the speech. Like the audience in *The Chairs*, so the citizens that Madeleine keeps referring to remain invisible; in fact, the dystopian seclusion that Bob and Madeleine have chosen for themselves renders the citizens' existence utterly implausible. In providing a representation of the dramatic alienation of individual from society through the metaphor of the popular middle-class habit of booking an escape, Crimp takes the symbolism to the extreme: Bob and Madeleine are the ultimate example of divorcing oneself from one's reality, and of isolating the private from the public. Such are the perils of extreme individualism, a concept that Crimp directs attention and critique towards. It is interesting that, as Dominic Cooke, who directed the premiere of *In the Republic of Happiness*, notes, for Crimp, too, there was an Ionesco connection, albeit to *Rhinoceros*, the play that he translated for a new production (2007) at the beginning of Cooke's Royal Court tenure (2014: 410). It is true that this link, established on the basis of debates around individualism, which Cooke specifically mentions (2014: 410), provides a critical path from one play to the other. However, as Cooke notes, whereas in Ionesco's text 'the threat to human survival was human beings' propensity to conform, for Crimp it was the myth of separation' (2014: 410).

With *In the Republic of Happiness* Crimp takes on existing dramatic forms and develops them further, advancing the broader genres we might classify them under. This is the revisionist element of Crimp's work, which acknowledges the importance of extant representational forms but also charges ahead to attack complacency and inaction. Therefore, there are aspects of *In the Republic of Happiness* that are neo-absurdist (Parts One and Three, with Part One also promising naturalistic emphasis on familial predispositions before slipping into absurdism) and others that are neo-expressionist (the five segments of Part Two). Crimp describes the benefit of the open text as facilitating active interpretation by an audience (Benjamin and Crimp 2013). The comment is highly relevant to the changes of form of *In the Republic of Happiness*, which invite us into a process of thinking and questioning without tying us to a rigid formal structure, as is Crimp's observation that his approach is very different from Brechtian alienation (Benjamin and Crimp 2013; see also Angelaki 2012: 121–152). As Crimp notes, engaging the spectator in the ideas of a play is not contingent on establishing objective distance from the events we see on stage, but in implicating the audience (Benjamin and Crimp 2013). The device of self-narration, as Crimp adds, serves this purpose (Benjamin and Crimp 2013). The comment is particularly significant for *In the Republic of Happiness*, where Part Two is entirely built on this principle, with speakers talking at length about themselves, without, however, really conversing with one another, as Crimp mentions (2014). Even though Crimp's method in Part Two of *In the Republic of Happiness* resolutely breaks with verisimilitude, this is not to say that Parts One and Three are conventional. Their strangeness and artificiality are implied throughout, with constant subversions of characters' life stories by other characters, sudden expositions of disturbing facts that point to underlying violence clashing with the image of family normality and, as in *Fewer Emergencies* and *The City*, breakdowns in speech and attempts to restore a compromised narrative.

Disorientation and complexity in form and content are Crimp's way of drawing attention to the absurdity of contemporary experience and the impotence at negotiating moments of radical crisis, produced by the micromanagement methods of a system that encourages us to indulge in self-treatment and individualism. Crimp's play suggests that rather than deal with the issue, or the disease at hand (mental, physical or political), the solution often taken is to deal with the symptom. This only prolongs and exacerbates the problem, leading to the post-apocalyptic scenario of Part Three. Here, Bob and Madeleine find themselves the leaders of their own state. They appear entirely suspended in space and time, disconnected from any plausible reality or idea of society, despite Madeleine's proclamations as to the existence of citizens depending on them. Bob's monologue is indicative of his burgeoning existential crisis, occurring as a result of his isolation:

Uncle Bob   What lectures? Where are the citizens?

[...]

You [Madeleine] talk about the world but I listen and listen and I still can't hear it. Where has the world gone? What is it we've done? – did we select it and click? – mmm? Have we deleted it by mistake? Because I look out of that window and I don't know what I'm seeing [...] And of course I'm happy but I feel like I'm one of those characters Madeleine crossing a bridge and the bridge is collapsing behind me slat by slat but I'm still running on – why? What's holding me up? (Crimp 2012b: 84)

Bob's monologue delves into contemporary obsessions with technology, which the play treats as an agent for alienation. Ironically, technology gives the impression of serving our own agency through unlimited choice, creating the illusion of control, when, in fact, it compromises this. Elsewhere in the play Crimp alludes to the significance of investing in the latest version of popular smartphones as validators of one's identity (2012b: 46). Meanwhile, as it reveals the dramatic consequences of the missing social thread, it is important that *In the Republic of Happiness* articulates its critique by revisiting a form traditionally used to deliver social commentary on the stage: the state of the nation monologue. Crimp upsets this form, infusing it with the abstraction and strangeness that broadly define his work. It is the same tactic that Crimp follows in Part One, where he teases a naturalistic approach. As Crimp observes, the device of a family at the dinner table is traceable in canonical traditions and most notably Chekhovian drama (Crimp 2013), but what it also facilitates is the extended confessional monologues that we encounter in this part of the play, delivered by different family members effectively out of context. Then, in Part Two, Crimp transforms the confessional monologue into fragmented, jagged confessionals symbolizing the lack of cohesion that has transpired by means of the dissipation of life values and coherent narratives.

Crimp's revisiting of naturalism is crucial, because of its enduring primacy as dramatic vehicle for the exposition of hidden traits of one's personality, their explication, but also the revelation of one's inherent rootedness in society and its key conditioning factors of class and family. In this contemporary play, naturalistic emphasis on such conditioning serves Crimp's exposition of how individualism is passed on from one generation to another like mental and sometimes also physical trauma. At the same time, Crimp's coverage of three different generations cast in prototypical family roles is an additional nod to traditional naturalistic structures, serving the concept of personal histories extensively intertwined with social context. In the following segment, Granny's defence of her lifestyle and the entitlements of class is indicative, the simple trigger for her long monologue having been Dad's remark on her disdain for public transport:

> **Granny** [...] I don't use the bus, I take taxis. I may be an ugly old granny – as you have so kindly pointed out – but I still like to sit in the back of a taxi and be driven through the streets – especially at dusk in summer with all the smells of plants and restaurants coming in through the window [...]. I like to watch the meter running. I like to think ah these two minutes in a taxi have already cost me what that man emptying the bins will take more than an hour of his life to earn – and oh the extra stink of a rubbish bin in the summer! Yes on nights like that the taxi is glorious and the fact I'm paying for my happiness makes my happiness all the sweeter – and the fact that other people are having to suffer and work just to pay for such basic things as electricity makes it even sweeter still. (Crimp 2012b: 14)

The disparity in the privileges that Granny has been able to enjoy as opposed to later generations (her son's; her granddaughters') reveals the spectacular social changes that have removed the net of steady income and security, while at the same time promising the alluring affluence of capitalism. Moreover, that Granny appears to have earned her privileges by collaborating with big pharma, as she goes on to reveal in passing, is indicative of the level of detail in Crimp's play, which – amongst a multitude of social concerns – also takes on contemporary trends of compulsive diagnosing and over-medicating. As in naturalist plays private trauma mirrors the public sense of ailment and discontent, so in *In the Republic of Happiness* Crimp suggests that the characters' individualist obsession conditions one generation after another, indoctrinating them in corrupt politics and practices. As the play alludes to, this ultimately comes to have direct bearing on a disjointed, fragmented society – very much like the family in Crimp's play, where the characters' attempts to communicate are tentative at best, as all they serve is personal benefit. Then, fragmentation acquires even greater dimensions when we witness the disjointed narration and broken life narratives of Part Two. Crucially, Crimp notes that the play began with what became its middle section (Crimp 2013). The social collapse and isolation emerging from corrosive individualism, further depicted in Part Three, is also reminiscent of Ionesco or Beckett. Radical disconnection from society combined with the obsessive need to establish the significance of oneself accounts for the confessional mode that persists, in different forms, throughout the play. It is an adept way of exposing the prevalence of therapy culture and its filtering through all aspects of life, from social and political structures to major private institutions, like family.

Crimp has previously discussed his reading of Frank Furedi and Richard Sennett, which has fed into his work (Angelaki 2012: 33–35, 217–218). *In the Republic of Happiness* delivers the optimal amalgamation of these sociologists' approaches and their application to theatre, with Crimp's critique at its sharpest. The work that Sennett and Furedi have produced in the context of how neoliberalist individualism encourages disengagement with society is of course distinctive to their respective focal points, but Sennett's *Together: The Rituals, Pleasures and Politics of Cooperation* (2012) speaks well to Furedi's work on therapy culture, and the prevalence of trauma discourses and victim mentality (see also Furedi 2004: *Therapy Culture: Cultivating Vulnerability in an Uncertain Age*). Sennett observes that 'A distinctive character type is emerging in modern society, the person who can't manage demanding, complex forms of social engagement, and so withdraws. He or she loses the desire to cooperate with others. This person becomes an "uncooperative self"' (2012: 179). For Sennett, this profile is the combined outcome of 'structural inequality and new forms of labour', where the individual 'occupies a middle ground between psyche and society' (2012: 179). Crimp's play stages this state of turmoil emerging from struggling to contend with the burgeoning crisis experienced at a personal level and feeling powerless, incapable of connecting to others and making the transition to the social, so that this crisis can be addressed collectively and effectively. The play therefore exposes the ultimately debilitating consequences and suspended experience of neoliberalist detachment and self-containment.

The most spectacular manifestation of this comes in Part Three and Bob's breakdown and eventual incapacity to sing his and Madeleine's '100% Happy Song', however much she prompts him. His failure is protracted and painful to observe; decontextualized from society, Bob as an individual is no longer sustainable. Cooke has remarked on the significance of this moment in an account worth quoting at length:

> Part Three shows [...] a nightmare vision of a world which has turned to ash. In the production we created an artificial room, with no sense of day or night, no comfort, no light or relationship to nature. [...I]t felt as if Madeleine was a kind of embodiment of capitalist individualism – always promising fulfilment and salvation to Bob but withdrawing it when he gets close. Madeleine has separated Bob from family, from any sense of a society or belonging and he is forced to sing her song [...]. He gives a performance of happiness but the experience of it eludes him. [...] As Madeleine detects his increasing dissent, she struggles to enforce her reality onto him. [...] She leads him back to the ritual of the happy song, but he can't remember the words. (2014: 411)

Sennett's discussion of paralysing individualism is particularly relevant to this scene and the play more broadly, as Crimp presents us with a range of individuals who operate as autonomous units irrespective of context. Sennett's comments on loneliness also resonate strongly.

He mentions the solitude of Beckettian figures as conveying 'existential anxiety' whereby 'absence is a basic ingredient of the human condition' (Sennett 2012: 183). If in Beckett the individual's separation from his/her world points to an essential truth of the inherence of loneliness in life, in Crimp we are dealing with the tension between the individual's assumed need to withdraw, and the radical disconnection from society that they experience as a consequence of this, which ultimately becomes destructive. As Sennett adds, there is no noble aspect to this isolation; it is merely an act of indulgence that is ultimately bereft of deeper significance (2012: 183). Sennett's observation concerning the individual's retreat from action and from public, or community life, is also helpful to consider at length:

> [...] voluntary withdrawals whose purpose is to reduce anxiety, don't have that existential or spiritual reach; they don't, indeed, arouse feelings of loneliness or lack. When the purpose is just to relieve anxiety in dealings with others, these withdrawals produce, instead of illumination, a kind of blindness. There are two psychological ingredients of this blindness: narcissism and complacency. (2012: 183)

Such is the case for Crimp's characters and anonymous speakers in this play, and particularly so for Bob and Madeleine who experience this 'withdrawal' physically as well as mentally. Sennett's nuanced analysis of narcissism, which proceeds from Freudian psychoanalysis, enables an understanding of it also as lack of empathy to a degree that does not include the self as the reflecting device for the understanding of the situations of others (2012: 183–186). This is the case with the self-absorbed, self-medicating individuals of *In the Republic of Happiness*. The link between narcissism and trauma that Sennett pursues via his Freud reference is important: continuous reliance on the past as processing device for all new experiences hinders progress and encourages retreat and regression (2012: 183). Then, there is the notion of imposed self-decontextualization: a form of warrior mentality that Sennett astutely describes in *Together*. This concerns the individual's disassociation from their social context for the purpose of fighting a solitary battle that they deem noble, even if it is ultimately transgressive, self-serving and self-preservational, undermining the well-being of others (Sennett 2012: 185–186). As his example Sennett draws on the actions of the financiers responsible for the dramatic market crisis of 2008 (2012: 185–186).

Furedi's work in *Therapy Culture*, but also in 'The Silent Ascendancy of Therapeutic Culture in Britain' (2002), is equally helpful for the better understanding of *In the Republic of Happiness*. Furedi specifically explores the wavering of British mentality, which, as he demonstrates, has recently crystallized into a new formation, redefining the entire national identity. Furedi's writing at times allows little space for empathy when describing the readiness with which society has given itself unto trauma discourse, indulging in frequent and extensive periods of grief. There is, however, an important vein of reason in Furedi's work in terms of how such ideologies have become pervasive, filtering through to all aspects of everyday life. Furedi describes this as a 'therapeutic ethos' engendered through 'the language of trauma', which has become the dominant lens for revisiting experiences in one's life (2002: 16–17). As Furedi characteristically notes, such is the extent of the phenomenon that any events that one might have previously treated as par for the course are now dealt with as injurious, in every imaginable context, from the classroom to the office; this has deeply conditioned everything, from how one reacts to triggers to how one frames their experiences (2002: 17–18). *In the Republic of Happiness* captures the new reality. In this section of Part Two ('The Freedom to Experience Horrid Trauma'), speakers have been adding to each other's intimate revelations, until they reach this composite:

> — My burning urethra, my chronic weight loss, diminished responsibility, stretch marks, broken nose and sex-addiction, addiction to morphine, addiction to shopping *plus* my post-traumatic stress *plus* my infertility *plus* my long long history of abuse.

> — My trauma! My horrid abuse!

> [...]

— My abusive father. My manipulative and abusive cat.

— My horrid abusive baby plus flashbacks of my abusive priest. Take blood.

— Take blood – scan my whole body – authenticate my abuse.

— Swab my mouth – authenticate my horrid trauma – offer me therapy.
(2012b: 55–56; emphasis original)

For Furedi the issue is both social and political. As he explains, government policy and rhetoric of the recent period, from Margaret Thatcher onwards and particularly under New Labour, have been deeply rooted in the lexicon and practices of therapy (2002: 19). It is interesting, however, that the result of such prevalent discourses and policies, which have generated a shift in the collective mentality, do not, as we have seen in Sennett's work, necessarily lead to a more empowered, but, rather, to a disempowered individual that further retreats unto the private realm. As Sennett notes, complacency stems from insecurity: whereas security can be a creative force, spurring on positive action, insecurity has a stunting effect, with the individual becoming risk-averse, for fear of loss of control (2012: 186).

Such is the reality that *In the Republic of Happiness* exposes: self-assertion is superficial, an internalized trait of popular culture rather than ideology based on principle that compels social action. As Furedi adds, with '[…] identity […] now recast on an intensely individualized foundation, which inherently contradicts wider notions of community, the political class has found a new role for itself as managers of people's emotional anxieties' (2002: 23). The irony is, as Furedi underlines, that to equate therapy mentality with individuation is a paradox: it becomes a doctrine so widely adopted, with such uniformity of treatment, that it eclipses the desired effect of feeling unique and autonomous (2002: 23). The lure of individualism is appealing, but the reality of mass culture is different. This is the issue that *In the Republic of Happiness* delves into in Part Two, where the anonymous speakers believe they represent themselves and their own beliefs, but, in reality, stories, experiences and treatment mechanisms are interchangeable. In Cooke's production, this was communicated by all cast members' preparedness to perform any part of the middle section in a given performance, alternating lines in different ways. This spontaneous delivery succeeded in involving spectators in the experience of those 'encouraged and rewarded for excavating their inner lives in public' in the model of a 'TV confessional' (Cooke 2014: 411).

The displacing of responsibility by diagnosis, which provides the option of dealing with any ailment or perceived discomfort with a prescription as the growing social symptom that Furedi recognizes (2002: 24), is of profound significance to Crimp's play. Characters, or speakers, constantly evade the confrontation of causes which demand profound ideological re-evaluation. Furedi's discussion of how diagnosis and subsequent treatment create the illusion of dealing with the issue at hand, when in fact they are treating the symptom, paving the way for emotional vulnerability that hinges on constant support (2002: 24), enables an understanding of the anonymous speakers in Part Two of *In the Republic of Happiness*. They are a chorus echoing sympathy with one another's plight while condoning the confessional expression of continuous vulnerability. Sennett's emphasis on narcissism and complacency, then, also becomes strongly relevant: the obsession of diagnosing and treating the self, which then offers a justification that does not involve any substantial introspection, or change, is part of the process that Furedi describes as the acceptance of an afflicted self (2002: 24). It can ultimately lead to self-satisfaction, and to the distancing of the individual from society.

In his earlier piece boldly titled 'New Britain—A Nation of Victims' (1998), Furedi reflects on the changing reactions of the British public to large-scale traumatic events (particularly concentrating on the death of Princess Diana) and the shift to collective attitudes that this has gradually produced. He suggests that outpouring of emotion became a new language for otherwise fractured societies; a means of exerting a modicum of community when there is no such connection on any substantial terms. That this grew in momentum, conditioning the population, Furedi classifies as a political act, which has delivered an overemphasis on performing emotion as substitute for implementing action towards change – and towards a significant way of bringing communities together. As Furedi observes, 'when politicised, the culture of victimhood can become a powerful force' (1998: 80). He adds: 'in New Britain, the combination of victimhood and the public acknowledgement of suffering represent a direct claim to moral authority' (Furedi 1998: 81). It is difficult to imagine a more apt representation of this condition than Part Two of *In the Republic of Happiness*. Particularly when it comes to major social crises, tragic events of violence, such as Dunblane, which Furedi specifically mentions, deflecting attention from the event and unto the public's reaction, and the extent to which it is performed with the anticipated emotion, is deeply problematic: it radically upsets social and political priorities and ultimately weakens, rather than strengthen, communities as potential pivots of action (1998: 81–82). Furedi concludes that the extent to which public expression of emotion and recognition of vulnerability have become marketed as an essential feature of the contemporary individual has effectively rendered therapy culture a religion – and that 'The religion of feeling and the worship of sentiment is an intolerant one' (1998: 84). The openness and even pleasure with which speakers perform themselves as partaking in a culture of precariousness, including surveillance mechanisms, is strongly expressed in 'The Freedom to Separate My Legs (It's Nothing Political)'. Beginning from a reference to airport security scanning, the segment expands unto a broad field of conditioning and disclosure:

— Cheese scans – deep scanning of my eyes plus click to explore my bank account plus click to identify my date of birth and current regime of drugs – I've nothing to hide.
— I've nothing at all to hide: my medication's in this bag – see for yourself – it's not political.
— My medication's in a transparent bag – it's not political – the deeper I medicate the safer we both feel – the deeper I medicate myself – the deeper I medicate my child.

— The deeper I medicate my own child, the safer we both feel. I have a right to identify the molecule.

— I have a right to scan my own child. I have a human right – yes – to identify the molecule that makes my child unhappy or stops my child concentrating or that makes him scream. (Crimp 2012b: 50)

The aggression with which speakers assert behaviours and broadcast emotions is paradigmatic of the compulsion to share. There is a genuine sense of rush, of feeling obliged to articulate the lines of confession, of this being the essential part of a soul-cleansing process of self-validation. This is embedded not only in the text's content – the urgency and openness of the lines themselves, but also its form: exchanges are swift and torrential; transitions from one thought and emotion to another occur at a dizzying speed; the lines effectively dangle over speakers, ripe for the picking. Who gets there first and succeeds in performing the traumatized yet self-aware individual in the process of healing is a race for time, an effect accentuated by Cooke's production. What Crimp's text also exposes, returning to Furedi, are the profound political implications of this behaviour and the degree of institutionalized control exercised on the individual, who effectively becomes trained to respond in certain ways to specific triggers.

Conclusion

As a nod to the reader/spectator, a playful comment on the assumed formal predictability of the play, which then escalates into complete subversion, Crimp introduces *In the Republic of Happiness* as '*an entertainment in three parts*' (2012b: 3), before listing the subtitles for the individual parts. With this play Crimp revisits his habit of providing epigraphs, and Part Three begins with a quotation from the third part of Dante's *The Divine Comedy: Paradiso*. The quotation reads: '*Tu non se' in terra, sì comme tu credi*' ('You are not on earth, as you believe') (2012b: 75). It is an apt choice for a play that feverishly pursues the hypothesis of how far our obsession with ourselves and with preserving what we deem necessary to procure our happiness might push us deeper into crisis. The extreme level of neoliberalist individualism that guides the actions of Bob and Madeleine, but also of all the characters and voices representing anonymous individuals that we encounter throughout this play cannot exist on earth, Crimp's final scene and this epigraph suggest.

It is understandable, then, why Crimp should delve into the metaphysical realm in the final part of this play. It allows an acknowledgement of the fact that in seeking a better world for ourselves alone, disconnected from our society, we are not on the path to a deeper state of contentment and awareness, but to extricating ourselves from the very fabric of life that is constitutive of our humanity: the membership of our society; the meaning of our actions in the context of others' existence; the prospect of collective progress. There is no profound truth and happiness in the mental and physical space of individualism, the play reveals. The extreme symptoms that Bob describes Madeleine as experiencing in Part One as he justifies their decision to leave, 'the horrid rash' and the 'hard lumps erupt[ing]' (Crimp 2012b: 25) when she reflects on his family, betray her *dysanexia* against any unit that might be deemed as collective, any sense of human partnership (however flawed the exchanges between family members have revealed this to be). It is a physical manifestation of extreme insularity: a psychosomatic metaphor for the manifold barriers the individual is willing to erect between themselves and their society once they have convinced themselves that a singular focus on one's own happiness, disconnected from the rest, is the sole viable and noble goal. As Crimp's play suggests, however, this is not paradise, but limbo – because happiness as a projected image of isolation, the island we create for ourselves even in a crowd, is untenable. As in the case of Bob, it merely throws the self into a state of terminal crisis, of disarray – ultimately, of burnout or collapse. With no moral satisfactions to be had, all other pleasures, as Bob and Madeleine come to find out, ultimately evaporate.

6

The Darkness within: Simon Stephens, Mobility and Melancholy

Simon Stephens's playwriting strives for a degree of discomfort; it stands at the sharp edge – like his solitary protagonist in *Song from Far Away* (2015) – and where it might move next is anyone's guess. This openness is conceptual (artistically and visually), thematic and formal. Stephens is prolific, and his plays range from esoteric monologues and dialogical pieces where characters intersect but fail to connect, to large-cast naturalistic expositions of humanity and hard-hitting social critique. He has also produced adaptations and versions of modern classics as well as contemporary texts, one of which, *The Curious Incident of the Dog in the Night-Time* (based on Mark Haddon's novel), has garnered significant attention since premiering at the National Theatre (2012). Stephens's theatre is as much representative of British culture as it has the capacity to translate culturally. His texts reflect our world of crisis back unto us, tracing how it is being inscribed into collective mentalities and performed through mobile bodies.

Stephens's work deals with fluctuating identities in a world of seemingly countless possibilities that prove surprisingly limited, leading to stagnation rather than progress. The combined prolificacy and astuteness of Stephens's theatre make it a practical impossibility to discuss it exhaustively in this chapter. But they also present the challenge of where we might trace the essence of his work. In order to pursue an analysis that is sufficiently in depth and representative of Stephens's playwriting more broadly, this chapter will concentrate on recent plays that have not been discussed extensively in existing publications: *Wastwater* (2011), *Carmen Disruption* (2014) and *Song from Far Away*.

These plays represent the three different forms (excluding versions and adaptations) that Stephens's playwriting has taken: naturalism; expressionism; monologue. Stephens has remarked that his work might even appear to be the product of different writers, an inevitability of responding topically to diverse social crises (2011a: ix). The plays analysed in this chapter capture a lot of what is immediate to Stephens's playwriting that ultimately renders his work irreducible to patterns. There is a core not readily revealed, which requires attention. This chapter, therefore, seeks to address the gap in existing interpretations of Stephens's work, tracing what it is that renders it so urgent.

Wastwater, Carmen Disruption and *Song from Far Away*: Music and mindscapes

Stephens's theatre explores the desolate mental, emotional and physical bodyscapes of characters who reflect the landscapes they inhabit. It has taken on social crisis at its extreme, evidencing how it seeps through all aspects of life. Capitalism is a major source of violence and grief in Stephens's work, repeatedly staged as ruinous for communities and individual lives. The degrees of crisis and violence that Stephens depicts differ from threatened to fully exacerbated, but even his quieter plays are permeated by the sensation of an imminent breaking point.

Often in Stephens's work, and certainly in the plays discussed here, a character's trials and tribulations unfold to a musical soundtrack, which, intense or more subdued, furnishes the play with a sense of urgency, depth and even danger. To date, five of his performed plays – *Country Music* (2004; in Stephens 2009), *Punk Rock* (2009; in Stephens 2011a), *Birdland* (2014), *Carmen Disruption* and *Song from Far Away* – even draw their titles from musical references. Stephens has spoken candidly about the importance of music, noting that it is a driving force in building the worlds of his plays (Stephens 2014b; 2015c). He cites the challenge of former Actors Touring Company Artistic Director Gordon Anderson to produce a play 'with the same spirit of juxtaposition as an album' (2009: xi) as an early call to an aesthetic that has persisted as a philosophy. Stephens observes: 'Often my intention at the start of conceiving a play will be to have the same impact on an audience member as a piece of music has on me' (2009: xiv). That Anderson extended his invitation while also suggesting to Stephens that he explore grief (Stephens 2009: xi) is significant. In Stephens's plays music is often lament, a tool for reaching into the soul and excavating what might be heartbreakingly impossible but also essential to release and confront. Considering this alongside an invitation to Stephens by Ian Rickson, former Artistic Director of the RCT, 'to write a play that had the same acerbic dissonant energy' (Stephens 2009: xv) of punk rock and adding to the mix the European infusion to Stephens's theatre through his collaborations and increased international presence in the late 2000s onwards, we begin to appreciate the disjunctions and ruptures in Stephens's forms, especially from *Pornography* (2007; in Stephens 2009) onwards. It is theatre that can lead to moments of explosion and then to post-apocalyptic anti-climax.

That music is so significant in the work of a playwright who is also intrigued by notions of place and belonging is not entirely surprising: concerns with mental, physical, emotional and geographical spaces feature prominently in Stephens's writing. The idea of home as location and identity that we carry with us and are conditioned by is also significant. In Stephens's plays, characters' bodies are often imagined as their only homes; at the same time, when they find themselves transient or displaced, by choice or necessity, their identity wavers. In such moments of crisis, characters face the need to establish themselves in their locale, which might, however, resist attachment, throwing their existence into further disarray. The driving forces of music and home mapping out the itineraries of Stephens's characters are summarized by his interviewer in the context of the Young Vic premiere of *Song from Far Away*:

> As in all of Stephens's work, at the play's heart there's a nagging concern with the notion of 'home' — with leaving one's origins behind and also with returning to them. He says this preoccupation comes

from having quit his own home town of Stockport when he was 18 and not having gone back [permanently]. It's striking that for many of his characters journeys offer temporary catharsis but no long-term salvation. Meanwhile, music promises to allow them to strap on new identities yet also links them to their losses. (Stephens 2015c)

The life paths of Stephens's characters emerge as vivid, often electrified, experiential soundtracks. These characters, always carrying the burden of their own individual crosses and trauma, both attracted to the pain and seeking to escape it, are on a quest towards redemption, an unofficial pilgrimage for exoneration.

Wastwater, directed by Katie Mitchell for its RCT premiere, carries a place name as its title. It alludes to a still but non-static liquid locale, much reflecting the emotional liquidity of the play's characters and the depth of their exchanges, not immediately perceptible. Wastwater, the deepest lake in England, acts as image and metaphor: a seemingly quiet landscape that harbours risk beneath the surface. It is an apt conceptual vehicle for a play where the characters' encounters take place in a certain stillness, but the truth and repercussions of their actions run deep. In three scenes, six characters, three women and three men, converse in pairs. There is a different kind of crisis in each segment and a sinking feeling that accompanies them, as characters are gradually subsumed in their inadequacies. The structure of the play is responsive to the landscape it draws its name from: it begins relatively innocently to immerse itself in ever greater depths of darkness and desolation.

Wastwater follows a reverse chronological order: its first scene takes place on '*June 25th, 9 p.m.*', and its second and third scenes both transpire on '*June 23rd, 9 p.m.*' (Stephens 2011c: 3, 20, 42). The first characters we encounter are Frieda and Harry, her foster son, about to embark on his longest journey for a job in Canada. The conversation takes place at the outdoor space of Frieda's property, '*A greenhouse on land adjacent to a large garden of a converted farmhouse outside Sipson in Middlesex*' (Stephens 2011c: 3). Next we see the awkward encounter between Lisa and Mark, who have taken '*A room at the Crowne Plaza Hotel, Heathrow Airport*' to have sex; they are both in other relationships (Stephens

2011c: 20). Mark is an art teacher; Lisa works for the police. Finally, we come to Sian and Jonathan, whose meeting has been scheduled at '*A deserted warehouse on the periphery of Heathrow Airport*' (Stephens 2011c: 42). There is nothing emotional or sexual about this encounter; it is a business transaction. Jonathan is going to buy a child from Sian. At the end of the scene – and the play – two more characters make a surprise entrance: Alain and Dalisay. He is Sian's partner; she, the child Jonathan has paid for.

Carmen Disruption is a product of Stephens's enduring collaboration with Sebastian Nübling, which stretches back to a 2003 staging of *Herons* (2001). Stephens has since created some of his boldest work in both form and content with Nübling. Before *Carmen Disruption*, *Pornography*, the open-form depiction of different urban and national mentalities in monological form, focusing on the 7/7 London bombings, and *Three Kingdoms* (2012), a relentless pursuit of good/evil boundaries in a fractured Europe through the lens of crime and sex trade, fired warning shots as to the degree of risk and experimentation Stephens is willing to engage in and of Nübling's catalytic force in furnishing this kind of result. Both plays had internationalism and mobility built into their very fibre as international co-productions, but also because they created an inter-European vehicle for assessing major crises of our contemporary moment as they have impacted our societies, with ripple effects extending beyond the borders of the singular nation-state. From national identity and belonging (*Pornography* exposes the Britishness of the terrorists, the remaining characters' ambivalence towards their city, communities and nation, and, in its emotional 'obituary' section, the ways in which immigrants have been the life-blood of British society) to the presumably free, open and equal Europe (*Three Kingdoms* depicts the preying of the sex industry on precarious social groups and the violent web it weaves across the 'civilized' West and the 'unruly' East), more recently (*Carmen Disruption*) Stephens and Nübling moved to another archetypal myth. This time it is a question of longing and its repercussions against a wholesome European background of grandeur under collapse.

Carmen Disruption began as a '*provocation*' to Stephens by Nübling (Stephens 2015a: 3) and it was Nübling who directed the premiere production at the Deutsches Schauspielhaus Hamburg. The play is like gun residue: if Bizet's *Carmen* fires a bullet, Stephens's text follows the directions in which its traces have travelled. *Carmen Disruption* shows fascination with the fractures of *Carmen*, taking on the different dimensions in which strands of the original plot might develop. If Bizet is concerned with entanglement, Stephens is preoccupied with detachment: the triggers in Bizet's text are picked up as solitary crises in the lives of disparate characters. Even though they might intersect briefly in their trajectories, these women and men are singularly absorbed in their own lives. This is *Carmen* for the twenty-first century and emotion is all but evacuated. That the play emerges as lyrical and elegiac, even, is testament to Stephens's skills to provide depth and emotion to what might seem as pure cynicism.

There are five characters: The Singer (a woman in her thirties, an opera professional), Micaëla (a young female university student), Don José (a female driver in her fifties), Carmen (a male prostitute in his twenties) and Escamillo (a male businessman in his thirties) (Stephens 2015a: 3). *Carmen Disruption* is subversive because it uses elements of *Carmen* but only insofar as it challenges them, taking an entirely counter-normative approach to the material. This includes substantial undermining of gender stereotypes and plot predictability. There is also the matter of the Chorus: in Nübling's production this involved '40 Hamburg Women and Hamburg Men' (*Carmen Disruption* 2014). In Michael Longhurst's Almeida production the Chorus was played by Viktoria Vizin (Stephens 2015a: 1), who, in stereotypical *Carmen* costume, stood not only as reminder of the source text but also as mirror image of The Singer, especially from the moment she changes into her performance costume and puts on her Carmen wig. The Singer will ultimately abandon her performance in the culmination of a long unravelling breakdown because of constant travelling and dislocation. The event produces a disturbing loss of distinction between art and life, while a meta-relationship eventually forms between The Singer and the Chorus/Carmen who mirrors her on the stage. The meta-intrigue deepens as Vizin is a mezzo-soprano herself. Nübling had achieved a similar effect by casting Rinat Shaham as The Singer. As Andrew Haydon's review noted, Shaham appears 'as a [...] postmodern version of herself who reflects on the experience of playing Carmen repeatedly across a globalised world' (2014). Then there is Carmen as a narcissistic sex worker, whose emotional pain is kept tightly under control until a violent sexual encounter with a client unleashes his anger propelling an existential crisis. Carmen's paths do not cross with those of Don José or Escamillo in any meaningful way. Don José is a mother who abandoned her family for a passion that would destroy her; she now finds herself the go-between in a criminal act so as to repay a debt. Escamillo is preoccupied with his own debt, albeit in high-stakes finance, visiting an acquaintance in a desperate effort to source essential funds for his professional survival. Micaëla moves in the margins of the play and of her own life: abandoned by her male professor lover she must endure the pain and continue their professional relationship, which aggravates a crisis of dependency on multiple levels. Given the intricacies of *Wastwater* and *Carmen Disruption* the plot of *Song from Far Away*, which involves one man in his mid-thirties, Willem, travelling from New York (where he lives) to Amsterdam (where he comes from and where his family still are) for his brother's funeral and back, might strike us as simple. It is only gradually that Willem's melancholia and the extent of his alienation are revealed.

Wastwater, Carmen Disruption and *Song from Far Away* all stage different negotiations of grief. This is the interconnecting thread between characters in *Wastwater* and also what mobilizes them: their processing of it may include a change of environment and lifestyle, or an overall hardening of their personality that leads to radical disengagement with the world. Harry is an example of the former. His unresolved grief for this friend Gavin, in whose death he feels complicit (a car accident where Gavin was driving), compels him to leave. He confesses 'Everything round this whole area is making me feel ashamed', adding, 'There's no way on earth I could possibly stay. I'd feel sick' (Stephens 2011c: 12). It is some time into Mark and Lisa's scene that we realize Mark's story is intertwined with Harry's. As he reveals to Lisa in the kind of inadvertent confession that only the sudden, accelerated connection to a stranger seems likely to precipitate in Stephens's work (the same experience she has with him, as she details her drug addiction and involvement in porn films), he has been severely affected by grief:

> **Mark** I've only started working again in the past six months. I stopped for about four years. Four and a half years ago the best student I ever taught was killed in a car accident. He was a boy called Gavin Berkshire. He was astonishing. He and a friend got drunk and got into a car and he drove it into a wall. He died. His friend didn't, which always struck me as a little unfair. After that I found it difficult to work at all. Just recently I've started again. My work's become quite figurative. I make paintings of people. This is very strange. (Stephens 2011c: 34)

Verbalizing grief is always a passing moment of humanity for Stephens's characters, who otherwise labour to retain their tough exterior. In this play, this is nowhere more strongly felt than in the case of Sian, who terrorizes Jonathan throughout their exchange, but occasionally reveals details about her life that suggest her own grief for a family she never had and for the loss of the only person she seemingly loved, her foster mother Frieda, because of poor choices, or, as she calls them, her 'many failures' (Stephens 2011c: 52).

Like Sian, most characters in *Carmen Disruption* do not associate grief with death, but with the road not taken and the relationships sacrificed. No character shows an upfront realization of their own shortcomings or allows for vulnerability: it is only through the seams that weaknesses become apparent. But there is also a broader sense of mourning in the play for a Europe that becomes an increasingly fluid concept, a generic term that leads to non-specificity as the European space and its metropolises are progressively branded by uniformity (the same grief for cities alienated from their character emerges in Willem's wandering in New York and Amsterdam in *Song from Far Away*). For some characters in *Carmen Disruption*, as for Willem, who mourns the death of his brother as well as the effective loss of his family, from whom he feels deeply alienated, the grief is manifold.

'I remembered Alexander [her professor and lover] and cried and cried', says Micaëla, before confessing the event that has aggravated her emotional trauma: 'My grandmother was buried, this morning, back in the town where I was born and I couldn't go because of my work and because I had no money and I was going to call my dad and ask him to bring me home in time for the funeral but I didn't' (Stephens 2015a: 6). Her grief is all-consuming as different emotional crises begin to converge dangerously. But Micaëla's mental health was already compromised before the latest events; she talks openly about her fragility, whether it is crying after intercourse or constantly craving security and physical intimacy (Stephens 2015a: 11). 'I'll have been preparing myself for weeks and weeks. I'll have re-read your email a million times. Your name echoes into my inbox and it's like a bomb goes off in the pit of my stomach. My son', says Don José, reminiscing of the family she left behind and reflects on constantly (Stephens 2015a: 9). As she finds herself in yet another temporary home as part of her constant touring, The Singer begins to absorb her new whereabouts before her vulnerability comes through in the shape of sadness for the transience of her own life, that, once again, has her interjecting into someone else's, as she takes her Airbnb lodgings. 'I cry for a little bit but only a little bit and then I stop', she confesses (Stephens 2015a: 15). For Carmen, the effort is to repress emotion and retain his tough exterior, all the while negotiating his turmoil after having been brutalized by a client. As he rides the train to visit his mother, he contemplates his options, before resolving to continue as if nothing happened: 'I could sit here and just cry. Let the tears fall down my face', he says (Stephens 2015a: 21). In Escamillo's self-centred, ruthless businessman world there may not normally be space for feelings, except on a day like this, which is somewhat of an anomaly. He finds himself in his hometown, which he has distanced himself from, at a critical juncture, his professional future hanging in the balance. So he allows himself an almost imperceptible moment of vulnerability, reeling not with homesickness but with the fragility his background has bequeathed him and the emotional hold it retains over him. Earlier we have heard him reveal that no one could have predicted his success; now he admits that, as he had to return, 'I start to remember exactly where I am. It starts to make me feel in some small way sad' (Stephens 2015a: 24). Then there is the grief associated with death that Carmen feels for his father, and Don José for her second husband; the more time we spend in their stories, the more it is revealed that emotions run deeper. Death, passion, love, abandonment – the archetypal truths that make Carmen mythical permeate Stephens's play, amounting to, as Micaëla puts it, 'a weight of sadness so profound' (Stephens 2015a: 34). It is only fitting that these characters should converge in the same city when there is a run of *Carmen* scheduled at the Opera, one in which The Singer is due to perform. In the Almeida production, as the audience took their places in the auditorium, we also took our places in The Singer's imagination, cast as the audience who always anticipates the permanent performance of *Carmen* that her life has become. Walking past the part of the set that represented The Singer's dressing room, to which she later refers (Stephens 2015a: 43), we feel her peering look; later we will realize she was merely trying to locate herself in a city that kept eluding her, somewhere between truth and fantasy.

The same dominant sensation of sadness emerges in *Song from Far Away*, where Willem carries its weight as his only companion in his solitary journey towards the city that used to be home, and the city that should have become home, but has not. Neither New York nor Amsterdam is familiar in any meaningful way; the connection runs no deeper than the mere recognition of landscape. Death is omnipresent in these plays and everyone is at risk. The motorcycle accident affecting an unknown man in *Carmen Disruption*, references to which recur throughout, indicates death circling characters as a lingering threat.

For Willem death is much more immediate, as he is wrestling with the sudden and untimely loss of his brother, Pauli. He faces a muted, unconquerable grief released in letters he now writes to Pauli. The play is an elegy, building up to a climactic finale. Willem does not perform his grief publicly or redemptively. As his father attacks him by saying "'You go to the funeral. You stare at everybody. You don't even try to look sad'", he offers no self-defence (Stephens 2015d: 18). But when Willem expresses his grief in the letters, its numbing effect turns to anger:

> **Willem** You know what's annoying? My brother died.
>
> I'm going to have to get used to saying that sentence out loud.
>
> My brother died last week. My brother died last month. My brother died last year. My brother died when I was thirty-four. (Stephens 2015d: 10)

Or:

> **Willem** We exist in the gaps between the sounds that we make.
>
> We all die interrupted.
>
> And you've got no more sounds left, Pauli. You've disappeared without trace. (Stephens 2015d: 13)

The links between Stephens's preoccupation with death and that with mobility, which this chapter explores as a perennial quest towards home and self-discovery, is transience. Grief and sadness in Stephens's plays are literal (see, for example, his intimate depiction of a child's death and a father's grief in *Sea Wall* (2008; in Stephens 2009)), but they are also metonymic. That is, they convey the feeling of exposure and vulnerability against a world in an unprecedented state of uncertainty where random acts delivering irretrievable blows to everyday life have become commonplace. In Stephens's work the personal is intensely political and his characters are permanently conditioned by the pervasive feeling he describes here:

> I grew up with a childhood terror of what form the Third World War would take. On days like this [Stephens references a terrorist incident] it feels like the Third World War started without anybody telling anybody else. (Stephens 2009: xx)

Or:

> we live in a time of profound safety but with a deeply troubling sense that something awful is about to happen. (Stephens 2015c)

It does not take an extravagant production to convey large-scale vulnerability and uncertainty. In the case of *Song from Far Away*, Ivo van Hove's subdued, visceral staging, which involved Jan Versweyveld's minimal set of Willem's apartment that might also stand in for his hotel room, or the multiple impersonal public spaces that he travels through in his life of constant motion, perfectly bared the depth of melancholia. Pauli is rendered present in his absence, but mostly it is Willem's vast emptiness that we are confronted with. He occasionally projects his thoughts and emotions unto a chair in his otherwise spare hallway, effectively personifying it so he can have something physical to address when he talks to Pauli and revisits the past. When Mark Eitzel's music and lyrics enter the frame, and especially as the play reaches its climax, Eelco Smits's rendition of Willem's physical and emotional exposure produces a moment of profound lament. It is a call to humanity against desolation, a primal cry from within to a distant universe. We have seen Willem bare his body as he enters the most fragile parts of his narration. As he prepares for the next stage, it is left ambiguous whether he excises death through his speech to Pauli and into the void, or he chooses to make his own exit. Having exposed his soul, he begins to wear his clothes again: his exterior, businessman armour. Willem then moves to the window ledge and climbs on it – perhaps to measure himself against the vastness, perhaps to fall into its arms, body out-stretched. In that moment, with Eitzel's song echoing, we are reminded of the intimate portrait of his brother that Willem had painted earlier with a reference to singing. In the context of a play so invested in music, the long quote is merited:

Willem You [Pauli] told me once that talking was just a peculiar
form of breathing. It was like posh breathing for humans, you said.
And that singing was something deeper and richer and stranger and
more incredible. You told me that scientists had started to think,
when they studied the vocal chords of the earliest human beings,
that hunter-gatherers sang before they spoke. They didn't live so close
together. There weren't so many of them. They needed to communicate
over long distances.
So we are animals born to sing more than we're animals born to
talk. It sounded unlikely, to me. But I liked the way you said it.
(Stephens 2015d: 23–24)

In these moments, song serves two essential functions: it creates, on
a metaphysical level, a bridge of communication between Willem and
Pauli, on the basis of Pauli's own conviction that song is a much more
honest, immediate, natural form of contact. That Willem has brought
Pauli's guitar back to New York with him is especially meaningful – it
is music that most strongly emulates the essence of Pauli now that he
is gone, as references to his fondness for it recur. Secondly, song is the
most affective means for practical and hardened Willem. It provides
an agent for accessing his feelings, which acquire deeper urgency as
they mix with the lines of the song. The song and music intimately
depict Willem and Pauli's bond; the love between them that transcends
emptiness is ultimately not lost.

Carmen Disruption and *Wastwater* also enable sharp insights into
characters by means of music. In these cases the shared language (aural
and verbal) of *Carmen* interconnects the plays and their themes of
death, anger and passion. There are references to Carmen throughout
Wastwater: Harry sings 'Habanera' in the beginning, so the first aural
contact we have with the play is established through embodied music
rather than speech (Stephens 2011c: 3). Later on, Lisa will sing the
same piece before revealing her history to Mark (Stephens 2011c: 27).
In *Wastwater Carmen* represents the corporeal and elusive Other,
the call to an impulsive, different life: an apt metaphor for a play
that slowly reveals its characters' deep-set desires while probing the

concepts of leaving and trying – and failing – to bury one's demons and transgressions.

There are references to other music in *Wastwater*, but 'Habanera' persists as a theme. In *Carmen Disruption* the entire play is underscored by *Carmen*, not least because of characters emulating the original structure. The Almeida production also featured two cellists on stage, whose music furnished verbal matter with tension, accentuating the high-strung behaviours and reinforcing the 'at risk' feeling and imminent dramatic denouement running through the piece. Stephens credits *Carmen Disruption* for his first foray into opera and classical music (2015b). Also fittingly for a play whose pivots are music and mobility, Stephens recounts the experience of listening to *Carmen* on a London Underground train on his way to Heathrow (a subtle nod to play histories, and especially to *Wastwater* and *T5*), Cologne-bound for a development meeting with the *Carmen Disruption* artistic team (2015b). He describes how *Carmen* on the Underground conditioned his impressions of fellow travellers who, in his imagination, became cast as an impromptu ensemble for the music (2015b). Stephens's comments bear direct relevance to The Singer's in *Carmen Disruption*:

> **The Singer**   I keep seeing the same four people. I see them everywhere.
>
> There's a moment when I realise exactly who they are. It's Carmen, the lover. And Don José, the fighter. And Micaëla, the lost girl. And Escamillo. (Stephens 2015a: 27)

The quotation is indicative for how music conditions The Singer's perception, framing her entire world. Even the password for the Wi-fi reception in her temporary accommodation is 'Habanera'. The fact that Stephens and Nübling interviewed Shaham extensively as a *Carmen* 'veteran' with whom Nübling had collaborated on a 2007 staging of *Carmen*, and then developed this material into *Carmen Disruption* is telling of the intricate layers in the play (Stephens 2015b). Stephens reveals that Shaham spoke candidly about her identification with the character she shared a long history with; the physical image of Shaham, as Stephens notes, is also strongly evocative of Carmen's physical presence (Stephens 2015b). The dark-haired Carmen with unruly curls recurs as a reference throughout *Carmen Disruption*, with characters encountering in their wandering the mysterious female figure that seems otherworldly and anachronistic, yet perfectly comfortable within the public space of her European urban habitat. In the Hamburg premiere Shaham played The Singer, further disturbing the binary between art and life. The image of the artist at a crossroads between music and experience, at the centre of a lived soundtrack which interblends the fervour and melancholia of the archetypal with the modern, emanates from the play. There is a lingering sense of anxiety for a Europe in search of its identity, intertwined with the characters' own fragile individualities. Such are the delicate balances of negotiating the everyday, and the awkward transitions between subjectivity and objectivity that come with adjusting to increasingly globalized, mobile lives.

Wastwater, Carmen Disruption and *Song from Far Away*: Mobilities and crisis

In Stephens's playwriting, 'home' persists, a place that can never be entirely reached, but whose pursuit tantalizes. Addressing this in the context of the internationalism of his writing, Stephens argues:

> All of the plays I've written have in some way been about travel. As a writer I'm fascinated by an interrogation of the idea of home. What it is to be at home. What it is to live at home or to leave home or to damage a home or reinvent a home or leave a home and return back to it. It is fitting then that the experience of having my plays produced in Germany and returning home to England to work has been so central to my thinking. When we travel abroad we see our home with a clarity that we may never have been offered before. This has happened to me in my work as much as in the lives of the characters I've created. (2011b)

The obsessive need to attach themselves to a place, or to other people that might act as an anchor (even though relationships in Stephens's plays also prove transient) that characters display is a combative action against insularity. The urgency for transcending isolation and attempting to connect is visible in two ways in Stephens's theatre: in his recurring international collaborations and in his characters' perennial travelling and attraction to the concept of travel. Why Stephens's work adopts this defence mechanism can be summed up in his statement:

> We're an island nation that looks largely inward, if not entirely geographically then culturally and linguistically when we programme our theatres. (2011b)

So Stephens's theatre has become pluralist, not only in how it has sought to redefine the notion of home and belonging, but also in how it has conceptualized its own home as non-fixed but mobile and located in collaborations.

In *Carmen Disruption* characters are static for much of the play. However, the intensity of their verbal matter and their narrations of journeys across cities and countries, occasionally matched by vigorous physical movement on stage, gives the impression of relentless mobility. It is a quest of 'Mobility [...because it] produces [mental] stability, or, a greater acceptance of internal instability' (Lorimer 2011: 24). Not so much a case of escaping the problem, but of attempting to deploy the pliable body as one's ally, reclaiming it from its own fixations and attachments. As John Urry notes, 'Walking is privileged, stimulated by a plethora of desires and goals stemming from the interrelations between bodily movement, fantasy, memory and the texture of urban life' (2000: 53).

The battleground of *Carmen Disruption*, symbolized in the Almeida production by the life-size prop of a bull that lies front- and centre-stage for the duration of the play and begins to bleed as the performance reaches its climax, is no longer Carmen's body, but the body of the city, and, more broadly, of Europe itself. This becomes embodied and embroiled in the characters' mobilities. The bull is the prize and sacrifice: whoever tames the wild continent with the fluctuating identity stands to stake a claim of permanence. It is significant that in Greek mythology Zeus abducted the female figure of Europe, or Europa (*Evrōpe*), the object of his lust, by taking the form of a bull that carried her away. Now is the time for a new conquest of Europe, the Almeida production of the play showed in its intuitive response to Stephens's text – this is the abduction of Europe in the post-capitalist apocalypse of transience and fluidity.

The significance of the city, and, in the case of these plays, the metropolis as the space of exchange, has been a recurring concern in sociological investigation and especially in the crossovers between studies of urban space, mobility and commerce. As Markus Hesse notes:

> Cities and urban regions have always been significant nodes for the exchange of goods. Trade and merchandising, wholesale and retail distribution have been closely connected with urban places and urban development. Cities have been a central place by definition, for both city and region, and a gateway for providing goods and services to a more distant hinterland. (2008: 13)

As this chapter discusses, the marketplace function of cities still involves urban centres and recurs across the world with minimal cultural differences in the spaces of trade and financial exchange, but it has also expanded beyond this. Cities have built extensions of themselves in the form of airports; or, from a different perspective, airports have had cities annexed to them as a means of facilitating commercialization.

In *Wastwater*, in the space between London and Heathrow, we witness exchanges of money (Frieda to Harry, who has also bought himself a ticket for a flight that will in turn buy him a better life; Jonathan to Sian, in exchange for a child), as well as commodities in the form of human bodies (Lisa and Mark have met to consume each other, while Lisa's history of drug consumption previously led to a double devouring of her body by substances and by the porn industry to which she sold herself; Dalisay is being sold to Jonathan for a lump sum). In *Carmen*

Disruption, ever-mobile characters converge in a city centre where one of them (Carmen) sells his body for money; another (The Singer) has become an international art commodity. The remaining characters are also defined by moral and financial debts. Moreover, all characters consume the myth of the city as space of activity and possibility, even if it has become so saturated by the logic of commerce that it fails to have any transformative effect on their lives. In *Song from Far Away*, Willem travels from New York to Amsterdam and back only to realize that he applies the same pattern of consumption to all aspects of life: he is a collector of people and moments that are ultimately discarded. His experience as a frequent traveller is a parable for the capitalist era. Willem's only journey is from his corporate office, to his apartment, to the airport, to the hotel – and back. In a life defined by the comforts of commercialism, home itself is unattainable. Ultimately, Willem has become a commodity of the capitalist system he serves.

The notable rise in mobility studies, responsive to the social context of motion, transience, widening communications and intersections helps us better understand what Stephens's theatre contends with. Although international travel and by extension flying is the most commonly encountered version of mobility in the plays discussed here, the body in motion, leaving, trying to reach home, on the verge of a discovery, travelling across a country and towards oneself is a recurring preoccupation in Stephens's theatre. *Port* (2002; in Stephens 2005), *Motortown* (2006; in Stephens 2009), *Pornography, Harper Regan* (2008; in Stephens 2011a), *Three Kingdoms* and *Birdland* are further examples of how Stephens has conceptualized the body in motion and transit, dwelling in the acts of walking in one's city, attempting to reconnect with the outposts of one's past, or navigating a foreign landscape. All acts carry degrees of risk: the routine and familiar easily becomes transformed into the wild and unfamiliar because of crises experienced individually, collectively or both. It is so in *Port* and *Harper Regan*, where the institution of family collapses in the face of social challenge and dissatisfaction; it is so in *Motortown*, where PTSD lingers when the war fades in the distance; it is so in *Pornography*, where 7/7 unleashes chain reactions in the characters' perceptions of their lives, and of their city; and it is so in *Birdland* and *Three Kingdoms* where crime and transgressions against fellow humans radically upset the concepts of good and evil, propelling mental breakdowns.

In a recent study of mobility as key component of individual freedom, but also as one that might be compromised, impeded or abused in a way that challenges its democratic roots, Tore Sager takes a nuanced approach to the subject of travel as promise (also in the sense of opportunity or right) and actuality. As Sager notes, 'the potentiality aspect of mobility means that the individual has a choice between travelling and not travelling. This is an essential aspect of freedom as mobility; freedom of movement implies the right not to move' (2006: 469). In Stephens's work we find individuals at different stages of mobility: they are experiencing it, they have become encumbered by it, they are on the verge of it. In *Wastwater*, Frieda, a staple for the children she has fostered through the years, is contemplating a move of her own and her home is presented as much as an essential part of her rootedness as a weight. It is particularly meaningful that it will be the enhancement of someone else's mobility that will allow Frieda to move: she is unlikely to travel long distance herself, to visit Harry in Canada, for example – but if Heathrow acquired its new runway, she would be expected to relocate due to redevelopment. She and Harry are both on the verge: he, on his way to a new life; she, with the promise of mobility ahead – and, in the meantime, with the option of convincing herself that staying might also be her choice. In any case, they are both weary of 'home' as a physical area (whether building or location) and willing to embark on the pursuit of what home might mean next. Sager's suggestion that 'mobility is created by overcoming friction measured as physical distance, costs, or other variables indicating inertia or resistance' (2006: 467) is relevant to other characters in limbo in *Wastwater*: for a play about mobility, the stasis is overwhelming. It points to the play's title: the more time these characters spend in their 'homes', whether we take these to be the places that accommodate them temporarily, or their permanent living situations, the more they become submerged in the depth of their circumstances. The underlying crisis of personal failure and dissatisfaction connects all three scenes, accentuated by the different social crises that each depicts: the potential tearing apart of a community for the purported improvement of others' quality of life through airport expansion; Lisa's transition from drug abuse and the porn industry to the obsessive consumption of sex; Mark's stagnation in his unsatisfactory life and the uncertainty as to whether he is able to move on, even though he has been given an opportunity for a new beginning overseas; the smuggling of humans of which Sian and Jonathan are equally guilty.

The space between stasis and movement has been a recurring concern in mobility studies, but it emerged urgently, and with a new set of parameters, following the ash cloud disruption of 2010, when the eruptions of Eyjafjallajökull grounded flights. One of the scholarly responses to the temporary crisis, which also highlights its consequences and potential dimensions towards more permanent action, is particularly noteworthy in drawing parallels between the volcanic eruption and John Cage's *4'33"*. Daryl Martin's bold associations between art and lived experience in 'Eyjafjallajökull 4'33": A Stillness in Three Parts' are remarkably relevant to *Wastwater*, but also to the other plays examined in this chapter. As Martin notes, providing dates for the three different periods of closure, 'the disruption to UK airspace similarly [to Cage's piece] took the form of a "three part movement"' (2011: 86–87). Martin's discussion of how Cage has upset the norm of what music represents – similarly to what the airport is seen to represent – as his artistic position more broadly 'attempts to evacuate content and disrupt expectations', in this case through 'evocation of silence, stillness and structure' which 'may serve as a point of departure for reflecting on the eruption [...], the immediate disruption this caused for the aviation industry in Europe and the long-term consequences for the practice of aeromobility as it has evolved in contemporary societies' (2011: 86), is a helpful reference point. Though certainly not silent, *Wastwater* pays attention to stillness and structure; it is metaphorically silent in that it alludes to the possibility of flight, it teases escape, but does not visualize it. *Wastwater* is a play of stillness in stark contrast to motion, because even though we hear characters talk about leaving, or we find them located in proximity to the major mobility hub of Heathrow Airport, we do not witness them in motion (with the exception of Sian who makes a quick getaway following her transaction with Jonathan – but this has been preceded by a torturous, protracted interaction that has involved very little physical movement). Even in *Song from Far Away* or *Carmen Disruption*, where characters experience mobility, we never see the locus of flight – it does not form part of the set. Stephens trusts the audience to visualize movement in its absence: characters create a stagescape for it as their bodies map, create and narrate the city.

What emerges from all three plays then is that in terms of conceptual depth, dramatic intensity and intellectual engagement stillness might be a more affective way to stage actual, projected or attempted movement and to mobilize the spectator's imagination. That is, 'stillness does not indicate that nothing of significance is happening for mobility. Instead, stillness, like silence, can be interpreted as a meaningful action [...] to be noticeable and accountable [...]' (Haddington, Mondada, and Nevile 2013: 32). Some of the most experimental and socially astute theatre, with Beckett being the most obvious example, has relied on stillness. It is therefore entirely reasonable that contemporary experimental playwrights like Stephens should revisit it today.

Wastwater, in particular, with its three movements, or scenes, can be understood in this context. It is a deceptively realist play, which in fact takes on a more experimental form as one scene ripples out to the next, until the deep-lying interconnections are laid bare. Mitchell's premiere production at the RCT captured this ripple effect, established through both form and content, with an intelligent use of the set (by Lizzie Clachan). The first scene made dense physical use of the space, the two actors front-stage in close proximity to the audience and each other; the second opened up to reveal a spacious hotel room, which allowed the characters more freedom of movement; the final scene surprised us with a vast, deserted warehouse. The notion that stillness generates more stillness, with three sets of characters unable to escape their lives and submerged into stasis by their past, echoes the play's title and manifests that still waters run deep. As Lisa remarks of Wastwater, which she visited as a child, 'It's terribly still. My dad told me that the stillness was a bit of a lie. "It looks still, Lisa, but you should see how many bodies are hidden under there"' (Stephens 2011c: 33). Like Cage's piece, and like the experience of the immobilized passengers during the volcanic disruption, the play also suggests that in physical inaction a lot can happen, with the experience of the moment, suspended in time, weighing all the more heavily.

Although Cooke's initial vision of the play was more adventurous than the end result, as he had imagined the three sections in different parts of the RCT, involving a mobile audience, the production did deliver an altogether different sense of adventure through the gradual subversion of expectations (Cooke 2011). The play did not pursue a forensic quest for answers; instead, it quietly submerged us into the problematics of its characters' lives and exposed the depth of crisis. If, as Martin argues, Cage's piece 'critiques [...] commercial expectations [...] [as] the musical content is emptied and we are left with only the outlines of a rhythmic structure' and the volcanic eruptions have invited us to 'attune ourselves to the temporary [...] stillnesses' (2011: 87), so Stephens's play enables us to feel the palpitations of mobility with minimal actual movement. Contextually, this theatrical study of stillness in the vicinity of an airport came only a year after the volcanic disruption.

The framing device of the airport is crucial in *Wastwater*, where it represents a space both dark and alluring. Other than Heathrow, reference is also made to Stansted, in a hotel room in whose vicinity Lisa first became involved in porn (Stephens 2011c: 30). The relevance of the airport as place and concept to *Song from Far Away* and *Carmen Disruption* is also significant. In the latter, the relationship between urban mobility and flying/airport mobility brings new dimensions to the enquiry. While Stephens's theatre retains the fascination with the act of travelling it does not build an emotionalist link to either leaving or returning. It is, rather, interested in the state of transit and wandering, and what this contributes to the journey towards self-awareness. It recognizes that travelling may be an instinctive reaction to personal crisis, or itself the catalyst for crisis and disorientation. Travelling, therefore, emerges as both symptom and cause of a transient identity. Ultimately, Stephens's theatre does not conceive of mobility as merely a neoliberalist state, but as the contemporary human condition compelling reflection.

Peter Adey writes of 'Airport sounds penetrat[ing] the airport boundaries. [...] Adverts and aircraft distribut[ing] the airport beyond itself', part of a strategy that enables airports 'to orientate bodies to them' (2011: 142, 145). He adds that 'Examining a mobile body moving through an airport [...], is to examine a mobility within an enormous wider context of mobilities travelling to the airport and aeromobilities across the globe' (Adey 2011: 147). As Sven Conventz and Alain Thierstein argue, 'Formerly planned as stand-alone facilities in the cities' periphery, airports – particularly those with a hub function – have gone through a morphogenesis into more or less urban-like entities' (2014: 77). They add that the widely used term '"airport city"' indicates this evolution (Conventz and Thierstein 2014: 80). Proceeding from such claims, I argue that these developments have not only conditioned our attitudes towards airports, but also our mode of inhabiting urban spaces. Stephens's texts are responsive to this new reality. The visual images that his characters' narrations produce construct the mental web of an ever-mobile, interconnected world. To be *of* the airport does not merely mean that one is physically present within the terminal, but that one gravitates towards it, that they find themselves in its vicinity, that they are conditioned by the presence of this potential gateway to elsewhere. Or they might find themselves in the shadows of the airport, both tantalized by its proximity and immobilized by their circumstances. Such is the case for most characters in *Wastwater*. The airport emerges as the building that lives converge upon, and it holds a certain allure: 'It's rather beautiful I think' (Stephens 2011c: 22), says Mark of Heathrow in *Wastwater*, gazing at it from his hotel room.

It is meaningful that specific airports emerge as the hubs of action in *Wastwater* and *Song from Far Away*. Heathrow has already been mentioned; in *Song from Far Away,* the primary airport in question is Amsterdam's Schiphol. It is significant that the play was a Toneelgroep Amsterdam production featuring Smits, a long-standing member of the company, as Willem. The reference to Schiphol is a nod to the play's own internationalism and hybrid identity. The airport is local to the company, familiar to the main character and, at the same time, a global hub. It serves as both a grounding and disorientating device, a staple of Willem's fluid belonging and convoluted experience. Willem describes Schiphol as 'a small suburb,' which commands long journey times even when one is already in the building, in transit between different parts of the airport (Stephens 2015d: 6). Conventz and Thierstein note that 'Although named and recognized as Amsterdam-Schiphol, the airport is actually located in the neighbouring municipality of Haarlemmermeer and not in the city proper of Amsterdam' (2014: 86). The reference serves the specific example, but it also provides a concise summary for how cities become equated to their airports regardless of the actual geographical divide, and for how airports stand in for and represent entire cities for passengers in transit, but also as the primary gateway, the first or final (depending on journey direction) image and outpost of the city. Conventz and Thierstein's analysis of the desirability of the broader Schiphol area for business aligned with how the airport has come to define the city creates a helpful narrative: for the gearing of action towards enterprise, for the shifting of action towards the airport rather than the city centre, for understanding how business and global capitalism – activities closely linked with international travel – impose their rhythms on actual city centres as well (merely an extension of the hubs that airports are) and, finally, for why people find themselves gravitating towards airports (2014: 86–88). These spaces embody both activity and escape, and, most often, provide the path to consumption. Tellingly, in the second scene of *Wastwater* Lisa establishes the connection between cities, airports and consumerism, making an otherwise unwarranted reference to Minneapolis and the Mall of America, which evidences how the prospect of escape and intimacy is, in our neoliberalist world, inevitably interlinked to consumption:

> **Lisa** [...] It's the biggest shopping mall in the world. Japanese tourists fly in just to go there. They go straight from the airport and then go straight back home again. We could go there.
>
> [...]
>
> **Mark** We could.
>
> **Lisa** Go shopping. Buy clothes for each other. [...] (Stephens 2011c: 39)

When increased mobility renders cities and their airports synonymous, and at the same time indistinguishable from other urban centres and their respective airports, confluence troubles perception. This is the state we witness in *Carmen Disruption*. The centre and grounding of one's experience forever shifts away from a specific locale, creating the impression of constant mobility. The accompanying piece to the playtext of *Wastwater*, the short monologue *T5*, culminates in a woman's discovery (such is the momentous feeling the place exudes) of Heathrow's newest, fifth terminal. Here, as well as in *Song from Far Away*, Stephens's approach to the concept of flight is poetic. The flight in this text, however, like the possible flight at the end of *Song from Far Away*, does not necessarily involve travel. Although the outcome is ambiguous, both pieces entertain the possibility of their respective protagonists' suicide. The airport invites and welcomes, but it also drains and taunts as part of its self-performance. The Woman in *T5* perceives of her journey to Heathrow, which takes her away from her afternoon routine, as an act of defiance, an escape from the family crisis and the alienating city with the unforgiving pace that she had been experiencing quietly and solitarily (other than her husband's adultery, she undergoes a motherhood crisis). Upon contact with the terminal building, the Woman reacts with wonder and awe, captured in the breathlessness of her congested speech:

> **Woman**   I get out at the station at Terminal Five and the rush
> and the chrome and the glass and the size and the sound and the
> air and the roar and the space and the space and the space and the
> swell and the oil and the roof and the light and the water and space
> and the space and the size and the space feels like nothing I've ever
> quite known. (Stephens 2011c: 73)

Her stillness juxtaposed with the promise of the surrounding space
is overwhelming. She has journeyed to the airport but will go no
further and Stephens's text describes a suspended moment with the
woman in flight, as she becomes elevated from her context to take
in her environment with extreme clarity. It is uncertain whether she
has leapt into the void, whether she is having a mental breakdown or
whether this is a lucid moment of profound insight. The metaphysical
aspect of Stephens's text perfectly contrasts with the concreteness of
the building that gives the text its title. Then again, that same building
embodies the possibility of being lifted above and carried away,
however temporarily, in space and time. The airport is as literal as it
is metaphorical.

The way in which constant travel regulates lives of speed and
transience is captured in both *Song from Far Away* and *Carmen
Disruption*, which conceptualize the mobile individual's failure to
connect as a primary crisis leading to alienation. Willem speaks of
his airport and flight experience like a seasoned traveller, revealing
his fondness of blending into anonymous crowds in the suspended
moments of the in-between hub, the airport, that ends up becoming a
destination in itself. The flight crew are, in a way, Willem's people; he
is their 'fellow nomad' (Stephens 2015d: 5). In *Carmen Disruption* The
Singer describes her travel experience, rendering evident the extent to
which this has become a permanent, corrosive lifestyle:

> **The Singer**   […] It tells me when to stand up from my seat and how
> long to wait before everybody else has got down from the plane. It tells
> me where the best place to wait for my luggage is. I've two cases. One
> full of work clothes and medicine. One full of the things that I need
> just to stay alive. (Stephens 2015a: 7)

Or even:

The Singer   In the past six months I've lived in three different cities.

I've stayed home on precisely five nights.

On three of those nights I was on my own. (Stephens 2015a: 10)

The position that 'mobility does not necessarily result in lack of local attachment' and 'one of the potentials of discussing mobile forms of belonging is to show how a mobile everyday life for many people necessitates varying forms of belonging to places' is, of course, also tenable (Arp Fallov, Jørgensen, and Knudsen 2013: 484). Displacement and detachment are not essential partners of mobility – and especially of the elective mobility we mostly encounter in Stephens's plays, as opposed to, for example, forced migration. However, alienation is the case when it comes to Stephens's characters, whose quest for elsewhere becomes a compulsion.

Stephens's work demonstrates that despite claims of freedom and access, mobility is not always a democratic process, nor is it necessarily a conscious choice. Even though 'We are [...] very often mobile with others, and even when we move alone we can very rarely do so fully independently, or without regard to others or what is happening around us' (Haddington, Mondada, and Nevile 2013: 3), idealized notions of implicit togetherness can be problematic. As the plays examined here show, space is often experienced singularly and far from entails a necessary connection to others. We see this in characters talking almost irrespective of one another in *Wastwater*, evidencing their distance even in an '*interactional space*', or 'space [...] configured by the arrangement and coordination of the mutual body positions of the participants' (Haddington, Mondada, and Nevile 2013: 22; emphasis original) and remaining transient in each other's lives. We also encounter this in characters caught off-guard by temporary and unexpected moments of encounter (with each other, and with other strangers in the streets of the city) in *Carmen Disruption*, that leave them bemused, or in Willem's awkward and fruitless attempts to reconnect with family members and a former partner who have been marginalized by his mobile lifestyle. The disappointment and occasional despair that these situations cause are the only real emotions to emerge from the characters' mobility, which has otherwise programmed them to treat everything – and everyone – as mere agents in transactions. Relationships may be collected and discarded with zero consequence; they do not provide the foundations of a life. As Escamillo readily admits, 'It is only through the things that you buy that you can ever feel at home any more' (Stephens 2015a: 23).

Urry's consideration of 'the material transformations that are remaking the "social", especially those diverse mobilities that, through multiple senses, imaginative travel, movement of images and information, virtuality and physical movement, are materially reconstructing the "social as society" into the "social as mobility"' (2000: 2) is particularly relevant. Stephens's characters create their social spaces by means of mobilities and itineraries; in fact, they become their own social spaces, more than attaching themselves to physical locales. Therefore, *Wastwater* is underpinned by an airport theme that underlines the impermanence and sensation that the only life for these characters is formulated in the here and now, with uncertain outcomes and futures. The communication clusters these characters form are only temporary and thereby tentative; rather than commitment to the social, there is only a commitment to the self. Even though in *Carmen Disruption* characters give us the impression of intersecting, in fact they are only carving their own individual courses while incidentally inhabiting the same urban physical space. It is unsurprising, then, that these characters do not communicate but rather perform their individual, fractured identities and speak their insular narratives in a contemporary Tower of Babel parallel.

The city in which the play unfolds is also incidental: it is filled with references to landmarks suggestive of a certain European landscape (the Old Town, a river, a cathedral with an adjacent square, a University, an Opera House, expensive hotels, all the major transportation hubs) but at the same time these are generic enough to be easily transferrable and applicable to any other major urban centre, not even necessarily

European. Carmen's description of a gay bar he frequents is indicative of the dispersed, non-site-specific experience:

Carmen [...] I like this place. I feel very at home here. I like that it exists in every city. And that wherever I am, in any country in the whole wide world there is always a Rudi's [the name of the bar] and I can always find it and I always, always, always feel at home. (Stephens 2015a: 14)

Through the insularity and urban isolation of his characters, as well as their constant drifting in airplanes, cars, trains, buses and city streets, Stephens's play remarks on the essential travelling nature of life. The business and gain approach that individuals motivated by materialism bring to urban centres means that, dominated by market principles, our cities have become more interchangeable than we might imagine them to be. At a time when debates on Europe are raging on, Stephens's play demonstrates that our unity might in fact be built on our growing erosion of unique urban/spatial characteristics, which global capitalism has inflicted. As Escamillo frames this:

Escamillo [...] For a moment I even forget which country I'm in.

[...]

Because the shops are all the same and the roads are all the same and the airports are the same and the hotels are the same and the drinks are all the same and the food is all the same and the music is the same and the cars are all the same and the films are all the same and the football is the same and the television is the same. Everybody has lost all real sense of landscape. All natural resources are commoditised and transportable. The only way we continue nowadays is by selling the selling of the selling of the selling of every last thing that we sell. And you can do that from anywhere. (Stephens 2015a: 23)

The varying degrees of mental crisis (and breakdown, in The Singer's case) are indicative of the characters' radical disorientation and split experience. They are only able to perceive of themselves as fragments materializing in isolated, insular moments in time and context is immaterial.

In *Song from Far Away*, Willem's awkward attempts to recreate his home by reviving family relationships in the aftermath of his brother's death proves a failure, evidence that he has been disinvested far too long for the relationships to be salvageable. The only connection Willem succeeds in establishing is the one that produces the monological form of the piece: the confessional letters to Pauli. At this moment of crisis, Willem attempts to unburden himself of his materialist lifestyle and appears compelled to root down his emotions in a form that is fixed, representing some form of permanence. That he disperses the sheets of paper containing his letters (not a stage direction but a directorial intervention in the Van Hove production) in the streets of his vast and alienating city in the finale of the play conveys the vast depth of his loneliness. It is also an act of sharing, not electronically but physically, his quest for an emotional home with the world as a final radical move. When Willem lets the pieces of paper slowly land unto the streets of New York and climbs on his window ledge we realize that he is – literally – one step away from eliminating the only home he has been able to sustain, which has accommodated his constant mobility: his very body. Willem's apartment conveys the 'one-size-fits-all' mentality that hinders individuality and banks on the fast turnover of homes and inhabitants. And so, for Willem, New York is Amsterdam and Amsterdam is New York; neither of his 'hometowns' manages to provide a home. Therefore, the crises of alienation, uniformity and assimilation are not presented as a European but as a global phenomenon in the developed world and Stephens shows how mobilities may eventually result in ideological, emotional and physical standstill.

Earlier in the play, Willem's preference of a hotel room over the family home in Amsterdam symbolizes his extent of alienation and that the only places that feel comfortable are impersonal spaces such as hotels and airports. Recounting his outward journey to Amsterdam, he speaks warmly of 'the lounge by invitation only' and the degree of comfort and homely feeling this otherwise anonymous space provides (Stephens 2015d: 4). He also refers to 'the smoking lounge at Murphy's Bar' with genuine fondness, a mark of the constant mobility conditioning his identity, describing his impression of it 'like the only real place left in the world' (Stephens 2015d: 6). Urry's description of '[...] lounges [... as] places of intense sameness produced by the global networks and immutable mobiles of the aviation industry and of intense hybridity as mobile peoples and cultures unpredictably intersect as they "dwell-in-transit"' resonates strongly (2000: 63). Even Willem's choice as to which hotel he stays at in Amsterdam is meaningful: he chooses the Lloyd, because it represents 'The place of embarkation', its history associated with that of emigrants awaiting departure (Stephens 2015d: 6).

Urry speaks of 'globalisation not as a borderless utopia but as a new dystopia' (2000: 13). His observation that 'it is inhuman objects that reconstitute social relations [...which] are made and remade through machines, technologies, objects, texts, images, physical environments and so on' and these 'inhabit most work and domestic environments' (Urry 2000: 14) is poignant with reference to Stephens's plays, where technology is a key conditioning factor for characters' mobility and displacement. *Carmen Disruption* captures this human condition expressly, for example in Carmen's obsessive attempt to connect, which is habitual impulse rather than genuine need for contact:

Carmen   [...] I check my Twitter feed.

I check my timeline.

I update my status.

I check my tumblr.

I check my emails. Delete three of them.

I check my Vine account.

I search for myself on Twitter.

There are twelve other people with my name ahead of me.

Nobody is talking about me.

I check out Tinder.

I check out Grindr. (Stephens 2015a: 31)

Other characters narrate similar moments, and the Almeida production also created the striking image of characters posing for selfies simultaneously, fixed in their stage positions as they attempt to capture a 'Europe crumbling' but 'Defiant' (Stephens 2015a: 48). The most poignant moment of human interface with technology, evidence of the disconnection that comes with living lives virtually and in transit, is Micaëla's reference to her dead grandmother. Micaëla regrets that her grandmother never joined Facebook or Twitter as she insisted, because, had she done so, 'she would still have been alive in a way' (Stephens 2015a: 13). The representation of Micaëla's grief, who craves the agency of technology that might mitigate her pain, is both realistic and disturbing: if there is a lack of understanding that the virtual image is hollow, it is all the more unlikely that Micaëla (or any of the other characters) will grasp that remote exchanges and the digitization of relationships are merely avatars for absence, symbols of an expanding crisis of disconnection.

Proceeding from Urry's comments on the impact of technology (2000: 14), the oxymoron is that its all-pervasive impact might seem to diminish distance, but it also subtracts from corporeal communication and enhances alienation. Urry's survey of nomadism (2000: 27–29) renders it evident that any positive associations would not apply to the confused state that Stephens's plays depict. Amongst Urry's references to the theorization of the nomad, Raymond Williams's concept of '"nomad capitalism"' (Urry 2000: 28) is particularly applicable. It identifies the fraught phenomenon of draining individuals, places and resources for gain and then simply moving on to the next target (Urry 2000: 27–28). The mental, emotional and physical burnout that Stephens's characters experience in *Carmen Disruption* and *Song from Far Away* is a manifestation of this. Ultimately, in Stephens's plays we witness the embodied practice of Urry's assertion that '[...] travellings [...are] constitutive of the structures of social life – it is in these mobilities that social life and cultural identity are recursively formed and reformed' (2000: 49). As Urry adds elsewhere, mobility – even on a constant basis – is the new normal; there is nothing eccentric or exotic about it anymore, and lives are being moulded by it (2000: 50).

Conclusion

Proceeding from three recent examples, this chapter has concentrated on how Stephens's plays problematize mobility, rather than treating it as a contemporary class marker, privilege and benefit. Further to the line of argument that this chapter has pursued, concerning the fractures to identity and to social cohesion that constant transience contributes to, there is, of course, an additional thematic strand in Stephens's work and his preoccupation with the ethics of mobility. This aspect is particularly prominent in *Wastwater*, and it concerns the environmental impact of frequent travel, the ease and relative low cost of flying that corrodes the questioning of its necessity and the eradicating of the ecology of local communities for the market-driven expansion of an airport. This play can therefore also be seen as a relatively early symptom of the environmental turn in new writing, given its juxtaposition of the awe-inspiring natural image of Wastwater with the urban and charmless landscapes where the action of the play unfolds. However, given the extensive attention that this book pays to environmental crisis in Chapters 2 and especially 4, here I have followed an approach that has enabled the cross-contextualization of different forms of Stephens's theatre under the thematic strand of global and urban wandering, pursuing a core, recurring concern in Stephens's work, which is, however, mostly overlooked: the inability to attach oneself to home and community as either a reality or an idea mostly owing to the pervasiveness of neoliberalist individualism.

Stephens's work confronts this uncontested, naturalized state, which breeds more distance and solitary crisis, even at the time when mobility stakes a claim to the very act of diminishing distance and alienation. The plays emanate as much the allure of the city as the site of 'restlessness, flexibility and nomadism' (Pinder 2011: 68), as they emit distrust towards this narrative, and what it has meant for identity. There is, in other words, 'a need to question the social and political ramifications of [...the] celebration of flow, flux and mobility' (Pinder 2011: 169). Proceeding from Gaston Bachelard, Urry argues that space needs to be 'lived' in with commitment for it to allow any durational experience (Urry 2000: 118). He develops the concept further with reference to Heidegger, ultimately contesting it, to argue that in our time the impermanence of our relationship with one place and state of inhabitation far from *de facto* evacuates the integrity in our intentions, or the importance of the experience (Urry 2000: 131–132). This is part of the complexity and conflict that Stephens's characters also encounter: they do not invest in duration, or, when they do, they are made uncomfortable by it; no singular place can accommodate their mobile desires. Their experience ultimately becomes fragmented, and they are uncertain how to process it. This ultimately culminates in varying degrees of crisis: from the pursuit of ephemeral solutions, as in *Wastwater*, to the public breakdowns that characters experience in *Carmen Disruption* and the untimely exit that Willem considers in *Song from Far Away* because, despite his countless mobility options, his mental and emotional experience has become so confined that he is left with nowhere else to go.

Stephens notes that he has often written material in the form of duologue or monologue because of 'an interest in dramatizing a world that seems to be more atomized and fractured than it has been in the past and subsequently scorched by a need and an inability to connect' (2009: xxi). If there is a conclusion that emerges from the fractures of mobility that Stephens's work depicts, these characters' 'roots and routes' (Urry 2000: 133), it is that

There are [...] a variety of ways of dwelling, but [...] once we move beyond that of land, almost all involve complex relationships between belongingness and travelling, within and beyond the boundaries of national societies. People can indeed be said to dwell in various mobilities; bell hooks writes: 'home is no longer one place. It is locations' (1991: 148) (Urry 2000: 157)

The plays discussed here, but also Stephens's work more broadly, show us that home may well be forever slipping away. Still, rather than accept this passively, these plays urge us to question our own agency and interrogate the degree to which mobility is a necessary, if not defining, feature of our contemporary lives, increasingly built into our constitutions. Unlike the mobile software that Stephens's characters are so drawn to, and that might locate us with precision and root us, locating ourselves and our identities may be more challenging; but these plays are invested in the effort nonetheless.

7

Residues of Violence: debbie tucker green's Desolate Selfscapes

'Normally my stuff starts with dialogue and I don't always know where it's going to go', stated debbie tucker green in a recent, rare interview given for the promotion of her film *Second Coming* (2015) (Marshall and tucker green 2015). When probed about the concealment and slow reveal tactic of her plays, tucker green does not acknowledge it as a technique, but rather as unintentional (Marshall and tucker green 2015). Similarly, when the interviewer attempts a connection to Pinter's resistance to providing an explanation for his work, including to collaborators trying to understand the play in a specific production, tucker green appears entertained but refrains from further comment (Marshall and tucker green 2015). Still, tucker green reiterates that she trusts the work and the spectators to have their own views of it, therefore attempting to impose a specific interpretation is ultimately irrelevant (Marshall and tucker green 2015). Rather than reticent, distant or even hostile to differing views of the work, tucker green emerges as invested in the journey of her plays, with the spectator the ultimate determiner. The playwright also rejects the notion that her writing is tailored to specific performers like Nadine Marshall (Marshall and tucker green 2015), a frequent collaborator who, other than her lead role in the *Second Coming*, delivered the monologue in the RCT premiere of *random* (2008) and was the protagonist in the National Theatre Shed opening of *nut* (2013). If the interview offers any glimpse at tucker green's method, it is that her work comes into being like that of any other writer who allows themselves to be surprised by the text that emerges and that it is much less esoteric than it has been imagined as.

The mention of Pinter in the context of tucker green's work is in a number of different ways justified. Further to the apprehension towards answering questions that might impose an explanation on the plays, the two playwrights also share an affinity for staging the personal as political and vice versa; for stage action that is borne through language; for elliptical and yet imagery-rich work. Defining the 'stuff' that tucker green mentions, therefore, is an intricate process. Familial (especially intergenerational) dysfunction, abuse, gender, power relations, alienation, mental illness, sex trade, racial segregation, genocide, AIDS, child soldiers, war crime, urban violence, punishment, governmentality, desensitization, therapy culture, have all found their way onto tucker green's stage. Occasionally there is also humour. As for what tucker green's stage (often directed by herself) has looked like, it has always been sparse, whatever the venue. In tucker green's work, characters collide forcefully and the fact that her plays tend to be rather short in duration with revelations made painfully slowly leads to a potent mix of first delayed and then suddenly accelerated, maximized impact. It is a method that serves the 'particular trope of her writing [...] a concern with highlighting how selfish individualism, apathy and inaction are complicit in continued violence and trauma' (Goddard 2013: 192).

Given the attention that tucker green's work has been receiving in an increasing amount of publications, even though this chapter is informed by her oeuvre more broadly, it concentrates on *truth and reconciliation* (2011), *hang* (2015) and *nut* (introduced above) so as to enrich and advance existing discourse which has tended to concentrate on tucker green's earlier work. For a playwright whose theatre is so multifaceted, what tucker green's plays share is their characters' vast emotional desolation, a reflection of their physical environment and often the by-product of mental and/or physical (self-)abuse. In *random*, the playwright combines the two most effectively to convey the grief of a family whose young son has sustained a fatal knife attack, the result of urban street crime. Even though with plays like *born bad* (2003), *dirty butterfly* (2003) or *stoning mary* (2005), to name but a selected few, tucker green had been receiving attention for the better part of the decade, *random*, an achievement in dramatic lyricism that blended disdain for the mundane with the deepest human tragedy of loss, delivered thunderously by Marshall on a bare RCT Downstairs stage, essentially confirmed tucker green as a household name. The powerful witnessing aesthetic in tucker green's theatre, which is often commented upon in critical discourse, was particularly poignant. As Mireia Aragay and Enric Monforte point out, *random* was the kind of play that 'clearly casts spectators as witnesses' (2013: 113). The experience is enhanced by the staging methods and form of tucker green's work, which serve to heighten the audience's sense of involvement and draw attention to the crises that the plays negotiate. Following on from Aragay and Monforte, I would therefore note that tucker green's theatre first and foremost casts us as citizens.

truth and reconciliation: Ghosts of justice

It is unsurprising that following *random* tucker green took a somewhat longer pause before her next play, *truth and reconciliation*. It was also the subject of the play that merited the pause and, one imagines, necessitated research. The plot concerns multiple encounters within the UN Truth and Reconciliation Committee framework, where victims and perpetrators face off in a quest for justice and redemption. This play, too, was staged at the RCT, albeit in a Theatre Upstairs production directed by tucker green herself. The subject tucker green chose allowed her to further engage with her already established concerns of human rights, race and civic awareness. Truth and Reconciliation Committees have received substantial scholarly attention, but the theatre has been slow to catch up. Therefore, paradoxically tucker green's text remains one of comparatively few examples of how playwriting has dealt with this political platform and the social and historical issues that it opens up for enquiry. The most well-known of the pre-existing texts, which has had international revivals, was Jane Taylor's *Ubu and the Truth*

Commission (1997). tucker green's play interweaves different time points, locations and stories of individuals affected by violence, but it is punctuated by one specific story with which it begins and ends. This concerns the murder of a young girl in 1976, Apartheid-era South Africa and the truth and reconciliation meeting that is scheduled for the family and the perpetrator in 1998. The storyline is revisited throughout performance. Other action unfolds (in order of staging) in Rwanda, 2005; Bosnia, 1996; Zimbabwe, 2007 and Northern Ireland, 1999.

In Rwanda, a widow who encounters her husband's murderer with her brother- and father-in-law demands to recreate her husband's final moments by asking what he was wearing, what his final words were, whether he cried. The perpetrator remains composed and resistant to providing answers, while tension develops between the woman and the family members who disagree with her questions. Eventually, the woman, Stella, is left alone with her husband's killer. He antagonizes her, fabricating a version of events that paints her husband as weak and frightened. While she resists this version of her husband, insisting that it is not consistent with her knowledge of him, it is only late in the play, when we witness an encounter between Moses – her husband – and his killer that it becomes clear that Stella was right. In this sequence, Moses shames his killer.

In the Bosnia scenes, two former Serbian soldiers, awkward with each other despite their former familiarity, are faced with a Bosnian woman in the advanced stages of pregnancy – a woman that, as we learn, has travelled a long distance to claim the right of confronting her rapist (it is implied that she was raped by one of the men, while the other was present). It is unclear whether the final interaction we see between the two men occurs before or after they are confronted by the Bosnian woman, but tucker green once more exposes the perpetrators' cowardice, showing the two men arguing as to who will assume responsibility. The callousness with which one man imagines himself as a functional member of society, attempting to coerce the other into coming forward so that he might preserve his status, delivers an ironic comment on the radically different marks that war leaves on victims and perpetrators. As the play implies, even the PTSD that the now alcoholic, unemployed former soldier appears to suffer from does not compare with the trauma his victim is forced to endure. Worse yet, neither man admits to be at fault, despite the woman's confident accusations.

The Zimbabwe segment concerns a couple that we first encounter in a private, domestic context, disagreeing over the woman's increasingly vocal political activity, which is exposing her to physical threat. When we come to see her husband in a committee later in the play, he is involved in a heated argument with a woman who refuses to be cast as the perpetrator in their conversation, although it is clear that she had some level of involvement in the disappearance – and death – of his wife. This is another occasion in the play when tucker green makes a case as to the strength and agency of women under duress: as with the Rwandan couple, we are dealing with a wife resisting passive and submissive stereotypes. At the same time, it is another powerful woman who accuses the husband of the disappeared Zimbabwean for being unable to control her actions. In the final committee, a Northern Irish mother becomes antagonistic against two men and one woman who confront her about the actions of her dead son. As Lynette Goddard notes, tucker green's investment in gender concerns is crucial to 'expanding the diasporic concerns of black British playwriting within a framework that pursues greater understanding of transnational issues' (2015: 154). We witness the struggle to (self-) articulate throughout the play, but in this case the process is notably protracted and aggressive, leading to a deeply hostile and aggressive exchange between the two women. Their sons are equally guilty of transgressions, but only one woman's son is seen as the instigator and she refuses to concede blame. As they release their wrath, an elemental instinct of defence emerges between the two mothers, both bereaved and in mourning, as well as wrestling with their own sense of emptiness, failure and inadequacy. In a play about communities shattered from within, a note of primal grief is struck through the matriarchal role that tucker green awards all her female characters, who emerge as the contesters of male political and/or military hegemonies that produced the radical crisis that they must now contend with.

As action travels from one encounter to the next, with some episodes introduced early in the play and others entering the frame later, we spend varying, but in all cases short spans of time in each scene/context, watching the action advance, but also stall. The stage directions make clear that '*Places and dates should be shown*' (tucker green 2011: 3), rendering the final, climactic segment, which takes place in 1976 South Africa, all the more poignant. This scene, which refers back to the 1998 South Africa segment, introduces two different characters from the ones we have seen thus far, adding to the metaphysical atmosphere of the play. These characters are the ghost of the black girl killed by the white South African police officer, who confronts him about his crime and ethically compels him to attend a hearing that will take place twenty-two years later. He accepts, even though we know, from what has transpired earlier in the play, that the officer does not attend.

Sarah Hemming described the play as 'a sombre, painful, patient piece, innovative in form in that it operates by accumulation and that it attempts to articulate inarticulacy' (2011). To call *truth and reconciliation* an agitprop play would not be accurate, because it functions more subtly than this. But it does serve to ignite the spectators' civic and political consciousness, simultaneously demonstrating the rousing power of language and its impotence in restoring peace and faith in a better future. It even manages to instil in the audience not only the impatience experienced by the victims but also their profound disappointment for a system established to diffuse conflict, which does not quite serve its imperative. Amidst all this, our position is not one of detached spectatorship and mere observation. In Lisa Marie Hall's arena of a set, the audience was placed in the same uncomfortable wooden chairs as the committee attendees, and these seats were arranged circularly around the pit where action took place. The proximity combined with Matt Haskins's lighting design, which delivered all-encompassing darkness, made for an immersive experience. This served a dual function: it emulated the setting of a committee hearing, rendering us participants; it reminded us, in our audience role, that we bore witnesses to the atrocities spoken of – and that we may bear witnesses to other incidents of cruelty, violence and bigotry by virtue of our citizenship in a globalized world. As we could not shut our eyes to and ignore the happenings within our physical range, in our presence, on the show's unconventional stage, so, the play implied, we cannot ignore any events constituting a breach of the freedom of others. As Goddard also observes, tucker green makes use of the distinct 'technique' of 'situat[ting] spectators in the position of a witness to promote an ethical and emotional response' (2015: 122).

Even though there are differences between the playwriting of tucker green and that of Pinter, it is important to recognize the shared sensibilities in their socially engaged theatres. These points of contact emerge particularly strongly in tucker green's more recent work. The technique of introducing a ghost to deliver justice for the crimes committed in the past in contexts of political subjugation is used, most notably, in Pinter's *Party Time* (1991; in Pinter 2011). Dusty, a young woman introduced early in the play, attends a private party at Gavin's home, which clearly involves an elite that has had a major role in an undemocratic political upheaval. Dusty inquires after her brother Jimmy, only to be rebuffed by Gavin and, without much effort, they transition into conversation topics that seem idle, concerning the lifestyle of the privileged few. In fact, they point to a membership of an exclusive group – one whose remit and actions are never revealed by Pinter since he keeps the references to a hegemonic oligarchy strictly vague. Each time Dusty – who has married into this dubious group and appears mentally unstable – returns to her question as to Jimmy's fate, she is silenced. As the play progresses, it becomes clear that incidents of political dissent are unfolding outside, only to be suppressed; by the end of the play we receive an answer as to what has happened to Jimmy. With all other action on the stage suspended and characters remaining motionless, as most lights dim one light brightens, marking Jimmy's appearance at the doorway (Pinter 2011: 313). In one of Pinter's most poetic stage moments, through a brief monologue Jimmy describes the loss of his life and identity, having faded into the mass of anonymous, missing victims of political, likely military violence:

> **Jimmy** [...]. I had a name. It was Jimmy. People called me Jimmy. That was my name.
>
> Sometimes I hear things. Then everything is quiet. When everything is quiet I hear my heart.
>
> [...]
>
> What am I?
>
> Sometimes a door bangs, I hear voices, then it stops. Everything stops.
>
> It all stops. It all closes. It closes down. It shuts. It all shuts. It shuts down. It shuts. I see nothing at any time any more. I sit sucking the dark. (2011: 313–314)

The way in which tucker green writes political suppression and inscribes the violence on the haunted – and haunting – human body is a continuation of the Pinter tradition. In *Party Time* we bear witness to Jimmy narrating his tortured, eliminated self, a defence against disappearing and being forgotten, erased from the face of national history. He is shown as oscillating between life and death, already a victim of blind cruelty. It was not Pinter's style to name the place or the time, but the lack of historical reference far from renders the play ahistorical. If anything, it strengthens its power of exposition and relevance. By tying her play to specific events, and even though *truth and reconciliation* is not a verbatim text, tucker green had the challenge of avoiding the limiting specificity of reference and also of emotionalism. When, in the final moments of the play we revert to 1976 South Africa, there is no ambiguity in the script or on the stage as to the status of the young girl, the 'Child' as tucker green's script identifies the 14-year-old girl who was killed by the white police officer (tucker green 2011: 75). It is understood that, as the text notes, '*The CHILD is dead*' (tucker green 2011: 75). As opposed to keeping the Child separate from the remainder of the action, tucker green's direction involves the girl and in her script the moment of oscillation between life and death is delivered by a dialogue between the Child and the police officer, as she confronts him about her murder and demands that he attend the hearing.

As the scene begins, the girl surveys the space, rearranging the chairs around where the officer is sitting to create a spatial semiotics of interrogation, the officer seated alone with three chairs pointed to his direction, anticipating the future reckoning of the committee (tucker green 2011: 75). In this way, the Child stages an informal version of a hearing, confronting her murderer as she commits him to a future of guilt. Eventually, after she has exposed the sequence of events that led to her arbitrary and unjustified murder, given no warning, apprehended at random, contained with physical violence and attacked with a deadly weapon almost immediately without having provoked, shot repeatedly even though she had expired after the first bullet (tucker green 2011: 75–79), the Child enters her indicting monologue:

Child Twenty-two years from now

you will sit opposite my mama

my nana

my brother

and my sister…

[…]

You will tell them

what happened.

To me.

What you did

to me.

Where what is left of me

is.

Now. (tucker green 2011: 79)

As the officer remains silent, the Child continues (tucker green 2011: 80), now establishing an eerie foreboding of what we have already seen unfold – the mother refusing to sit or cry and retaining her dignity and strength throughout, the grandmother expressing dissatisfaction with the uncomfortable chairs. There is only one major difference contrary to what the Child expects and demands, to which the officer also agrees. That is, he does not, as we have witnessed, appear:

Child   [...]

You will go.

You will go.

You will not be late.

You will not be willing.

But you will go.

And you will tell them.

[...]

Officer ... Ja

I will go. (tucker green 2011: 80)

The play closes with this final exchange, the officer and the ghost of the girl interlocked in what strikes us as an eternal fight for justice against oppression that the committee has not resolved. It is the same in other cases, where the surviving victims are not able, willing, or both, to file their trauma into the past, much as they might strive to move on and overcome. In their recent survey and historical overview of the practice and critical literature developing in the field of performance and ghosts, Mary Luckhurst and Emilie Morin rightly observe that 'the ghost has been increasingly deployed as a powerful political device', noting that 'numerous wars, genocides, natural disasters and acts of terrorism in recent times, have proliferated the device of the ghost [...] and on stage the ghost of more modern times is not so much the revenge figure of previous eras but often a cipher for signifying trauma, violence and otherwise hidden human rights abuses' (2014: 1–2). As Luckhurst and Morin also find, proceeding from a reference to Marvin Carlson, the notion of ghosts in the theatre is multifaceted and profoundly linked to memory; this is also the aspect of ghosting that most concerns us here (2014: 3).

In tucker green's plays, ghosts, in their different manifestations, have been crucial to rendering the concept of lived history visible in a way that has acted as interconnecting thread in much of her work and certainly in the most recent plays that this chapter concentrates on. Even though Christina Wald has written on plays of different focus and aesthetics from tucker green's, her observation that ghosts both externalize the protagonist's longing and 'suture the perception of audiences [...] with the perception of the melancholic protagonist' bears considerable merit (2007: 212). In a short piece on ghosts and theatre, which briefly refers to *truth and reconciliation*, Rachel Clements acknowledges the lack of explicit didacticism in the piece and, referring specifically to the ghosts of the Rwandan man and the South-African girl, argues that these 'physically realised' characters 'become the specific [...ones] whose deaths haunt both relatives and perpetrators, and the vectors through which tucker green asks whether and how reconciliation, peace, truth, forgiveness might be possible' (2013b: 27). Clements adds that the play 'never suggests that it is itself doing any reconciliatory work – it is always clear that it is looking at, not intervening in, the questions it raises' (2013b: 27). The complexity of the play is such that, even though the embodiments of these two, not so much characters, as notional touchstones of violence and oppression, might be particularly striking, tucker green's method ensures that the sense of ghosting and haunting lingers throughout the play. Each committee plays a pivotal role in contributing to this affect from a different angle, so that the stage becomes dense with the absence/presence of those talked about, before we come to see two of them materialize on the stage. We are in the company of ghosts throughout the play: once in reverse, in the case of the Zimbabwean woman who is first seen as a living person and then disappears, her life implied to have been taken, all essence of her becoming a mere ambiguity when her husband is in the position of asking for answers; once in their presence, as in the case of the Bosnian woman whose trauma becomes ghosted and deferred even in the company of her perpetrators, two present/absent non-entities, who exist in parallel to the woman in that scene, refusing to acknowledge her; once via proxy, as in the case of the Northern Irish mothers defending the memory of their dead sons in their absence and holding firm in their ideologies. The absent person is bodied forth, rendered present by means of a speaking agent's corporeal intervention. Luckhurst and Morin note that 'The modern theatrical imagination has long teemed with mediums and ghostly voices, and the inception of the telephone, the gramophone, the telegraph, the wireless and contemporary digital technologies have all given an added dimension to theatrical representations of haunting' (2014: 5). As we will see with reference to *nut* and *hang*, the playwright's representation of ghosts and haunting is intricate and a part of her structural building of the play; even though we might occasionally find ourselves in the presence of ghosts – or visions – this is not the only way in which tucker green utilizes them to achieve her highly politicized affect. The fact that she does not intervene as far as a message does not mean that tucker green is not producing interventionist theatre by questioning the validity of established political/therapeutic practices for the handling of collective trauma. Her characters' stuttering and wavering and the sudden unimpeded flow of words when it is least expected create powerful moments. tucker green's ghosts linger. Rather than merely set up the verbal and physical battleground of her characters and observe, tucker green is an involved playwright, fiercely in search of truth and justice.

nut and *hang*: Fragile mental states

In production, *nut* established its dark and oppressive atmosphere from the beginning, adding to spectatorial discomfort as a means of creating a sensory understanding of the unease that haunts the play's protagonist. Smoking is a recurring theme in the play, pointing to addictive behaviours both mentally and physically constituted. The same is true of the lifestyle that Elayne and those close to her are submitted to: a vicious cycle of unrewarding lives and relationships played out in a hostile and anonymous urban environment, which is not so much a backdrop as an intrusive and coercive force in these characters' lives. The smell of fake cigarettes used throughout the performance takes hold early on and hovers for the remainder, creating an atmosphere of asphyxiating enclosure. The Shed, a dark, makeshift space, significantly smaller than the National Theatre's main auditoria, was conducive to this. The sensory trigger of discomfort in an enclosed space created a corporeal metaphor for the mental state and living conditions of the play's protagonists. We were effectively entering someone's mind and however claustrophobic it might have seemed, it would become even more so once we realized how densely inhabited this territory actually was. The realization that Elayne's mind and home are ghosted by personas of oppressors that she has created to defer her compulsive and self-destructive behaviour only comes very late at the end of Act One. In the meantime we have witnessed Elayne have conversations with Aimee, later also with Devon; towards the finale of the first Act, she speaks with Trey, who has also been present, singing to himself without participating in the conversations. Elayne is a black woman; Aimee a white woman; Devon a black man; Trey a black boy. Trey, we understand, later, represents the purest aspect of Elayne's self: her singing and the repressed desire to once again spend time with the niece that no longer visits, the child who once used to sing with her. He is the voice that she has been deprived of, and a manifestation of the grief for that loss.

We know that there is intimate familiarity and a passive-aggressive element in Elayne and Aimee's relationship from observing their conversation, which at first focuses on the possible content of Elayne's eulogy, before moving to Aimee's and then to how their respective deaths would be experienced by the people in their lives. In the Shed production transitions between scenes that were part of the same Act were seamless, so when we move to the next stage and Devon has also entered the conversation, we have not noticed a shift. Devon, it appears, is more abrasive than Aimee, wielding character accusations at Elayne for failing to replace the batteries on her doorbell. Devon is also more extroverted and so the dialogue soon escalates as the combined judgmental voices of Aimee and Devon descend on Elayne to accuse her of her own loneliness. They reinforce the social stigma of failing to connect, to have friends, to have visitors. Aimee, Devon and Trey are a manifestation also of this: they do not only account for the different aspects of Elayne's personality, but also for the physical absence of people; so she concocts different types to address the void.

The slow denouement of the first Act begins when Aimee, Devon and Elayne start to argue and, once more, circle the topic of death. As in *truth and reconciliation, random, dirty butterfly* and *stoning mary*, tucker green's work suggests that there is nothing noble about death; no claim to dignity; no sense of celebrating the life that was. It is merely a blow that the vulnerable – mentally, physically, politically – are destined to endure prematurely, even though it may be entirely preventable. The atmosphere in the scene grows darker still when the conversation specifically moves to cause of death – options ranging from suicide to accident – and flirts perilously with tragedy. When Trey finally speaks, he represents lucidity, reason, resoluteness and fleeting hope. He confronts Devon about his smoking, which, as he says, is harmful to him and against Elayne's wishes, and asserts that when he dies the only attendees he would expect in his funeral would be loved ones, however few. Trey is also the voice of defence against Aimee and Devon's subjugation of Elayne and their invitations to self-harm. But Trey fails: Devon has already instigated the victimization of

Aimee and Elayne, smoking and inviting them to self-harm using the ash of the burning cigarette. As Trey exits in disappointment, Aimee begins to blow the ash of her cigarette into Elayne's palm, coercing Elayne into daring her to burn her with the cigarette. At that moment, the action is interrupted because Elayne has a guest, this time an actual one, waiting at the door.

Elayne's guest is her sister, though in a style that is typical of tucker green's work, she is only described as 'Ex-Wife', to designate her generic, normative function, unlike Elayne, who is given a name in the list of characters, along with her multiple personalities, as the eccentric, isolated individual. The unidentified victim of circumstance, the marginalized Other, therefore, receives an identity and is reclaimed from mental illness statistics and anonymity as a human being. On the contrary, Elayne's sister merely becomes a member of an average anonymized mass and it is only a role that she has acquired by means of her personal relationships – failed, no less – that distinguishes her in any way. The same is true of her 'Ex-Husband', with whom she shares the second Act of the play. This segment acts as a disjoining device, a realist fracture interrupting Elayne's haunted mindscapes. The play asks what is more destructive: the tedious conflicts recycling themselves in the everyday, such as those between a divorced couple awkwardly sharing custody in a life riddled with compromise, or inventing a reality as distraction to the tedium of actual life. tucker green's work, therefore, invites the spectators to consider why one option should be seen as more harmful than the other and whether there is an alternative to such crises.

As we approach the end of the second Act, amidst the bitterness and resentment, the former couple seem to regress to a kind of tenderness; the issue is, however, that this is predicated on co-dependency, no different from the kind that Elayne develops with her split selves. The Ex-Husband lights a cigarette; the Ex-Wife – who has quit – disapproves but soon succumbs and joins in. As with Elayne's ghosts, any false pretences of empathy are disproved as soon as latent aggression begins to stir. As Devon and Aimee invade Elayne's space, imposing their routine, much to the discontent of Trey, who represents Elayne's attempts at strength and resilience, so the Ex-Husband violates the parameters that the Ex-Wife has set for her life – and she enables this. Addiction to substances and lifestyles is not easy to break, shows *nut*, regardless of whether the intruders come from outside or within, ghosts of a past life or of unfulfilled desires, persistent trauma and present fears. The third and final Act of the play merges the realism of the second with the illusory world of the first, as Elayne attempts to negotiate the conflicting aspects of her life. Her sister is visiting. At first their dialogue is fairly mundane, but it soon becomes apparent that they are both attuned to each other's indulgences and self-destructive tendencies. Eventually, Elayne's sister notices the cigarette burns on her arms; it is at that point that Elayne's ghosts become visible, albeit only to her and the audience, not her sister. They interject in the conversation, voices in Elayne's head that cannot be silenced. The final segment of the play offers a moment of mutual recognition, this time taking place between Elayne and her sister alone; they are smoking together, probing past traumas: the distance in their relationship; their similarities. But it becomes clear that the only connection Elayne is able to establish is by sharing the physical trauma along with the mental, and so she invites her sister to partake in self-harming, reproducing the earlier scene between herself, Aimee and Devon. When her sister fails to submit to this, or to intervene, Elayne retreats into her world and any connection between them hangs in the balance. The lack of intervention from Elayne's self-assured sister represents the self-contradictory principle of neoliberalist behaviour–asserting one's agency but failing to assume any responsibility:

> **Elayne**   You watchin you / watchin?
>
> **Ex-Wife**   Hurt your hands I ent gonna do / nuthin.
>
> **Elayne**   Dare me to / do it?
>
> **Ex-Wife**   Bu'n up y'hands I ent gonna do / nuthin. (tucker green 2013: 81)

In her review of *truth and reconciliation*, Hemming also notes: 'The chairs are a running theme, with characters shifting them or refusing to sit on them, seeing them as symbolic of guilt or acceptance [...] the audience [is] likewise seated on hard wooden chairs, as if witnesses to the proceedings' (2011). Further to poignant uses of set design, discussed earlier, the significance of the chairs extends to the absent body that fails to inhabit them; to those victims and perpetrators that, for different reasons, will not partake in what is predicated as a moment of justice and recognition. The density of the empty space waiting to be filled, which is physically represented by the empty chairs, is an important theme for tucker green more broadly and one that she returned to for *nut* as well as *hang*, two plays that, notably, she also directed herself.

In *nut*, chairs are prolific on the set; they even hang from its semi-abstract metal structure, anticipating, like the multiple pairs of shoes lined up on the floor, the body, or bodies, that might inhabit and utilize them. In *hang*, they seem innocuous – mere tools for an office; but they are the triggers for discomfort and coercion. In *Ghosts: Death's Double and the Phenomena of Theatre* Alice Rayner discusses the function and signification of chairs extensively. Rayner observes that the chair as object represents the past and present simultaneously: it emulates the one who occupied it, it frames a future act of inhabitance; it emanates the sensations and relationships that the bodies it accommodated formed to each other; it *has* happened and is waiting *to* happen as a protagonist in its own right (2006: 112). The epigraph for the chapter that she dedicates to the topic cites a line from Ionesco's *The Chairs*, which Rayner also goes on to discuss (2006: 110, 118). There is hardly a more paradigmatic reference than the specific text, which revolutionized the concept of absence/presence as attested by a physical stagescape clashing with an aural one. Ionesco's play depicted the everyday object as highly significant, lifting it from habit and obscurity, and casting it as an agent producing the compelling need for inhabitance through its mere existence. The hypothesis of the play is simple enough: an (implausibly) elderly couple are hosting a multitude of guests in anticipation of an orator, who will deliver a crucial message. The couple behave as though the eccentric guests are arriving, frantically, at times, struggling to keep up with how fast they are expected to bring in a minimum of forty chairs – the chairs are, as Ionesco notes, taking over the entire stage, populating it aggressively (Ionesco 1997: 59). The audience sees no one at all other than the two protagonists. As we become convinced that the guests are a figment of the delusory couple's imagination, so the end of the play challenges the hypothesis. Before the final curtain, we are suddenly confronted by a cacophony of sounds pointing to the presence of a crowd, starting softly and becoming increasingly loud before evaporating (Ionesco 1997: 57–58). Our perception is challenged and doubt sets in. Ionesco's play, then, stages a ghosted public event, which at first strikes us as not having been attended by those it was meant for until it goes on to subvert the assumption. All the way we are left contemplating whether what we have experienced was the product of the couple's terminal mental crisis, or whether Ionesco was implying his audience's own metaphorical moral and civic blindness.

The work of tucker green may not be paradigmatically absurdist like Ionesco's, but it persists in its exploration of the mind's inner world and the metaphysical, making periodic use of the tools of the Absurd. The humour is mostly absent – with tucker green we find ourselves in a darker territory. Of the plays discussed in this chapter, the one where the device of ghosted presences projected onto and materializing through chairs has the strongest political significance is *truth and reconciliation*. On Rayner's terms, this would also be the play that would come the closest to a parallel of her case study analysis with reference to the Oklahoma City National Memorial, dedicated to those affected by the events of the 1995 Oklahoma City bombing – specifically Field of Empty Chairs (2006: 110–136). Rayner concludes regarding this paradigm and the chair as memorial more broadly: 'The chairs individualize each loss with a name and a place, making no claim on universality, only on the rift that separates and connects the living and the dead. The chairs remain there, as onstage, as the sites of death's power and life's vulnerability' (2006: 136). The poetic terms on which Rayner describes the reverberations of loss and survival in the site of memory, the physical record of the atrocity and the celebration of human life against violence, match the tones of tucker green's most lyrical work. In *truth and reconciliation* we are confronted with traces of absence and presence in a public event, left to question whether the fact that the encounters between Child and officer, or the Rwandan man and his killer, happen not in a realist but a conceptual space, renders them any less impactful – especially given their vast emotional affect on the audience – or plausible, by means of an act of metaphysical haunting: the *Erinyes* gathering over a guilty conscience. In *nut*, we are dealing with a different process. We begin with, and go on to spend a substantial amount of time in the physical company of characters presented to us as fully real. Only very gradually, and once we have transitioned to a different part of the play, does it become evident that they are the mere manifestations of a mental ailment. Again, tucker green undermines the assumptions of presence and absence as she creates a context whereby empty chairs are anticipating bodies. Except, in this case, she works in reverse, not offering a metaphysical sense of retribution, but of subverting that which we have taken for granted to expose it as imaginary – and then move us into the sphere of realism having highlighted the extent of the trauma.

Rayner rightly identifies a function in any chair we might encounter as part of a theatre set that can be understood on phenomenological terms, particularly as objects in the space of art – and in lived experience more broadly – recur in phenomenological discourse (2006: 112). As part of her analysis of *The Chairs*, Rayner arrives at an observation which is also helpful to understanding how *nut* functions. She proposes:

> Such fear [stemming from isolation and mortality] is a great creator of frightful ghosts, because it is a further dimension of the isolation of the individual. Without the corrective realities of a material, social context, such isolation generates the kind of subjectivity in which the imaginary dominates actuality or, rather, begins to constitute the doubling of reality as a subjective one. (2006: 121)

As opposed to the geographical and physical isolation that Ionesco's characters experience and Rayner delves into as metaphor (2006: 118, 121, 124), *nut* reflects how this form of isolation, in our time, has acquired more disturbing dimensions. In a context where playwrights have been depicting isolation as part of a neoliberalist cocoon, or as lack of empathy, in tucker green's work we are given a different kind of insight as to how class conditions isolation and mental health. In this case, the isolation that Elayne experiences is not a side effect of the lack of 'the corrective realities of a material, social context', which, in turn, produces an errant subjectivity. Elayne does live alone, but in the urban centre that both play and production made clear she inhabits, Elayne is not socially isolated in the material sense. She is, however, isolated in the sensory, emotional and mental sense, unable to connect to those who form part of her immediate family circle and concocting variant personas which her imaginary casts in the role of co-dependent, coercive 'friends', who escalate her self-destructive behaviour.

nut demonstrates how someone might be living their life as part of society, while being excluded from it at the same time: a process in which the trauma of social class and impaired mental health enter a vicious circle of co-determination, with whose detritus the individual must contend. Therefore, *nut* ultimately operates somewhat differently from the process that Rayner identifies in *The Chairs*, whereby the objects represent the characters' need to attach the absent human body to a present inanimate agent that embodies and signifies it (2006: 125). However, there is also a key similarity: in *nut* Elayne invites in the personas that are essentially split fragments of her own self in order to fill not an externalized vacant space, onto which she has projected her desolation, but an internal one, which has absorbed the isolation inflicted on the self by an alienating world. Elayne is therefore now developing mechanisms of accounting for her existence and choices to imaginary others, given that her chronic social subdual means she is unable to be assertive in 'real' life. An alternate reality is therefore crafted, where, proceeding from Rayner (2006: 125, 128, 129), it is a question of perspective whether it is the individual that has been rendered a socially hollow shell that is the ghost, inhabited by its fractions, or the personas that inhabit the individual as manifestations of its own needs, fears and obsessions. Whichever option we take, we are confronted with a profoundly social problematic, whose roots, the fissures in society that are impacting the individual, are entirely political.

In *nut* and *truth and reconciliation* respectively we are dealing with spectres of the self as she is felt and experienced by the afflicted subject and with spectres of the self as s/he once was, before the impact of loss. *truth and reconciliation* also presents us with the spectre of the one who is absent, but whose presence is felt. *hang* returns to ghosting from a different perspective. As in *truth and reconciliation*, a horrific crime has been committed. This time, again, the onus is placed on the individual to decide how to deal with the trauma of the past in an institutional context of mediation, in a neoliberalist state dystopia where the victim has the power to choose their perpetrator's punishment, debating the advantages and disadvantages of different options. However, the crime this time is not a product of political subjugation, but of raw urban violence.

The premise of the play is striking, even if it ultimately lacks the dramatic power of earlier work by tucker green. After much evasion, in dialogue that once more is 'repetitive' and 'circular' (Hemming 2011), more indulgently so than in previous work, we understand that the protagonist, named Three, is called to make a decision on the fate of the man who terrorized her and her family, inflicting unspeakable physical and mental trauma. Other than revealing her family's recovery struggle in terms that suggest a particularly heinous transgression, Three does not state the exact nature of the crime; nor do One and Two, the administrators who liaise with Three as she deliberates which form of the death penalty the criminal is to receive. Even though Three also has the authority to grant him immunity, the play never offers any compelling evidence that Three is amenable to entertaining this option; her resolve holds firm and by the end of the play she has made the choice that the perpetrator should be hanged.

The play offers a shrewd take on the practices of a penal system that deflects guilt from the perpetrator to the victim, leading to mental and emotional conflict that adds another layer to the trauma already sustained. The right to anger, grief and self-preservation becomes displaced, deemed somehow secondary to the human rights of the one who so brutally violated the human rights of others. Even though *hang* wavers in its dramatic affectiveness, it does pose this bold and urgent question. In an emblematic act of exposing the individuation of therapy culture, *hang* shows how the single subject – in this case the victim – is being forced to choose; to feel solely responsible; to deal with the problem on a personal level, subdued by a system that claims to protect her but is merely forcing her hand, diverting responsibility from the state. Three, therefore, has been doubly failed by the system: firstly for suffering the effects of a lack of community and empathy, which breeds violence; then by being systematically coerced by those managing her case into developing feelings of empathy for her attacker, as an act of progress and civilization. Neoliberalism emerges as the driving force of the crises we witness in both *nut* and *hang*, which depict the effects of the individual devolving into a singular unit deprived of any sense of community. Elayne and Three cut stark, desolate figures who, despite interactions with real and/or imaginary others, must ultimately endure their mental, emotional and physical journeys alone.

Issues concerning mental health and self-assertion are conceptualized in *nut* and *hang* as products of disjunction in the relationship between individual and society, or proceeding from Sennett, in the roles that the individual will be expected to perform publicly and those that s/he will experience intimately, the 'masks', as he characteristically writes that s/he will wear to perform in different situations (2003: 35; see also 33–43). The two plays capture the crisis that occurs as a product of this conflict. Even though we might think of neoliberalism as a contemporary phenomenon – and certainly it is such if we place it within the specific political context from which it emerged in our time – its roots are historically traceable. This explains how behaviours have become institutionalized, and how the most recent neoliberal political framework provided a model for a pattern that was already nascent. This pattern, Sennett argues, dates back to attitudes historically encouraging the individual to withhold emotion in public and to experience crisis in private. As he notes:

> The paradox of visibility and isolation which haunts so much of modern public life originated in the right to silence in public which took place in the last [19th] century. [...] To speak of the legacy of the 19th Century's crisis of public life is to speak of broad forces such as capitalism and secularism on the one hand and of these four psychological conditions on the other: involuntary disclosure of character, superimposition of public and private imagery, defense [*sic*] through withdrawal, and silence. The obsessions with selfhood are attempts to work out these conundrums [...], by denial. Intimacy is an attempt to solve the public problem by denying that the public exists. As with any denial, this has only made the more destructive aspects of the past the more firmly entrenched. (Sennett 2003: 27)

The proposition provides a context for the suppression of public emotion that detonates as private grief and mental health affliction, or as repressed angst and aggression. *nut* and *hang*, respectively, offer manifestations of this. In *nut* we are dealing with a protagonist for whose frustration and dissatisfaction there is no outlet in the public realm, which marginalizes that which is deemed non-normal and encourages its exclusion.

We observe this, for example, in the angry, honest exchange between Elayne and her sister in the play's finale. Here, the sister represents the normative force that is unwilling to bend to the understanding of the Other having embraced the system herself, and Elayne represents the aberration, the one who learns to anticipate criticisms as to her erratic behaviour, effectively a social pariah. Elayne's sense of exclusion from her family and the broader social norm is exemplified in this extract, where the normative hegemony exercised by her sister's husband becomes evident:

Elayne   He made you not wanna come.

Ex-Wife   We was married.

[...]

Elayne   He made you not wanna be here.

Ex-Wife   we've done / this.

Elayne   he still does (tucker green 2013: 72)

Similarly, Elayne's mental retreat is shown as a symptom of chronic desolation:

Ex-Wife   Your [Elayne's] mistakes is involving – are involving – draggin me / in –

Devon   Who asked her to come?

Ex-Wife   Draggin me / down.

Aimee   Don't get involved.

Devon   Who asked her to come?

Aimee   Tell her to fuck / off.

Devon   Don't get involved.

Aimee   Why is she even here?

Trey   I didn't ask her.

Devon   No one asked her to come –

Elayne   I never asked her to / come (tucker green 2013: 68–69)

The ghosts Elayne concocts are a side effect of the externally imposed haunting that occurs and that Sennett identifies, one that forms behavioural patterns that become 'entrenched' and taken as the norm, when they ought to be radically questioned. When Elayne is unable to develop intimacy with the real people in her life – the sister who visits rarely, the niece who has been kept away from her – she retreats within, formulating alternative means of intimacy with the disparate versions of herself, personified. In *hang*, Three is similarly forced to retreat into a private experience of a crisis that is public and of a trauma that is the repercussion of generalized sociopathy. The stigma and shame of the victim are such that they escalate the withdrawal into silence and desolation: first comes a failure of communication amongst family members, then the belief that the system is incapable of providing any helpful solution. So it asks the individual to become the punisher: to forgo any belief in a more effective solution, any investment in the mending of society, for the sake of a temporary measure that treats the symptom rather than the problem.

The significance of Three being, as one reviewer observed (Wicker 2015), resolute and unwavering from beginning to end in her commitment to punish her tormenter is better understood if we take into account Sennett's observation on the roles we perform in public and the rift between these and the emotions we experience privately (2003: 37). Three's aggression is a manifestation of the utter powerlessness, disbelief and anger that she has been negotiating with her broken family, and that only she has intimate knowledge of. The playwright's cyclical style of dialogue occasionally frustrates, flirting with tedium, but it is, ultimately, a symptom of the individual painfully awkwardly and gradually adapting to their quasi-public role as punisher. In other words, we witness Three's tentative efforts to develop a moral ruthlessness that matches the physical ruthlessness of her transgressor. As part of this, she must discipline her body to refrain from emotional signs of weakness, as the perpetrator was bereft of any compassion towards his victims. Therefore, Three refuses to sit throughout the play, a primary instinct to preserve her physical control. In a room haunted by her attacker, who is rendered present through the device of a handwritten letter, pleading for her magnanimity, it is she who once more runs the risk of being handled against her will, this time by the state, which is passive-aggressively encouraging the option of absolution while displacing its own agency; a radical form of governmentality. Three's resolve mirrors that of the South African mother who refuses to sit and concede any power to the officer, who never arrives. In *hang*, Three is aware that responding to violence with more, this time state-administered violence of which she is the agent, is not the answer to crisis, but she also knows that it is a method of managing it; cruelty is the kind of self-defence the system tasks her with choosing, while, at the same time, having failed to mitigate her own suffering. tucker green affords her protagonist several monologues, of which the following most strongly expresses her wrath towards governmentality:

> **Three** […]
>
> Your developments affect my sleep
>
> *how* I sleep
>
> that I don't sleep. Can't sleep. Still.
>
> It affects *their* schooling
>
> affects their schools
>
> their grades
>
> their prospects
>
> their future.
>
> Fucked their future.
>
> Affects where we live
>
> fucked where we lived. (tucker green 2015: 29)

The very names of the characters, in this and most plays by tucker green, empty of any specific identifiers, reflect her concern with a world where subjects are expected to act singularly, even though they are no longer individuals but mere cogs in a problematic system and its methods of subdual. The above monologue also clearly exemplifies the abrasive reach of systemic failures that tucker green's play contends with, from the physical to the emotional and the mental to the material, as we have seen these concerns recur across her work.

Conclusion

In her most recent appraisal of the field, Goddard describes tucker green as 'undoubtedly the leading black British woman playwright of the early twenty-first century' (2015: 69). She locates the importance of tucker green's work in her handling of 'aesthetic *and* social aspects [...] to create the overall impact [...and highlight] concerns about selfish individualism, apathy and complacency towards world events and current affairs' (Goddard 2015: 70; emphasis original). The character of Elayne in *nut*, like the Child in *truth and reconciliation*, embodies a primary innocence that takes tucker green into the more emotional veins of her writing. The same is accomplished in the monologues of Three in *hang*, which reveal a previously underexplored strand in tucker green's theatre: bare emotion against injustice that expresses itself quite simply in language drenched in despair, with vulnerability overtaking anger. In these characters we see the depths of pain, the recesses of fear, but also the possibilities for hope and change. Elayne's illness is paradigmatic of the conflict in a society at odds with itself, where mental health crisis is endemic because of the crisis in ideology and of the irreconcilable demands on civic behaviour. For those more fragile, these demands become debilitating and lead to retreat; others, like Three in *hang*, compensate for their fragility with yet more violence. The generic room of a set that could be anywhere and the administrators who are merely perfunctory accentuate the irony: the person is expected to act alone, under a guise of individuality, yet their mere function is to catalyse a system that is already in place but refuses to acknowledge its role, or take responsibility. With *nut* tucker green delivered her most abstract play yet, but this is not to say that the actions the play depicts are removed from the realm of the possible. With a play like *hang* tucker green also asks to what lengths we are willing to go, if acting to preserve one's own interests is the core guiding principle, however much we may feel morally compelled. That tucker green does not sermonize is a fact; but in all her work, and especially in plays from *truth and reconciliation* onwards, she retreats further away from detail and disclosure to empower the spectator as a thinker and the play as instigator of debate. If *truth and reconciliation* and *hang* reveal the failure of institutional justice, they are also a call to dialogue, to consider the societies we *have* lived in and those we *might* live in – and to decide collectively what options could still be available to us.

8

Trials of Happiness: Lucy Prebble and the Human Experiment

Lucy Prebble is not a prolific playwright. Since her 2003 debut play *The Sugar Syndrome* (RCT Upstairs, director Marianne Elliot) she has only had two plays staged, although she has, in the meantime, also written for television. Her most well-known play, *Enron* (2009, Minerva Theatre, Chichester, director Rupert Goold), is an extravagant performance event depicting spectacular corporate collapse. It was a long time in the making, with Prebble dedicating two years to research (Editorial 2010). *Enron* enjoyed a long touring life and became a major success in Britain. Prebble's next – and to date most recent – play arrived in late 2012, when *The Effect* opened (National Theatre, Cottesloe, director Rupert Goold). As with *Enron*, Prebble had once more given herself a vast topic to tackle: this time it was big pharma and its impact on the malleable masses as witnessed through private lives. The research was again rigorous – from consultation with UCL Professor of Cognitive Neuroscience Sarah-Jayne Blakemore to first-hand exposure to a drugs trial (Woolman 2012) – but also effective. As this chapter will go on to show, Prebble's meticulous method has been worthwhile, leading to potent work producing narrative explosions. Her theatre is rightly ambitious, investigative, topical, knowing, funny and large-scale, and with *The Effect* Prebble proved that it could also be poetic, conceptual and tender.

The Sugar Syndrome was eerily ahead of its time in how it dealt with the skewed reality of online identity and self-misrepresentation. Even though the play came years before the era of carefully edited life narratives and the allure of social media that we would come to experience in the late 2000s, it displays a prescient intelligence and a certain intuitiveness in the depiction of difficult, multifaceted topics. Judged in its original context as opposed to what we know now about how our virtual world has evolved, *The Sugar Syndrome* must be seen as a cutting-edge statement on the depths of isolation experienced, ironically, when using technology as a means of connecting. The play was also a precursor of how Prebble's work would retain an interest in profound human crises of different forms, from Jeffrey Skilling's megalomania and loneliness in *Enron* to the unmitigated depression experienced by characters in *The Effect*. Regardless of how we represent ourselves to others, Prebble's work has suggested, there is an intimate space of grief that can never be entirely communicated or overcome. In all three plays, therefore, Prebble is invested in exposing the process of how, first, we immerse ourselves into our own crises and how, later, we might attempt to dissect and manage them. The investigative and methodical element of Prebble's writing emerges noticeably throughout.

Prebble's innovation must also be understood within the context of how cybercrime more broadly and issues relating to online grooming and paedophilia specifically have come to the fore through recent theatre. Prebble's *The Sugar Syndrome* was a proto-text, an attempt at navigating the unchartered waters of a world that was yet to manifest the extent to which it had the power to prey on vulnerability, undermine humanity and provide forums for the indulgence of sordid desires. More recently, Jennifer Haley's *The Nether* (2013) offered a sophisticated counterpart to the early play benefitting from hindsight infused with – far from implausible – rich imagination, whereas Prebble's play had anticipated a still impending crisis. The staging of the two plays was also markedly different: since Marianne Elliott's bare production of *The Sugar Syndrome*, playwriting transitioned to motifs that often became much more visually imposing and increasingly conceptual, making a resolute departure from realism. Prebble's later work benefitted from this through her collaboration with Headlong, the same company whose aesthetics shaped the UK premiere of *The Nether*. The approach that Headlong have brought, combined with the intuitiveness of Prebble's writing that stems from her resistance to oversimplifying the problem at hand, fleshed out, from *Enron* onwards, the fluidity of boundaries, which has always been present in Prebble's theatre. In her later work, this found a visual representation in the grotesque humanity and accentuated physicality of the Headlong productions, which added intrigue and disruption to the textual narrative. Prebble's challenging of binaries has been a natural partner to the company's work, immersing spectators in the given play's problematics. What Billington recognized early on as lack of moralizing, emerging from Prebble's penchant for 'compelling sympathy for damaged people' and 'exud[ing] a strange solitariness' that in her work appears 'the natural human condition' (2003) and Cavendish as 'captur[ing] [...] adroitly the mixture of motives' (2003), have remained the defining features of Prebble's theatre.

Enron: The corporate God complex

Enron is characteristic of how Prebble's playwriting defies binaries not only in its subversion of the primal 'good' versus 'evil' categories, but also of another classical divide: tragedy versus comedy. Like Kelly in *The Gods Weep* and *The Ritual Slaughter of Gorge Mastromas*, Prebble identifies mega-corporations as the ideal arena for her drama. It is not surprising, then, that *Enron* emulates the epic staging proportions and emotional range of the classical canon. The affinity to nuance and the lack of hesitation towards embracing difficult, even unappealing themes, is not surprising for a writer who names Caryl Churchill's *Icecream* (1989) as a touchstone and source of inspiration (De Angelis et al. 2004). Prebble commends Churchill's ability to produce a play that avoids facile 'farce, crude jingoistic comedy, satire' and manages to diffuse the severity of its life-and-death subject matter with considered humour (De Angelis et al. 2004). Prebble's fascination with personal histories and domino effects of actions, which emerges through her reference to *Icecream*, hints at the path that this writer, then at the early days of her career, would go on to follow (De Angelis et al. 2004). Considering the crises that her work has delved into, it is necessary to recognize that Prebble's emphasis on the 'beautiful, chaotic moments pepper[ing] a play that refuses to explain or punish actions, but portrays people hurtling into strange encounters and conundrums' rings very true in choices she has made in her own theatre (De Angelis et al. 2004). All her work has dealt with ethical, and sometimes also legal entanglements – but whatever the crime committed, Prebble's playwriting refuses to punish. It does not facilitate the audience's moral judgement, but is more invested in the individual behind the choice, however public the repercussions. The constant wavering between past, future and being true to oneself, which so moved Prebble in *Icecream* by virtue of its thematic depth and aversion to social messages (De Angelis et al. 2004), is present in the moral and visceral dilemmas of her characters. They are forever reaching forward, only to find out that the past cannot simply be deleted and personal histories, littered with limitations, carve out trajectories rendering them forever liable, even though they might strive to transcend them.

Prebble's investment in the human condition takes the shape of investigating the God complex – archetypal hubris brought on by excessive arrogance – as well as its contemporary manifestations and repercussions. If hubris was the ingredient that exacerbated war and brought boundless catastrophe in the myths and tragedies we have known, Prebble's theatre asks how, today, it pushes the trigger for vast economical and humanitarian crisis; for wars waged not in the battlefield, but the boardroom. The implications of the actions that *Enron* depicts are so extensive that it led to a rare phenomenon: it transcended theatre reviews to feature in finance columns. One of these articles, dating back to 2009 and the height of the recession aftermath, notes:

> In a way, the Enron collapse was a precursor of the recent crisis, since it used complex vehicles to disguise unprofitable deals – in its case, overseas power plants and broadband trading rather than subprime

mortgages. What is still striking is how much we depend, as investors and commentators, on executives to report accurately the financial conditions of their firms, when those managers have every incentive to gild the lily. Indeed, on many occasions, they may believe their own rhetoric – after all, the executives at Lehman and Bear Sterns lost small fortunes when their companies went under. (Buttonwood's Notebook, 2009)

Enron occupied a strange territory of being both reality and metaphor; both self-referential, about a major corporate collapse, and representing a historical moment that, in 2009, provided a vehicle through which to reflect on the causes and effects of the 2008 recession that was all too recent. If reflecting on the present through current affairs were too painful, then refracting the reference to the recent past and to an event that served as a precursor allowed for some critical distance, as well as humour. Combined with musical interventions and 'vaudeville' depictions of human greed, as Rupert Goold described them (Hemming 2009), Prebble's play achieved a neo-Brechtian, but also neo-expressionist effect.

The megalomania and 'emperor's new clothes' analogy that journalists recognized (Buttonwood's Notebook, 2009) are shown in Prebble's play as originating in top-down greed. This produces a corporate mantra trickling through the various layers of the company, executed by those who people the corporation and labour to its targets and philosophy. The main figure is Enron President Jeffrey Skilling, rising through the ranks to amass exceeding power and ultimately become one of the primary perpetrators of the Enron collapse and scandal. The text, therefore, is as much a playful – yet stinging – dissection of ruthless industrial greed, as it is the study of one man's ambition. Where *Enron* shines is in its ability to capture Skilling as multifaceted: intelligent, fearless, self-serving, deluded. That Skilling succeeds in branding his ambition and blind experimentation with people's earnings – and lives – as an attractive vision, gathering acolytes and suppressing the voices of dissent, is testament to Prebble's skill of capturing the absolutist hegemony of big business without disregarding human agency. Prebble's work has always 'demanded both comedy and empathy' (Prebble 2009b). She achieves this by crafting a story of corporation as cult: a form of religion with its very own leader. That Prebble adopts the form of a comic parable inciting emotion and involving frequent direct address, again forging a Brechtian parallel, underlines the astuteness of the play in form and content. On the one hand, there is the link to reality; the play may not be verbatim, but it is strongly informed by actual fact. On the other hand, Prebble offers us a language to be applied more broadly, so we may begin to assess our most recent collective social, political and historical failures through a story that is close to ours – but not quite the same. Therefore, it facilitates a humorous encounter with crisis, a way of acknowledging the trauma without disturbing the wound, or disrupting the healing process. Recovery is mostly encountered as a financial term in the context of the recession, but a play like *Enron* is geared towards mental recovery from crisis exhaustion as well.

As we see Skilling rise to power with the support of Enron CEO Ken Lay and the scheming of CFO Andy Fastow, it becomes apparent that the megalomania of corporations like Enron serves as social paradigm. It is a reflection of the business narrative and the readiness with which unrealistic targets are presented to the masses as plausible, triggering a process of desire for well-being that seems attainable through a canning masterplan by those claiming to have the right formulae. All that is expected by the masses subscribing to the narrative is, as we also see in *The Effect*, suspension of disbelief. *Enron* provides us with insights into the free reign given to Skilling, the partner-in-crime relationship he developed with Fastow, but also the complicity of the industry, from employees to observers and facilitators – analysts, for example. Amidst all this, Prebble gives the occasional nod to history from Clinton to Bush and an evaluation of the political context that facilitated industrial growth. Prebble also balances the dramatic with the satirical foraying into surrealism: this emotive aspect of the play is accomplished through the images of Skilling and his daughter. The girl's purity renders her part of a world from which Skilling is excluded and his influence on those closest to him is shown as limited. However, Prebble's expressionism is not only symbolic and spiritual, but also brutally satirical as in the visceral delirium of the raptors representing Fastow's dark transgressions or the image of Lehman Brothers as conjoined twins. As Prebble mentions: '[...] Fastow called them [the companies which absorbed Enron's debt] "raptors" in his accounts, and I wanted a theatrical way for them to exist on stage. Jurassic Park [*sic*] and Enron both felt very '90s. It was ridiculous enough to maybe work' (Prebble 2012b). Then, there are the musical segments – a self-aware nod, this time, that such harsh criticism of the corporate world cannot take itself too seriously, that the play is unapologetically treading popular theatre territory because of its populist subject matter and that it is formally attuned to the fact that to tackle a crisis so severe experimentation is expected. Since we are, socially, in unchartered waters, none of the old genre rules apply. One of the defining characteristics of *Enron*, through which it attacks the hysteria of widespread crisis and criminally inflated egos, is that it is entirely irreverent, delivering its attack through utter disregard for political correctness.

Therefore, Goold's invitation to Prebble to consider the play as 'a classical tragedy', which she acknowledges as a turning point (Prebble 2009b), made its mark not only on the structure of the piece but also on its theme: the central character takes it upon themselves to create a superhuman narrative in defiance of all else. In so doing, they incite first the wrath of the gods (in this case the authorities) and then of the people, the masses who had initially responded with adulation. The protagonist's fall, as in a tragedy, accompanied by moralizing and lament by those unable to counter the protagonist's actions, is guaranteed and spectacular (Prebble 2009b). But what has preceded it, as Prebble notes, was '"a system of belief"' (Prebble 2009b). As Megson observes, 'The play is important because it casts belief as the key alchemical agent within the citadels of global capital. [...T]he corporation has replaced the cathedral [...]' (2013: 43). *Enron* is littered with language that reinforces the sentiment: early on, the opening of the market for trading is described by Claudia Roe, Skilling's nemesis whose influence he gradually curbs, as a moment of glorious possibility and global interconnection as she utters the words 'the world is waiting' with a sense of awe and epic grandeur (Prebble 2009a: 11). Before long we hear Lay use even stronger terms: 'I believe in God, I believe in democracy and I believe in the company' (Prebble 2009a: 15). The statement is significant for two reasons: firstly, because it creates a false, misguided association between two of humanity's most aspirational concepts and a capitalist one, entirely rooted in greed and materialism; secondly, because by listing 'the company' in the context of 'God' and 'democracy', two concepts that have often been contested, frequently seen as abstract, fluid and certainly extending beyond the realm of the material, 'the company' becomes one such concept as well: its own inner workings, too, are framed as transcendental, more difficult to judge and to define and ultimately unaccountable. As Skilling notes in his pseudo-philosophical capitalist delirium, 'There's a dignity to giving people something they *can't* touch' – a statement promptly derided by Roe, who points out the fallacy of Skilling's 'calling', as he attempts to instil a cult of faith into trading so that he may widen his corporate influence (Prebble 2009a: 19).

The image of Skilling as a cult leader is not only built verbally but also visually. For example, when he becomes the subject of '*yet another magazine cover*', he is captured in a '*god-like*' pose of physical assertion (Prebble 2009a: 53). At the same time he is shown as spiritually bereft, a consequence of his neoliberalist faith in the religion of self, extricated from the experience of others, for whom he claims to speak. *Enron* captures this in Skilling's awkwardly funny attempt to join Lay in prayer, which for Skilling becomes a mere performance as he appears entirely disconnected from the ritual with which he is, however, '*fascinated*'; it inspires the same kind of piety and devotion that he is cultivating for the company as it is created in his form (Prebble 2009a: 65). This and Skilling's 'crucifixion' in the later stages of the play, part of a sacrificial process that culminates in his resignation, are two of the most religiously evocative moments. The 'crucifixion', a part-Christian and part-heathen stage parable of a moment, creates an image of primal tragedy of the human versus the divine – in this case the unyielding market. Emulating tragedy once more, this is Skilling's moment of ultimate humiliation as he sustains penance for his hubris: his abuse of the market, a capitalist crime against humanity. In that moment, like any other tragic hero in radical crisis whose world is collapsing, he is reminded of those he neglected to pursue his blind ambition. Skilling realizes that the damage the Enron stock is sustaining is irreparable; in a personification of the 'divine', in this case the market force, Prebble has her protagonist enter a direct exchange with the stock, leading to Skilling demanding of it: '[...] You want me? Is that it? Is that what you want?' as '*He ends, his arms outstretched, crucifying himself before the market*' (Prebble 2009a: 92). We might be forgiven in thinking that for a brief moment Skilling is shown to regain his humanity when he declares his love to his daughter, but this is undermined by the fact that in the same phone call he asks his child to warn her mother, advising her to sell all her Enron shares (Prebble 2009a: 92).

Prebble's play revels in such contradictions, denying the audience a crystallized moral message. It toys with tragedy rather than strictly follow its forms and resists catharsis: those who have been victimized by Skilling's power lust are not vindicated and the perpetrator remains unrepentant. *Enron* is also a product of its time, infused with the technological advances of the 2000s. As a writer, Prebble has displayed a consistent and intuitive understanding of such issues: from the very topic of *The Sugar Syndrome* to the disconnected lives rendered in stunning visuals in *Enron* and *The Effect*. As she takes on issues of acute social crisis, Prebble collaborates with stage artists who are able to match the distinctive aesthetic her work creates. Prebble's fascination with video games, a subject on which she has written a column in *The Guardian*, is relevant here: it comes with an understanding of structure, gradual build-up and visuality. When an interviewer points out that Skilling 'played high-risk games with energy supply, made accountancy a fantasy of future growth [...] reinvent[ing] the world on his own terms' (Prebble 2009b), the comment resonates. The recognition of this trait in Prebble's work speaks to its video game aesthetic: dubious morals in high resolution, high stakes, large scale and staged in a way that enables uninterrupted scrutiny for the audience (including multi-angle, or occurring on different platforms), as well as protagonists who believe nothing is outside of their control. Prebble's work is as exciting as it is popular – and this guarantees her a wide audience for the major debates she engages in.

The Effect: The doctor God complex

If *Enron* had been a desirable project for Goold because it was responsive to Headlong's agenda of "'big ideas, big dialectic and bells-and-whistles theatricality'" (Hemming 2009), it might be difficult to imagine at first what drew the company to *The Effect*, 'A play for four people, in love and sorrow' as Prebble's opening note states (Prebble 2012a: 1). The experience of the play in performance, however, made clear that Headlong contributed a cinematic effect, through meticulous precision emanating from all parts of the play: from the stunning visual symmetry to immaculately choreographed verbal and visual dialogues. *The Effect*, a play about the human mind and body filtered through the human heart, went upon attacking its main subject with scientific systematicity engaging the audience in a visceral process of three-dimensional scrutiny. For spectators seated at the lower level, the proximity to performers was striking; for those occupying higher levels, the angle of vision was akin to observation in an operating theatre. The scientific through-line of the play is indicated clearly, as Prebble's directions list not only character names and ages, but also height and weight. Characters are presented to us as real humans, but also as specimens, especially as the first stage direction reads: '*Experiment begins*' (Prebble 2012a: 5).

An experiment it is, with the coalescence of theatre and medicine at its very core. The four characters of the play, two male and two female, two doctors (Dr Lorna James and Dr Toby Sealey) and two participants

(Connie Hall and Tristan Frey) are brought together in the context of a pharmaceutical trial. Goold's fascination with the stage depiction of 'uneasiness [...] anxiety, cultural as well as personal' (Hemming 2009) is revelatory when it comes to better appreciating *The Effect*: this is the feeling it attempts to capture, but also to instil affectively within the audience, creating a corporeally dialectical spectacle whereby what we see on the stage correlates to our contemporary experience. As others observe, spectators 'cannot evade the living body on a stage that (almost) invades their space. [...] *The Effect* is more than a mere "pharma play" [...] juxtaposing the private and the political as well as the social' (Drautzburg 2013: 382). Buether's malleable arena of a set ensured that this was the case as the stage became a testing and battleground for bodies and emotions, the densely inhabited space where human crisis unfolds leading to unpredictable results, scientific and otherwise.

As this book has shown in previous chapters, and proposes in the current one, a trend is becoming consolidated: to address the extremes of multiple crises as they are experienced, simultaneously playwrights and companies are performing a distinct turn into the broader realm of science, seeking the truth and explanation that they embark upon communicating to the audience. It is a process of mutual understanding, in which the playwright learns as much as s/he enlightens, seeking to engage the audience in a process of asking questions extending beyond the play. Carina Bartleet and Kirsten E. Shepherd-Barr argue that we are dealing with an expanded field of theatre production in what I term a sub-genre of crisis theatre by being confronted with increasingly multifaceted material taking on the issue of 'how science and theatre bisect each other' (2013: 292).

The '*Experiment begins*' with Connie (26) and Tristan (30) answering invasive questions determining their health status as they enter the clinical trial. From that moment a chain reaction of scientific and personal developments ensues and *The Effect* blurs the line between the two categories. The drug is an anti-depressant, giving Prebble the opportunity for topical and poignant social commentary concerning the marketability of the illness, as well as its treatment. Prebble also creates a framework that enables her both to juxtapose the pairs of the trial participants and doctors and to set them up as a continuum: the same issues of mistrust, indebtedness and dependency arise in both sets of relationships between Connie and Tristan, on the one hand, and Dr James (Lorna) and Dr Sealey (Toby) on the other. The sense of treading morally and ethically dubious territory is also shared amongst all four characters, with the added complication of sexual relationships developing (Connie and Tristan) or having developed in the past (the two doctors) leading to an impressive denouement. Despite showing Lorna as in complete control of the trial, Prebble allows glimpses at her wavering, both in terms of her stability and her belief in the integrity of the process she is overseeing. This is later confirmed when Lorna suffers an episode leading to her hospitalization. Her weaknesses are her personal relationships and sense of failure. Even though she confronts Toby on his shortcomings, ultimately he retains power in their personal and work relationship dynamic. The turning point is the revelation that Lorna was misinformed as to the fact that Tristan was not administered the drug but a placebo. Lorna's collapse, triggered by undermined authority, is mirrored in that of Tristan, who, likewise, appears both in utter control of his trial experience (he has been a participant on multiple occasions) and his relationship with Connie. Despite his initial bravado and carefree disposition, his confidence is shaken when Connie wonders whether their relationship is a side effect of the drug, or a genuine emotion. Tristan's insecurity, exacerbated by learning from Connie – who has extracted this wrong information from Lorna – that he is taking a placebo, borders on paranoia when he compares himself with Connie's older, wealthier partner. Meanwhile, Connie and Toby, for all their differences, appear mostly practical, in a better position to negotiate needs and emotions. Overall, the fact that the characters' emotional crises escalate as the trial peaks in dosages and effects accounts for the play's increasingly feverish atmosphere.

Furedi discusses the increasing regularity with which terms relating to mental affliction and treatment, including 'heal', 'trauma' (and various derivatives), 'distress' or 'closure', have been added to everyday discourse (2004: 2). The observation is crucial for understanding the formation of normative narratives in how we frame emotion without questioning the implications of our vocabularies and their impact on how we perceive ourselves. As Furedi adds, terms that the general public would not previously use regularly and might not even be aware of have in our time become part of everyday discourse; examples include 'disorder', 'anxiety', 'phobia', 'self-esteem', 'stress' and 'syndrome' and/or their derivatives, as well as their changing use through time – semantic and discursive developments emerging from the proliferation of a 'therapeutic vocabulary' (2004: 2–4). Furedi notes that to understand what this strong emergence of such a lexicon denotes is not only to appreciate that we are dealing with a turn towards emotionalization, but with a state specifically suggestive of affective disenfranchising, or what Furedi calls 'emotional deficit' (2004: 4). In Prebble's play, the sense of 'emotional deficit' persists, impacting all characters in different ways. It is 'depression' that becomes the catchphrase, the pivot around which the play revolves as far as both its primary plot (the trial) and the sub-plots (the characters' individual emotional turmoils) revolve. Furedi discusses depression extensively, remarking on its rise as diagnosable illness amongst children, which effectively renders it the adult affliction of the future (2004: 5). This is in a context where, as Furedi notes, depression is already seen to impact a significant portion of the population – and case studies concern Western so-called affluent communities rather than deprived societies (2004: 5). The inscription of depression as a contemporary illness, in the sense of the recognition and attention it is receiving, is, as Furedi's research reveals, tied to an endemic frequency amongst the young (2004: 6). It is a meaningful observation for *The Effect*, where the anti-depressant tested is framed as a necessity. Consider, for example, this extract, where Toby discusses diagnosis and medicating when challenged by Lorna:

> **Toby**   Don't hide behind this fashionable trashing of it all. Every
> time you have an episode, every time, the brain is altered and makes
> the next one longer and deeper. The sooner you start to medicate, the
> more you protect yourself. (Prebble 2012a: 79)

Connie and Tristan are young and in different ways unfulfilled in their
lives before entering the trial. Even though in their cases we are dealing
with erstwhile – seemingly – healthy bodies, it is fascinating to observe
how the trial releases underlying anxieties, triggering a process of
cause and effect. By the end of the play we cannot be certain whether
it was the mutual realization of their undiagnosed malaises that has
produced symptoms of depression, or whether it was their exposure to
the drug that lulled them into submission to their bodily and mental
subdual. This is especially noticeable for Tristan, a broken man in
the finale, due to the double dosage he ingests at the culmination of
the trial, especially as the crisis in his relationship with Connie has
elevated his stress levels.

The degree to which emotions are constructs is a driving factor in
the play, both in terms of trial side effects and predictable behaviour
patterns that accompany significant psychological events. Adopting
a textbook analogy, Lorna informs Toby that even though their
relationship added to other personal events, solidifying her depression,
it was not the direct cause of it. Toby reassures her that he was not
the cause of her depression, but the depression was the catalyst for
his choice to leave her (Prebble 2012a: 83). At no point is Lorna's
depression doubted, even though she consistently expresses serious
reservations that the condition can be treated chemically and resists its
facile categorization as yet another illness, for which it is appropriate to
prescribe medication that subdues the subject's faculties. She makes the
point particularly strongly for mild and moderate cases, citing figures
evidencing exponential growth in medicating (Prebble 2012a: 80–
81). Furedi considers the degree to which the over-eagerness to label
certain behaviours depressive disregards the fact that disappointment,
dejection and distress are common symptoms of emotional crisis
propelled, for example, by failure, grief or undesired developments

(2004: 110–112). *The Effect* implies a wider social crisis predicated on growing detachment from others, retreat into the individual and eventual desensitization: a crisis that is private as much as public, and personal as much as social. The play suggests that believing this can be treated medically might be a 'numbing down' process, precluding us from taking active steps towards mending a situation, or transforming what ails us and our societies. The position is consistent with Furedi's notion that '[...] therapeutic culture [...] [aids] not so much the promotion but the distancing of the self from others [...] crystallis[ing] the contemporary mood of individuation' (2004: 21). More recently, to establish a link between concerns such as the ones emerging from Furedi's study and Bauman's work, Ole Jacob Madsen's observation on Bauman's emphases is significant:

> an ideological reinforcement of individualisation [...is seen to have] taken place in the course of recent decades, [...] connect[ed] to late capitalism and neoliberalism, whereby individualisation becomes an obligatory process in which people's capacity for codetermination through their own life choices appears to obscure any opportunity for influence at a structural, collective level. (2014: 12)

Of course there are different types of influence and to argue that decisions made individually preclude public influence is only one part of the equation; the other is that what might appear as individually driven and self-serving has broad implications. One such example is the strategy of Skilling and Fastow in *Enron*, devised on the basis of own interests and ambitions, but impacting the fates of many. The way in which the trial is handled in *The Effect*, similarly, as both a personal bid for medical success (Toby's) and for financial gain by testing the limits of one's body, even though the product it will result in – the anti-depressant itself – will impact the lives of many, is strikingly similar. Although they might appear different, *Enron* and *The Effect* are in fact rather close in their central hypothesis. In both plays we witness the main characters handle personal deficiencies in a way that generates public repercussions. Various modes of therapy or self-therapy (from medicating to defence mechanisms) are shown as equally problematic in addressing inner lack emerging from disenfranchised agency in a radically individuated neoliberalist society. To quote Furedi, 'the therapeutic imperative is not so much towards the realisation of self-fulfilment as the promotion of self-limitation' (2004: 21). *The Effect* frames depression both as a response to social crisis and as a crisis in itself – and hints at the fact that neither of the two is necessarily being managed in a way that might deliver a solution.

The key to appreciating where the two plays intersect, which also facilitates a better understanding of the ideology in Prebble's theatre, is to return to the root of these behaviours that generate new forms of crisis, tracing the crisis back unto itself. Bauman observes: 'The trade in life meanings is the most competitive of markets, but with the "marginal utility" of the commodities on offer unlikely ever to shrink, the demand prompting competitive supply is unlikely ever to dry up' (2001: 4). The concept of competition is crucial: it determines action in all high-stakes fields, regardless of whether we are dealing with big business or big pharma. It is conducive to the 'God complex' that we witness in Skilling when he decides that his method of revolutionizing industry will inject new meaning to how corporate progress is achieved, creating acolytes who will subscribe to the narrative for the purposes of their own financial prosperity. It is also a catalyst for the development of new chemical solutions for handling illness in a way that will deflate other, typically considered superior branches of medicine. As Toby argues in one of his speeches, which also serve as business pitches, all the while clutching a human skull as an accessory:

> **Toby** [...] Depression is fast becoming the biggest cause of disability in the world. This is why medical intervention is so important. My father used to say about surgery that it's only love makes it anything except the act of two madmen. I feel that way about medication. It's love that means we treat people so they can live at home, in the community, rather than locked away. And it's love and it's trust that means that people don't lose their jobs or their children when they have a bout of depression. The psycho-pharmacological revolution is the most important occurrence in medicine in my

lifetime. And I'm *proud* to have been part of that. (Prebble 2012a: 30; emphasis original)

The quotation is reminiscent of Ken Lay's proclamations on Enron as a concept inciting high emotion. Linking back to Bauman, it becomes apparent how the neoliberalist argument is framed in quasi-socialist, community, public-benefit discourse. Because, of course, as Toby goes on to admit in his climactic confrontation with Lorna, he is highly aware of the 'sell[ing] things' aspect of his job, of the fact that he is part of a private industry market (Prebble 2012a: 80). However different the method, the remit is one and the same – to achieve personal fame and success predicated on the basis of serving the needs of others. It is indeed the most competitive market, as Bauman notes above. In these two plays, therefore, the megalomania in the boardroom is shared by that in the lab, leading to the same hubristic transgressions.

Bauman extends his enquiry to isolation as another major trope of neoliberalism. If we are taught to function as singular units, Bauman notes, it follows that any failures or adverse developments must be dealt with at the level of the individual too, processed exclusively as one's own fault, leading to vulnerability and crisis (2001: 5). It is revealing that when making the distinction between depressed and healthy minds, Lorna frames it as 'People prone to depression, Connie, they tend to attribute success to external causes and failure to internal ones', whereas 'the healthiest mind would think if things go well it's down to me' (Prebble 2012a: 21). While both accounts describe a neoliberalized state of mind with the individual at the centre, they also describe two different types of people: those who are able to metabolize neoliberalism into a positive and those who find it suffocating. Ambivalence towards oneself, as Bauman notes, is intensified further because we are bombarded by contradictory doctrines of what self-improvement is and how it might be accomplished (2001: 1–15). Prebble's nuanced depiction of aspirational, megalomaniac personalities alongside afflicted minds and bodies delivers a robust representation of extreme internal conflicts proliferating crisis.

Through this method, she also highlights the problematics of binarism between individual and society.

Discussing *The Effect*, Prebble locates love and depression within a purely individualized and neoliberalist framework, reflecting on the legacies of the Thatcherite 1980s. The quotation is worth citing at length:

> [...] One thing that binds that era [the 1980s] and those ideas [depression and love] is our focus on individualism, which [...] has exacerbated since the 1980s. [...] I think love as an idea is something we've defined as being individual, [...] as being everybody deserves a soul mate, and they are searching for that person and that quest is sacred and if somebody or something isn't making you happy anymore, then you move forward and you find the person who is your true love. And these things are embedded in the idea of you as an individual finding that person who will complete *you*, which is still a very individual idea. [...] Depression has [...] become a very individual state since the eighties, since we medicalized it, [...] within the confines of your own skin [...] that a person deals with as a disease, or an illness. In other cultures, both depression and love are thought of as part of a much bigger network of family and of society and would be treated in different ways because of that. [...] I think the eighties has been very instrumental in giving my generation an idea of love and depression as things that you are individually responsible for and [...] can therefore find or solve yourself. (Prebble 2015; emphasis reflecting Prebble's speaking tone)

Prebble's observation is in agreement with Mattheys's proposition that in 'dominant discourses around mental health', 'social and structural determinants are marginalised in favour of a focus on the individual' (2015: 477; Mattheys references M. Morrow, 2013). Returning to *The Effect*, understanding love and depression as not only states that each person, given their cultural conditioning, is indoctrinated into treating as a singular unit, but also as commodified because of this is crucial. The search for the one perfect partner who will fill an emotionally stunting gap is a shared characteristic amongst all four characters in *The Effect*. Even Connie, who is desperate to determine the reality of her relationship's emotional foundation, wavers between Tristan and her older, professionally successful (in contrast with Tristan) partner.

When Toby is alerted to the fact that falling in love might be one side effect of the drug, unsurprisingly, given his casual references to 'love' in his sales pitch, he entertains the idea of marketing the drug on that premise (Prebble 2012a: 46). The issue of managing one's needs, ailments and so on, on a self-contained basis is a recurring concern amongst theorists working at the crossover between sociology and psychology, especially when discussing individualization. Madsen returns to 'self-government', or 'governmentality', to argue that 'Through individualisation, the [...] subject becomes a manageable entity, which, ideally, will govern itself' (2014: 131–132). As Madsen adds, the feeling of entitlement that comes with neoliberalism, when challenged and discredited – as in cases of failing to accomplish what one might have felt was rightfully theirs – is not unreasonably linked to feelings of dissatisfaction leading to depression (2014: 132; see also 122). *The Effect* captures the consequences of self-regulation and self-medicating, which become the same as any other kind of business, given that depression is framed in terms of neoliberalist insularity.

If, as Madsen notes, we are conditioned to consumer behaviours (2014: 122), choice of therapy is no exception, nor is it necessarily much different from deciding which stock to invest in, with the hope that it will yield benefits, as we see in *Enron*. The downside of the self-medicating process that Toby describes as so desirable in his speech is, of course, that such courses of treatment that look to avoid social stigma, promoting self-management, may lead to further isolation and self-exclusion. The need to share the problem is undermined and eventually removed and instead of empowerment, the product is crisis. *The Effect* also serves as example of a further ramification that sociologists have pointed out when probing the links between neoliberalism and behaviour conditioning: governmentality and self-disciplining. Foucault's discourse on the Panopticon becomes the ideal schema (see Bauman 2001: 224) through which to describe self-managing on the basis of internalized rules that ultimately render body and mind subservient to the prevailing system. Through its depiction of a clinical trial operating on the constant monitoring of every (re)action,

The Effect manifests the extent to which choice is but an empty term and self-disposition only becomes a synonym for self-submission. Upon entering the trial, Connie and Tristan may believe that they will derive benefits, be that money, or service to science. In reality, they become mere specimens deprived of freedom. Even when they attempt to fool the system of surveillance, they are apprehended – or they voluntarily confess. Testing the limits of the body may be framed as yet another option at a time of de-sensitization, but, however attractive it may be, as Prebble's play reveals, to believe that the subject has any control over the process is a fallacy and merely another state of servitude.

Conclusion

When *Enron* flopped on Broadway, closing twelve days after it opened (Jones 2010), it may have been a partial surprise given its extraordinary success in the United Kingdom, but all things considered, the failure of the play to translate to US audiences was not altogether shocking. After all, it had taken on a topic that, however universal it might have become by the time *Enron* premiered in Britain due to the global financial crisis and the recession, it was also 100 per cent part of the American experience and arguably too close to home. This meant it was too soon to be treated in the United States with the same appetite for satire it had been greeted with in the United Kingdom, where, as I noted earlier, it served as a non-culturally specific metaphor for a wider problem. The failure of *Enron* in America happened for reasons not dissimilar to those that prevented Stephens's 7/7 play *Pornography* from receiving a British production until 2008, a full year after its premiere in Germany, where it was commissioned. Another example would be the treatment of the 2011 UK riots on British stages: a major work outside of the verbatim genre (see Gillian Slovo's *The Riots*, 2011; Alecky Blythe's *Little Revolution*, 2014) has yet to happen. Simply put, our own, viscerally experienced rather than remotely observed crises are harder to watch and different cultures have different recovery times and processes. In a statement following the US failure of *Enron*, Goold, amongst other factors, attributed it to the play's '[...] attack on different kinds of faith, not just our faith in finance [...]. It finishes with a quote from the Bible that is then twisted into a reference to finance: there, we were attacking twin American totems' (Goold 2010). While the observation may be accurate, it is also fair to say that faith and finance are far from American identity staples only. At the time of neoliberalism, finance still reigns supreme globally as we have seen time and time again, with narratives of austerity appearing infrangible. As for faith, it is a concept that as *Enron* itself demonstrates so aptly, is very flexible and far from tied to religion only, let alone one specific religion.

It is understandable, then, that in *The Effect*, a play that is also about faith and finance, except this time in science and pharmaceutical corporations, the relationship between form and content was made somewhat more abstract, enhancing the universality of the play. There are still long, naturalistic dialogues in *The Effect*, which turn into major disputes on relationships, depression or scientific integrity – but in the overall impression it makes on the spectator, *The Effect* is a very different play from *Enron*. The humour is subtle and even suppressed; the atmosphere is darker; the characters' incentives are much more ambiguous. Ultimately though, the plays are explorations on a theme: how happiness, whether material or emotional, is a business product engineered through mega industry. It is fascinating that both of Prebble's large-scale plays, *Enron* and *The Effect*, place controversial male characters at the centre of the developments, who appear to be contending with their own feelings of insecurity, leading to an abuse of power. Skilling admits to his contempt for the discrimination against intelligent people, as he perceives it, early on in *Enron* (Prebble 2009a: 11). In his market pitch, Toby clearly sets up himself as the opposite of his heart surgeon father, because he is representing a strand of medicine not taken as seriously (Prebble 2012a: 28–30). Nicky Marsh specifically makes the point that 'the sexual languages of the financial economy provide evidence of an aggrandizing heroic masculine individualism, an explicit abandonment of the collective demands of the social' (2011: 303). Insecurity, a symptom of the neoliberalist (male) pathogeny that ails, conditions and fragments lives, is also the driving force behind the God complex: a complex of lack internally developed and outwardly manifested.

Critics responded well to *The Effect*, which is already beginning to carve out an international path of its own, as new productions emerge. The *Wall Street Journal* correspondent called the London production 'Utterly superb', commending Prebble's ability to take on another high-profile topic following *Enron* (Levy 2012) and others have since praised Prebble for producing work that is nuanced, responsible and open to interpretation (Brantley 2016). The British press had reacted similarly, and the play was seen as the product of 'vivid, provocative intelligence', 'moving [...] and [...] tenderly [...] delivered' (Hemming 2012), a view that many critics shared. *The Effect* was an important step forward in contemporary theatre's relationship with science, not least because its premiere production played to big audiences in a staging that was artistically ambitious and resistant to sensationalism. It also opened up major questions that it did not pretend to answer conclusively, but that it showed it could measure up against with scientific knowledge and creative vision, utilizing Prebble's research (Woolman 2012). Bartleet and Shepherd-Barr are right to identify experiment as equally significant for theatre and science (2013: 293, 2014: 203). A play like *The Effect* shows how the schema of the experiment comes to be crucial for new form development, not only in the sense of the artist exploring new avenues, but also in the literal application of the structure of a medical experiment to a piece of performance. Ultimately, where Prebble's work succeeds in capturing contemporary crisis, is in her understanding of the importance of taking multiple angles of vision to the problem. Prebble's epic studies of human behaviour, of individualism and society, are involved in the lives of their subjects, but they also retain critical distance; never is the critical compromised for the emotional, even though the latter is a very tangible aspect of her work. But when it is all said and done, and the intense ride of the play is over, like a video game whose phantasmagoria fades, so the experiment ends – and what the finding was, is up to the audience. However tempting given her subject matter, public indictment is not Prebble's game.

Epilogue

This book has taken on one of the most pervasive and yet elusive terms – crisis – at a time when the word alone has become the staple of our contemporary experience. It has, defiantly, perhaps, suggested that crisis does not have to be a destructive experience. The work of the artists discussed in this book allows us to conceptualize our present moment as one that casts us in the role of an agent, a participant, and not merely a passive observer. The interdisciplinary sociological perspectives that the book has pursued have corroborated the hypothesis: however great the challenge – and it is – and however crucial our historical moment, in critical thinking and in performance practice there is a persistent, committed faith in humanity and community that refuses to surrender to narratives of pessimism and retreat; that still invests in the power of the individual to make a difference to society; that has the time to explore the conditions that make us alike despite different challenges. This book was written before the UK referendum that delivered a marginal majority vote for Brexit in June 2016. It entered its production process with the long-term consequences of the vote still uncertain. For this reason, Brexit does not feature as a concern of this book – how it will change our social, political and theatrical landscape remains to be seen.

Theatre and theory, represented by different strands of philosophy and sociology, have been natural partners for each other. As our social challenges intensify and our experience becomes transformed in ways unprecedented, so our methods have had to adapt. This book has reflected this with a critical language that has been responsive to our theatre's own natural turn towards ambitious representation, which has not treated any topic as unmanageable or any minutiae of everyday experience as too indifferent. As the book concludes, I am reminded once more of the following invitation by Richard Sennett, which resonates powerfully: 'We have at least to attempt to make the way we live', he writes (2012: xi). The plays that this book has focused on are considerate attempts, invested in enquiry and change. There may be no certainty or guarantee, the road may be long and difficult, but surrender to fate and isolation cannot be our only option. The plays echo the sentiment, even in their bleakest moments. The darkness never prevails; the light of cooperation and the optimism towards the prospect of achieving better – together, collectively – quietly sets in.

The book has chosen playwrights in whose work certain thematic preoccupations persist, matched with forms that push boundaries and redefine innovation. These artists dedicate their practice to the stage experiment, vehicle and metaphor for the unknown potential not only of theatre but also of life more broadly, which needs to be probed and unlocked. The book has contended that playwriting is not only alive as a genre of urgent socially and politically motivated theatre, but also in fighting form. The popularity of British theatre outside of the country and especially on other European stages consistently renders it evident that there is something special about this work, that it is attuned to the problematics of our time in ways that appeal to different cultures and transcend borders, geographical or otherwise. The theatre of crisis does not take one uniform shape: it embodies the multitudes of the different writing sensibilities, styles and approaches that may diverge in their aesthetics but converge upon the need to confront humanity with honesty and with hope. The field is constantly growing, but the purpose of this book has not been merely to catalogue; it has, rather, aimed to enter a dialogue with these plays, devoting space and time to them, treating them, I would hope, with the care and attention they have paid to the issues at hand. As the book went into production, and as is the nature of our field, more work was added to the discussion. I am keen to observe how the dialogue curated by Siân Adiseshiah and Louise LePage in *Twenty-First Century Drama: What Happens Now* (2016) might create more avenues for enquiry. It may be redundant to say that my book has not intended to be exhaustive in its coverage, because this is not its remit. It has, however, aimed for a meaningful discussion that may set the tone for others, especially at a time when 'crisis' is emerging in theatre scholarship with increasing regularity. Again, then, I hope that with this book I have investigated, with the reader, essential paradigms of the social and political theatre of our time using tools that have shed light on what renders them significant interventions.

In a recent reflection on contemporary British theatre specifically concentrating on new writing, Aleks Sierz wondered whether growing numbers of new plays are what we need to ascertain the health of the field before considering the hypothesis that, even if this were the case, numbers of hard-hitting new plays written today, for and about the present moment, were dwindling (2013: 250–251). There is value in the argument, although I cannot ultimately agree with Sierz's suggestion that tastes and forms became more conservative and the once sharp edge of playwriting softened in the recent period, a sign of a crisis within the theatre itself (2013: 250–251). If anything, the work of the playwrights that this book has discussed, a body of work whose volume is substantial, revealing depth and breadth rather than isolated occurrences, shows that playwriting has in fact accelerated in rigour. Not all of it, certainly, but enough of it to be shaping an active field, electric with the energy of debate and exposure. While Sierz ponders whether anger has all but disappeared from our stages (2013: 251), this book has proposed that the anger, the indignation, the disbelief and the appetite for change are all there – but their forms have changed. The theatre of discontent is different today. Plays can be introspective and subdued and still be quite angry; they can be demanding of change without pointing an accusatory finger; they can express their rage without demonstrating and teasing its every nerve – in the case of Churchill, simply by articulating the very word, in fact (2016). Sierz asks whether austerity has meant that theatre is undergoing a crisis analogous to that of the late 1980s, when conditions actively hurt experimentation and growth (2013: 251). But as I hope the reader agrees, the theatre out of a crisis that we are experiencing today is, in fact, a theatre moving out of austerity: even in economical structures, there is resistance; and in other kinds of more expansive structures, the sheer pluralism compels. Then, again, work like *Love and Information* shows us that theatre can be maximalist and minimalist at the same time: our experience is both augmented and fragmented. Nothing about this type of theatre implies retreat. Quite the opposite: it charges on, forward.

Bibliography

Adey, P. (2011) 'Airports: Terminal/Vector', in Merriman, P. and Cresswell, T. (eds.) *Geographies of Mobilities: Practices, Spaces, Subjects*. Farnham, Surrey: Ashgate Publishing, pp. 137–150.

Adiseshiah, S. and LePage, L. (eds.) (2016) *Twenty-First Century Drama: What Happens Now*. London: Palgrave Macmillan.

Alberts, P. (2011) 'Responsibility towards Life in the Early Anthropocene', *Angelaki: Journal of the Theoretical Humanities*, 16(4), pp. 5–17.

Angelaki, V. (2012) *The Plays of Martin Crimp: Making Theatre Strange*. Basingstoke: Palgrave Macmillan.

Angelaki, V. (2013) 'Politics for the Middle Classes: Contemporary British Theatre and the Violence of Now', in Angelaki, V. (ed.) *Contemporary British Theatre: Breaking New Ground*. Basingstoke: Palgrave Macmillan.

Appelbaum, R. (2014) 'Sunken Treasure: The Cultural Logic of Austerity', *symplokē*, 22(1–2), pp. 77–95.

Aragay, M. and Monforte, E. (2013) 'Racial Violence, Witnessing and Emancipated Spectatorship in *The Colour of Justice, Fallout and random*', in Angelaki, V. (ed.) *Contemporary British Theatre: Breaking New Ground*. Basingstoke: Palgrave Macmillan, pp. 96–120.

Arp Fallov, M., Jørgensen, A. and Knudsen, L.B. (2013) 'Mobile Forms of Belonging', *Mobilities*, 8(4), pp. 467–486.

Bachelard, G. (1994) *The Poetics of Space*. Translated by Maria Jolas. Boston: Beacon Press.

Bartleet, C. and Shepherd-Barr, K.E. (2013) 'Editorial', *Interdisciplinary Science Reviews*, 38(4), pp. 292–294.

Bartleet, C. and Shepherd-Barr, K.E. (2014) 'Editorial', *Interdisciplinary Science Reviews*, 39(3), p. 203.

Bartlett, M. (2008) *Contractions*. London: Methuen Drama.

Bartlett, M. (2009) *Cock*. London: Methuen Drama.

Bartlett, M. (2010a) *Earthquakes in London*. London: Methuen Drama.

Bartlett, M. (2010b) *Have the Baby Boomers Messed the World Up? Rising Playwright Mike Bartlett Talks about Earthquakes, His New Play at the National*. Interview by Dominic Cavendish. Available at: http://www
.telegraph.co.uk/culture/theatre/theatre-features/7909474/Mike-Bartlett
-anger-on-a-seismic-scale.html (Accessed: 28 December 2015).

Bartlett, M. (2010c) *Love, Love, Love*. London: Methuen Drama.

Bartlett, M. (2010d) *Mike Bartlett on Earthquakes in London*. Interview by Dominic Cavendish. Available at: http://www.theatrevoice. com/audio/mike-bartlett-on-earthquakes-in-london/ (Accessed: 28 December 2015).

Bartlett, M. (2011a) *Mike Bartlett: Earthquakes Everywhere*. Interview by Maddy Costa. Available at: http://www.theguardian.com/stage/2011/oct/18/mike-bartlett-13 (Accessed: 24 October 2013).

Bartlett, M. (2011b) *13*. London: Methuen Drama.

Bartlett, M. (2013) *Bull*. London: Nick Hern Books.

Bartlett, M. (2014) *King Charles III*. London: Nick Hern Books.

Bartlett, M. (2015) *Game*. London: Nick Hern Books.

Bartlett, M. (2016) *Wild*. London: Nick Hern Books.

Bauman, Z. (2001) *The Individualized Society*. Cambridge: Polity Press.

Bauman, Z. and Bordoni, C. (2014) *State of Crisis*. Cambridge: Polity Press.

BBC (2010) *BBC News – UK Economy Emerges from Recession*. Available at: http://news.bbc.co.uk/2/hi/business/8479639.stm (Accessed: 7 April 2016).

Bean, R. (2011) *The Heretic*. London: Oberon Books.

Benjamin, G. and Crimp, M. (2013) 'George Benjamin and Martin Crimp in Conversation in King's College London', 11 October 2013.

Billen, A. (2012) *Conceptual Theatre Is Hard to Watch and Even Harder to Make*. Available at: http://www.newstatesman.com/culture/art-and-design/2012/09/conceptual-theatre-hard-watch-and-even-harder-make (Accessed: 5 February 2016).

Billington, M. (2003) *The Sugar Syndrome*. Available at: http://www.theguardian.com/stage/2003/oct/21/theatre (Accessed: 30 June 2015).

Billington, M. (2009) *Royal Court Theatre Gets behind the Gaza Headlines*. Available at: http://www.theguardian.com/stage/theatreblog/2009/feb/11/royal-court-theatre-gaza (Accessed: 9 November 2015).

Billington, M. (2010) *Earthquakes in London*. Available at: http://www.theguardian.com/stage/2010/aug/05/earthquakes-in-london-michael-billington (Accessed: 20 December 2015).

Billington, M. (2011a) *The Heretic – Review*. Available at: http://www.theguardian.com/stage/2011/feb/11/the-heretic-review (Accessed: 12 February 2015).

Billington, M. (2011b) *13 – Review*. Available at: http://www.theguardian.com/stage/2011/oct/26/13-review (Accessed: 20 December 2015).

Billington, M. (2013) *The Ritual Slaughter of Gorge Mastromas.* Available at: http://www.theguardian.com/stage/2013/sep/12/ritual-slaughter-gorge -mastromas-review (Accessed: 11 June 2015).

Brantley, B. (2016) *Review: 'The Effect,' about Falling in Love while Taking Antidepressants.* Available at: http://www.nytimes.com/2016/03/21/theater/ review-the-effect-about-falling-in-love-while-taking-antidepressants.html (Accessed: 31 March 2016).

Brown, M. (2009) *Royal Court Acts Fast with Gaza Crisis Play.* Available at: http://www.theguardian.com/stage/2009/jan/24/theatre-gaza-caryl -churchill-royal-court-seven-jewish-children (Accessed: 9 November 2015).

Buffini, M. (2015) *Caryl Churchill: The Playwright's Finest Hours.* Available at: http://www.theguardian.com/stage/2015/jun/29/caryl-churchill-the -playwrights-finest-hours (Accessed: 24 November 2015).

Buffini, M., Charman, M., Skinner, P. and Thorne, J. (2011) *Greenland.* London: Faber & Faber.

Buttonwood's Notebook (2009) *Enron on Stage.* Available at: http://www .economist.com/blogs/buttonwood/2009/09/enron_on_stage (Accessed: 6 July 2015).

Carmen Disruption (2014) Available at: http://schauspielhaus.de/de_DE/ archiv/carmen_disruption.951088 (Accessed: 19 October 2015).

Cavendish, D. (2003) *A Dangerous Affair.* Available at: http://www.telegraph .co.uk/culture/theatre/drama/3605176/A-dangerous-affair.html (Accessed: 30 June 2015).

Cavendish, D. (2009) *Seven Jewish children – A Play for Gaza at the Royal Court, Review.* Available at: http://www.telegraph.co.uk/journalists/ dominic-cavendish/4601683/Seven-Jewish-Children-A-Play-for-Gaza-at -the-Royal-Court-review.html (Accessed: 9 November 2015).

Charlesworth, S.J. (2000) *A Phenomenology of Working-Class Experience.* Cambridge: Cambridge University Press.

Churchill, C. (1988) 'The Common Imagination and the Individual Voice', Interview by Geraldine Cousin, *New Theatre Quarterly*, 4(13), pp. 3–16.

Churchill, C. (1990) *Caryl Churchill: Plays Two.* London: Methuen Drama.

Churchill, C. (2000) *Far Away.* London: Nick Hern Books.

Churchill, C. (2002) *A Number.* London: Nick Hern Books.

Churchill, C. (2006) *Drunk Enough to Say I Love You?* London: Nick Hern Books.

Churchill, C. (2012a) *Ding Dong the Wicked.* London: Nick Hern Books.

Churchill, C. (2012b) *Love and Information.* London: Nick Hern Books.

Churchill, C. (2015) *Here We Go*. London: Nick Hern Books.

Churchill, C. (2016) *Escaped Alone*. London: Nick Hern Books.

Clapp, S. (2006) *Flopping and Ducking*. Available at: http://www.theguardian
.com/stage/2006/nov/05/theatre (Accessed: 9 April 2015).

Clapp, S. (2016) *Escaped Alone Review – Small Talk and Everyday Terror from
Caryl Churchill*. Available at: http://www.theguardian.com/stage/2016/
jan/31/escaped-alone-caryl-churchill-review-royal-court (Accessed:
1 April 2016).

Clements, R. (2013a) 'Framing War, Staging Precarity: Caryl Churchill's *Seven
Jewish Children* and the Spectres of Vulnerability', *Contemporary Theatre
Review*, 23(3), pp. 357–367.

Clements, R. (2013b) 'Ghosts', *Contemporary Theatre Review*, 23(1),
pp. 26–28.

Conventz, S. and Thierstein, A. (2014) 'Hub-airports as Cities of Intersections:
The Redefined Role of Hub-airports within the Knowledge Economy
Context', in Conventz, S., Derudder, B., Thierstein, A. and Witlox, F. (eds.)
Hub Cities in the Knowledge Economy: Seaports, Airports, Brainports.
Farnham, Surrey: Ashgate Publishing, pp. 77–94.

Cook, M. and Gardner, L. (2013) *Much Ado about Nothing, 1984, The
Herd: What to See at the Theatre This Week*. Available at: http://www
.theguardian.com/stage/2013/sep/06/this-weeks-new-theatre (Accessed:
24 October 2013).

Cooke, D. (2011) *SkyArts Interview with Dominic Cooke, Artistic Director*.
Available at: https://www.youtube.com/watch?v=yNj__Pc7ifU (Accessed:
29 October 2015).

Cooke, D. (2014) 'Backpages – Bringing *In the Republic of Happiness* to the
Royal Court Stage', *Contemporary Theatre Review*, 24(3), pp. 410–411.

Crimp, M. (1997) *Attempts on Her Life*. London: Faber & Faber.

Crimp, M. (2000) *The Country*. London: Faber & Faber.

Crimp, M. (2004) *Cruel and Tender*. London: Faber & Faber.

Crimp, M. (2005) *Fewer Emergencies*. London: Faber & Faber.

Crimp, M. (2008) *The City*. London: Faber & Faber.

Crimp, M. (2012a) *Play House and Definitely the Bahamas*. London: Faber &
Faber.

Crimp, M. (2012b) *In the Republic of Happiness*. London: Faber & Faber.

Crimp, M. (2013) 'Martin Crimp in Conversation with Dan Rebellato',
Dealing with Martin Crimp Conference, Royal Court Theatre, London,
12 January 2013.

Crimp, M. (2014) 'Martin Crimp in Conversation with Vicky Angelaki', University of Birmingham, 9 December 2014.

Crosthwaite, P. (2010) 'Blood on the Trading Floor', *Angelaki: Journal of the Theoretical Humanities*, 15(2), pp. 3–18.

De Angelis, A., Penhall, J., Prebble, L. and Ravenhill, M. (2004) *Life, Death and Estate Agents*. Available at: http://www.theguardian.com/stage/2004/jun/16/theatre2 (Accessed: 6 July 2015).

Diamond, E. (2009) 'On Churchill and Terror', in Aston, E. and Diamond, E. (eds.) *The Cambridge Companion to Caryl Churchill*. Cambridge: Cambridge University Press.

Diamond, E. (2014) 'Love and Information by Caryl Churchill', *Theatre Journal*, 66(3), pp. 462–465.

Donkers, M. and Orthia, L.A. (2014) 'Popular Theatre for Science Engagement: Audience Engagement with Human Cloning Following a Production of Caryl Churchill's *A Number*', *International Journal of Science Education, Part B*, 6(1), pp. 23–45.

Drautzburg, A. (2013) 'Lucy Prebble's the Effect, the National Theatre, London, 2013', *Interdisciplinary Science Reviews*, 38(4), p. 382.

Dymkowski, C. (2003) 'Caryl Churchill: Far Away ... but Close to Home', *European Journal of English Studies*, 7(1), pp. 55–68.

The Economist – The Data Team (2016) *Worldwide Cost of Living Survey*. Available at: http://www.economist.com/blogs/graphicdetail/2016/03/daily-chart-4 (Accessed: 7 April 2016).

Editorial (2010) *In Praise of ... Lucy Prebble*. Available at: http://www.theguardian.com/commentisfree/2010/jan/01/in-praise-of-lucy-prebble (Accessed: 30 June 2015).

Editorial (2014) *The New Poor: The Social Demography of Poverty in Modern Britain Is Changing Fast – and Tackling It Will Take More than Slogans*. Available at: http://www.independent.co.uk/voices/editorials/the-new-poor-the-social-demography-of-poverty-in-modern-britain-is-changing-fast–and-tackling-it-will-take-more-than-slogans-9878794.html (Accessed: 22 April 2015).

Emmott, S. (2013) *Ten Billion*. London: Penguin.

Emmott, S. and Mitchell, K. (2012) *Entretien avec Katie Mitchell et Stephen Emmott*. Interview by Jean-François Perrier. Available at: http://www.festival-avignon.com/lib_php/download.php?fileID=714&type=File&round=256295528 (Accessed: 26 January 2015).

Foucault, M. (1997) *Ethics: Subjectivity and Truth. Essential Works of Michel Foucault, 1954–1984*. Vol. 1. New York: New Press.

Frank, R.H. (2013) *Falling Behind: How Rising Inequality Harms the Middle Class.* Berkeley: University of California Press.

Furedi, F. (1998) 'New Britain—A Nation of Victims', *Society*, 35(3), pp. 80–84.

Furedi, F. (2002) 'The Silent Ascendancy of Therapeutic Culture in Britain', *Society*, 39(3), pp. 16–24.

Furedi, F. (2004) *Therapy Culture: Cultivating Vulnerability in an Uncertain Age.* London: Routledge.

Gardner, L. (2009) *Caryl Churchill's Play for Gaza Is a Prompt for Theatres to React Quickly.* Available at: http://www.theguardian.com/stage/theatreblog/2009/jan/26/caryl-churchill-play-gaza-theatre (Accessed: 9 November 2015).

Gardner, L. (2011a) *Earthquakes in London – Review.* Available at: http://www.theguardian.com/stage/2011/oct/04/earthquakes-in-london-review (Accessed: 24 October 2013).

Gardner, L. (2011b) *Lungs – Review.* Available at: http://www.theguardian.com/stage/2011/oct/25/lungs-crucible-sheffield-review (Accessed: 24 October 2013).

Gardner, L. (2012a) *DNA – Review.* Available at: http://www.theguardian.com/stage/2012/feb/14/dna-review (Accessed: 18 October 2013).

Gardner, L. (2012b) *Roundabout – Review.* Available at: http://www.theguardian.com/stage/2012/sep/26/roundabout-lungs-review (Accessed: 24 October 2013).

Gobert, D.R. (2014) *The Theatre of Caryl Churchill.* London: Bloomsbury.

Goddard, L. (2013) 'debbie tucker green', in Rebellato, D. (ed.) *Modern British Playwriting: 2000–2009: Voices, Documents, New Interpretations.* London: Bloomsbury, pp. 190–212.

Goddard, L. (2015) *Contemporary Black British Playwrights: Margins to Mainstream.* Basingstoke: Palgrave Macmillan.

Goold, R. (2010) *Why Broadway Didn't Like the Financial Satire Enron.* Interview by Laura Barnett. Available at: http://www.theguardian.com/global/2010/may/05/enron-broadway-financial-satire-american (Accessed: 31 July 2015).

The Guardian (2011) *Theatre of War.* Available at: http://www.theguardian.com/theguardian/2011/mar/04/antisemitism-feeding-homeless-cctv-hamlet (Accessed: 9 November 2015).

Haddington, P., Mondada, L. and Nevile, M. (2013) 'Being Mobile: Interaction on the Move', in Haddington, P., Mondada, L. and Nevile, M. (eds.) *Interaction and Mobility: Language and the Body in Motion.* Berlin: Walter de Gruyter.

Haley, J. (2014) *The Nether*. London: Faber & Faber.

Harvey, D. (2005) *A Brief History of Neoliberalism*. Oxford and New York: Oxford University Press.

Harvie, J. (2013) *Fair Play: Art, Performance and Neoliberalism*. Basingstoke: Palgrave Macmillan.

Haydon, A. (2014) *Carmen Disruption Review – 'Delights in Being Counterintuitive'*. Available at: http://www.theguardian.com/stage/2014/mar/18/carmen-disruption-review (Accessed: 19 October 2015).

Hemming, S. (2009) *'Enron', Royal Court, London*. Available at: http://www.ft.com/cms/s/0/fc18290a-9e61-11de-b0aa-00144feabdc0.html#axzz3fNxg3V4o (Accessed: 10 July 2015).

Hemming, S. (2011) *Truth and Reconciliation, Jerwood Theatre Upstairs, Royal Court Theatre, London*. Available at: http://www.ft.com/cms/s/2/d90d2748-d943-11e0-884e-00144feabdc0.html#axzz3hwUYUaBB (Accessed: 5 August 2015).

Hemming, S. (2012) *The Effect, National Theatre, London*. Available at: http://www.ft.com/cms/s/2/46d6de78-2e56-11e2-8bb3-00144feabdc0.html (Accessed: 31 July 2015).

Heppekausen, S. (2012) *Die Opferung von Gorge Mastromas – Christoph Mehler bringt Dennis Kellys neues Stück bei den Ruhrfestspielen zur Uraufführung*. Available at: http://www.nachtkritik.de/index.php?option=com_content&view=article&id=6918:die-opferung-von-gorge-mastromas-christoph-mehler-bringt-dennis-kellys-neues-stueck-zur-urauffuehrung&catid=38:die-nachtkritik&Itemid=40 (Accessed: 15 July 2014).

Hesse, M. (2008) *The City as a Terminal: The Urban Context of Logistics and Freight Transport*. Aldershot: Ashgate Publishing.

Higgins, C. (2009) *Is Caryl Churchill's Play Seven Jewish Children Antisemitic?* Available at: http://www.theguardian.com/culture/charlottehigginsblog/2009/feb/18/israelandthepalestinians-religion (Accessed: 9 November 2015).

Ionesco, E. (1997) *The Chairs*. Translated by Martin Crimp. London: Faber & Faber.

Ionesco, E. (2007) *Rhinoceros*. Translated by Martin Crimp. London: Faber & Faber.

Jones, K. (2010) *Enron Falls Again; Broadway Run of Acclaimed London Play Will End May 9*. Available at: http://www.playbill.com/news/article/enron-falls-again-broadway-run-of-acclaimed-london-play-will-end-may-9-168192 (Accessed: 31 July 2015).

Kelly, D. (2007) *Dennis Kelly: Plays One*. London: Oberon Books.

Kelly, D. (2008) *DNA*. London: Oberon Books.

Kelly, D. (2009) *Orphans*. London: Oberon Books.

Kelly, D. (2010) *The Gods Weep*. London: Oberon Books.

Kelly, D. (2012) *Dennis Kelly Opens the Stückemarkt*. Available at: http:// theatertreffen-blog.de/tt12/2012/05/10/dennis-kelly-opens-the -stuckemarkt/ (Accessed: 14 April 2015).

Kelly, D. (2013a) 'I *Thought that Drinking Was All I Had to Offer'*. Interview by Maddy Costa. Available at: http://www.theguardian.com/ stage/2013/sep/10/dennis-kelly-gorge-mastromas-interview (Accessed: 11 September 2013).

Kelly, D. (2013b) *The Ritual Slaughter of Gorge Mastromas*. London: Oberon Books.

Konings, M. (2016) 'The Spirit of Austerity', *Journal of Cultural Economy*, 9(1), pp. 86–100.

Lawson, M. (2012) *Caryl Churchill, by the People Who Know Her Best*. Available at: http://www.theguardian.com/stage/2012/oct/03/caryl -churchill-collaborators-interview (Accessed: 6 November 2015).

Lawson, M. (2015) *Brief Is Beautiful: How Caryl Churchill Conquered British Theatre*. Available at: http://www.theguardian.com/stage/2015/ nov/20/caryl-churchill-conquered-british-theatre-here-we-go (Accessed: 24 November 2015).

Levy, P. (2012) *Trials and Celebrations*. Available at: http://www.wsj.com/ articles/SB10001424127887324352004578136973413940646 (Accessed: 25 October 2013).

Lorimer, H. (2011) 'Walking: New Forms and Spaces for Studies of Pedestrianism', in Cresswell, T. and Merriman, P. (eds.) *Geographies of Mobilities: Practices, Spaces, Subjects*. Farnham, Surrey: Ashgate Publishing, pp. 19–33.

Luckhurst, M. and Morin, E. (2014) 'Introduction: Theatre and Spectrality', in Luckhurst, M. and Morin, E. (eds.) *Theatre and Ghosts: Materiality, Performance and Modernity*. Basingstoke: Palgrave Macmillan.

Macaulay, A. (2006) *Love and Money, Young Vic Theatre, London*. Available at: https://next.ft.com/content/e2a69300-7b03-11db-bf9b-0000779e2340 (Accessed: 18 October 2013).

MacInnes, T., Aldridge, H., Bushe, S., Tinson, A. and Barry-Born, T. (2014) *Monitoring Poverty and Social Exclusion 2014*. Available at: https://www.jrf .org.uk/report/monitoring-poverty-and-social-exclusion-2014 (Accessed: 4 June 2015).

Macmillan, D. (2011) *Lungs*. London: Oberon Books, 2011.

Macmillan, D. (2013) 'Backpages – Duncan Macmillan's Theatre of Luminous Motion', Interview by Caridad Svich, *Contemporary Theatre Review*, 23(3), pp. 450–454.

Macmillan, D. and Rapley, C. (2015) *2071*. Available at: http://www .royalcourttheatre.com/mmlib/includes/sendapplicationfile.php?id=5026 (Accessed: 7 February 2015).

Madsen, O.J. (2014) *The Therapeutic Turn: How Psychology Altered Western Culture*. London: Routledge.

Marber, P. (1997) *Closer*. London: Methuen Drama.

Marsh, N. (2011) 'Desire and Disease in the Speculative Economy: A Critique of the Language of Crisis', *Journal of Cultural Economy*, 4(3), pp. 301–314.

Marshall, N. and tucker green, d. (2015) *Front Row – BBC Radio 4*. Interview by John Wilson. Available at: http://www.bbc.co.uk/programmes/ b05w4jdb (Accessed: 3 August 2015).

Martin, D. (2011) 'Eyjafjallajökull 4'33": A Stillness in Three Parts', *Mobilities*, 6(1), pp. 85–94.

Mattheys, K. (2015) 'The Coalition, Austerity and Mental Health', *Disability & Society*, 30(3), pp. 475–478.

Megson, C. (2013) '"And I was struck still by time": Contemporary British Theatre and the Metaphysical Imagination', in Angelaki, V. (ed.) *Contemporary British Theatre: Breaking New Ground*. Basingstoke: Palgrave Macmillan, pp. 32–56.

Mellbye, A. (2003) *A Brief History of the Third Way*. Available at: http://www .theguardian.com/politics/2003/feb/10/labour.uk1 (Accessed: 8 April 2016).

Merritt, S. (2014) *Climate Change Play 2071 Aims to Make Data Dramatic*. Available at: http://www.theguardian.com/stage/2014/nov/05/climate -change-theatre-2071-katie-mitchell-duncan-macmillan (Accessed: 16 January 2015).

Milmo, C. (2014) *The Young Are the New Poor: Sharp Increase in Number of Under-25s Living in Poverty, while Over-65s Are Better off than Ever*. Available at: http://www.independent.co.uk/news/uk/home-news/the -young-arethe-new-poor-sharp-increase-in-the-number-of-under25s -living-in-poverty-while-over65s-are-better-off-than-ever-9878722.html (Accessed: 22 April 2015).

Mitchell, K. (2014) *I'm Fighting to Save Night Trains – The Ticket to My Daughter's Future*. Available at: http://www.theguardian.com/

commentisfree/2014/sep/18/save-night-trains-ticket-daughter-rail
-greenest-travel-europe-sleeper-services (Accessed: 19 September 2014).

Moore, S. (2013) *The Death of the Middle Class Will Undermine
Our Democracy.* Available at: http://www.theguardian.com/
commentisfree/2013/aug/28/death-middle-class-undermine-democracy
(Accessed: 22 April 2015).

Morrow, M. (2013) 'Recovery: Progressive Paradigm or Neoliberal
Smokescreen?', in LeFrancois, B.A., Menzies, R.J. and Reaume, G. (eds.)
Mad Matters: A Critical Reader in Canadian Mad Studies. Toronto:
Canadian Scholars' Press, pp. 323–333.

Oxford English Dictionary (2016a) 'Austerity, n.' Access provided by
University of Birmingham. Available at: http://www.oed.com.ezproxyd
.bham.ac.uk/view/Entry/13269?redirectedFrom=austerity& (Accessed:
14 March 2016).

Oxford English Dictionary (2016b) 'Crisis, n.' Access provided by University
of Birmingham. Available at: http://www.oed.com.ezproxyd.bham.ac.uk/
view/Entry/44539?redirectedFrom=crisis& (Accessed: 14 March 2016).

Payne, N. (2012a) *Constellations.* London: Faber & Faber.

Payne, N. (2012b) *Playwright Nick Payne: Master of the Multiverse.* Interview
by Maddy Costa. Available at: http://www.theguardian.com/stage/2012/
nov/02/nick-payne-playwright-constellations (Accessed: 2 April 2015).

Peck, J. (2012) 'Austerity Urbanism', *City,* 16(6), pp. 626–655.

Pinder, D. (2011) 'Cities: Moving, Plugging in, Floating, Dissolving', in
Merriman, P. and Cresswell, T. (eds.) *Geographies of Mobilities: Practices,
Spaces, Subjects.* Farnham, Surrey: Ashgate Publishing, pp. 167–186.

Pinter, H. (2005) *Nobel Lecture: Art, Truth & Politics.* Available at: http://www
.nobelprize.org/nobel_prizes/literature/laureates/2005/pinter-lecture-e
.html (Accessed: 18 June 2015).

Pinter, H. (2011) *Betrayal* and *Party Time,* in *Harold Pinter: Plays Four.*
London: Faber & Faber.

Prebble, L. (2003) *The Sugar Syndrome.* London: Methuen Drama.

Prebble, L. (2009a) *Enron.* London: Methuen Drama.

Prebble, L. (2009b) *'I hate to be told somewhere is out of bounds for women.'
Enter Enron ....* Interview by Tim Adams. Available at: http://www
.theguardian.com/stage/2009/jul/05/lucy-prebble-playwright-interview
-enron (Accessed: 10 July 2015).

Prebble, L. (2012a) *The Effect.* London: Methuen Drama.

Prebble, L. (2012b) *Lucy Prebble Interview*. Interview by Joe Ideas Tap. Available at: http://www.ideastap.com/ideasmag/the-knowledge/lucy-prebble-interview (Accessed: 9 July 2015).

Prebble, L. (2015) *Entrevista a Lucy Prebble autora de 'L'efecte' A la Sala Beckett del 04/02/2015 al 08/03/2015*. Interview by Sala Beckett. Available at: https://vimeo.com/118921664 (Accessed: 20 June 2015).

Radosavljević, D. (2013) *Theatre-Making: Interplay between Text and Performance in the 21st Century*. Basingstoke: Palgrave Macmillan.

Rayner, A. (2006) *Ghosts: Death's Double and the Phenomena of Theatre*. Minneapolis: University of Minnesota press.

Rebellato, D. (2007) 'Backpages – New Theatre Writing: Dennis Kelly', *Contemporary Theatre Review*, 17(4), pp. 603–608.

Rebellato, D. (2013) 'Exit the Author', in Angelaki, V. (ed.) *Contemporary British Theatre: Breaking New Ground*. Basingstoke: Palgrave Macmillan, pp. 9–31.

Rose, N., O'Malley, P. and Valverde, M. (2006) 'Governmentality', *Annual Review of Law and Social Science*, 2(1), pp. 83–104.

The Royal Court Theatre Presents Seven Jewish Children (2009) Available at: http://www.royalcourttheatre.com/whats-on/seven-jewish-children-a-play-for-gaza (Accessed: 9 November 2015).

Sager, T. (2006) 'Freedom as Mobility: Implications of the Distinction between Actual and Potential Travelling', *Mobilities*, 1(3), pp. 465–488.

Sennett, R. (1999) *The Corrosion of Character*. London and New York: W. W. Norton.

Sennett, R. (2003) *The Fall of Public Man*. London: Penguin Books.

Sennett, R. (2008) *The Uses of Disorder: Personal Identity and City Life*. New Haven: Yale University Press.

Sennett, R. (2012) *Together: The Rituals, Pleasures and Politics of Co-operation*. London: Allen Lane.

Sierz, A. (2013) 'Backpages – A New Crisis in New Writing?', *Contemporary Theatre Review*, 23(2), pp. 249–251.

Spencer, C. (2010) *Earthquakes in London, National Theatre, Review*. Available at: http://www.telegraph.co.uk/culture/theatre/theatre-reviews/7929004/Earthquakes-in-London-National-Theatre-review.html (Accessed: 20 December 2015).

Spencer, C. (2012a) *Ding Dong the Wicked, Royal Court Theatre, Review*. Available at: http://www.telegraph.co.uk/culture/theatre/theatre-reviews/9594624/Ding-Dong-the-Wicked-Royal-Court-Theatre-review.html (Accessed: 10 November 2015).

Spencer, C. (2012b) *The Effect, National Theatre, Review*. Available at: http://
www.telegraph.co.uk/culture/theatre/theatre-reviews/9675660/The-Effect
-National-Theatre-review.html (Accessed: 31 July 2015).

Spencer, C. (2013) *Ritual Slaughter of Gorge Mastromas, Royal Court,
Review*. Available at: http://www.telegraph.co.uk/culture/theatre/theatre
-reviews/10301519/Ritual-Slaughter-of-Gorge-Mastromas-Royal-Court
-review.html (Accessed: 11 June 2015).

Stephens, S. (2002) *Simon Stephens: Plays One*. London: Methuen Drama.

Stephens, S. (2009) *Simon Stephens: Plays Two*. London: Methuen Drama.

Stephens, S. (2011a) *Simon Stephens: Plays Three*. London: Methuen Drama.

Stephens, S. (2011b) *Skydiving Blindfolded*. Available at: http://
theatertreffen-blog.de/tt11/2011/05/09/skydiving-blindfolded/ (Accessed:
5 October 2015).

Stephens, S. (2011c) *Wastwater and T5*. London: Methuen Drama.

Stephens, S. (2012) *Three Kingdoms*. London: Methuen Drama.

Stephens, S. (2014a) *Birdland*. London: Methuen Drama.

Stephens, S. (2014b) *Simon Stephens: The Tracks of My Plays*. Available at:
http://www.theguardian.com/stage/2014/apr/21/simon-stephens-tracks
-plays-playlist-birdland (Accessed: 6 October 2015).

Stephens, S. (2015a) *Carmen Disruption*. London: Methuen Drama.

Stephens, S. (2015b) *How Bizet's Carmen Became a Male Prostitute*.
Available at: http://www.theguardian.com/music/2015/apr/13/carmen
-as-male-prostitute-simon-stephens-carmen-disruption (Accessed:
28 October 2015).

Stephens, S. (2015c) *Simon Stephens on Musical Cravings and New Ways of
Tackling Theatre*. Interview by Henry Hitchings. Available at: http://www
.standard.co.uk/goingout/theatre/simon-stephens-on-musical-cravings
-new-ways-of-tackling-theatre-and-life-s-disappointments-a2922366.html
(Accessed: 6 October 2015).

Stephens, S. (2015d) *Song from Far Away*. London: Methuen Drama.

Taylor, J. (1998) *Ubu and the Truth Commission*. Cape Town: University of
Cape Town Press.

Taylor, P. (2010) *Earthquakes in London, National Theatre: Cottesloe, London*.
Available at: http://www.independent.co.uk/arts-entertainment/theatre
-dance/reviews/earthquakes-in-london-national-theatre-cottesloe
-london-2044606.html (Accessed: 20 December 2015).

Taylor, P. (2012) *In the Republic of Happiness, Royal Court, London*. Available
at: http://www.independent.co.uk/arts-entertainment/theatre-dance/

reviews/in-the-republic-of-happiness-royal-court-london-8412800.html (Accessed: 29 September 2015).

tucker green, debbie (2003) *dirty butterfly*. London: Nick Hern Books.

tucker green, debbie (2005) *stoning mary*. London: Nick Hern Books.

tucker green, debbie (2008) *random*. London: Nick Hern Books.

tucker green, debbie (2011) *truth and reconciliation*. London: Nick Hern Books.

tucker green, debbie (2013) *nut*. London: Nick Hern Books.

tucker green, debbie (2015) *hang*. London: Nick Hern Books.

Ullmann, K. (2009) *Liebe und Geld – Stephan Kimmig bringt Dennis Kellys fatale Liebesökonomie auf die Bühne*. Available at: http://nachtkritik.de/index.php?option=com_content&view=article&id=2562:liebe-und-geld-stephan-kimmig-bringt-dennis-kellys-fatale-liebesoekonomie-auf-die-buehne-&catid=37&Itemid=100190 (Accessed: 15 July 2014).

Urry, J. (2000) *Sociology beyond Societies: Mobilities for the Twenty-First Century*. London: Routledge.

Van Oosten, R. (2014) 'Backpages – Writing Music for *In the Republic of Happiness*', *Contemporary Theatre Review*, 24(3), pp. 411–412.

Von Mayenburg, M. (2009) *The Stone*. London: Methuen Drama.

Wald, C. (2007) *Hysteria, Trauma and Melancholia: Performative Maladies in Contemporary Anglophone Drama*. Basingstoke: Palgrave Macmillan.

Waters, S. (2009) *The Contingency Plan: On the Beach, Resilience*. London: Nick Hern Books.

Wicker, T. (2015) *Hang*. Available at: http://exeuntmagazine.com/reviews/hang/ (Accessed: 28 August 2015).

Wolf, D. (2011) *Thoroughly Modern Mike*. Available at: http://www.prospectmagazine.co.uk/arts-and-books/mike-bartlett-13-modern-british-theatre (Accessed: 28 December 2015).

Woolman, N. (2012) *Love Is a Drug: Lucy Prebble Explores the Effects of Chemical Romance (wired UK)*. Available at: http://www.wired.co.uk/magazine/archive/2012/12/play/love-is-a-drug (Accessed: 30 June 2015).

Index